The Dodecanese:
Further Travels
Among the Insular Greeks

Selected Writings of
J. Theodore & Mabel V.A. Bent,
1885-1888

Mabel Virginia Anna Bent (1847-1929)

J. Theodore Bent (1852-1897)

The Dodecanese: Further Travels Among the Insular Greeks

Selected Writings of J. Theodore & Mabel V.A. Bent, 1885-1888

Travel Writings of J. Theodore & Mabel V.A. Bent from their Expeditions to the Eastern Mediterranean

Edited by Gerald Brisch

Also available in the Archaeopress 3rdguides Series (in printed and e-versions):

J. Theodore Bent: *The Cyclades, or Life Among the Insular Greeks*

The Travel Chronicles of Mrs. J. Theodore Bent:
Volume I   *Greece and the Levantine Littoral*
Volume II *The African Journeys*
Volume III *Southern Arabia and Persia*

The Dodecanese: Further Travels Among the Insular Greeks
The Selected Writings of J. Theodore & Mabel V.A. Bent, 1885-1888
Edited by Gerald Brisch

© Archaeopress Ltd and Gerald Brisch 2015

Unless specified, this transcription and all material © Gerald Brisch 2015

Preface © Marc Dubin 2015

3rdguides is an imprint of
Archaeopress Ltd
Gordon House, 276 Banbury Road
Oxford OX2 7ED, UK
www.archaeopress.com
archaeo@archaeopress.com

All rights reserved. No part of this publication may be reproduced, stored in a retrieval system, or transmitted, in any form or by any means, electronic, mechanical, photocopying, recording or otherwise, without the prior permission of the publishers.

ISBN: 978 1 78491 096 6
ISBN: 978 1 78491 097 6 e-pdf

3rdguides series editor: Gerald Brisch

Cover photograph © Gerald Brisch (Ayíou Pandelímona, Tílos)

Printed and bound in Great Britain by Marston Book Services Ltd, Oxfordshire

It seems to me that I have to choose between two extremes of affection for nature – towards outward nature that is – English or southern – the former, oak, ash and beech, downs and cliffs, old associations, friends near at hand, and many comforts not to be got elsewhere. The latter olive – vine – flowers, the ancient life of Greece, warmth and light, better health, greater novelty, and less expense in life. On the other side are in England cold, damp and illness, constant hurry and bustle, cessation from all topographic interest, extreme expenses...

Edward Lear, c. 1860

The subsequent history of the [Dodecanese] has not been an enviable one. After a period of comparative independence as a province of the Byzantine Empire, they eventually fell a prey to the land-hunger of the ubiquitous Norman Crusades, and were consigned, in 1310, to the rule of the Knights of St John of Jerusalem... In 1532...they were forced to admit suzerainty of the Turk; and Rhodes, once the cultural centre of the civilized world, the cradle of painting and sculpture and the sciences, of medicine and navigation – Rhodes, the most splendid of cities...where once had dwelt half a million citizens, was left stripped of her treasures...

Robert Byron, c. 1925

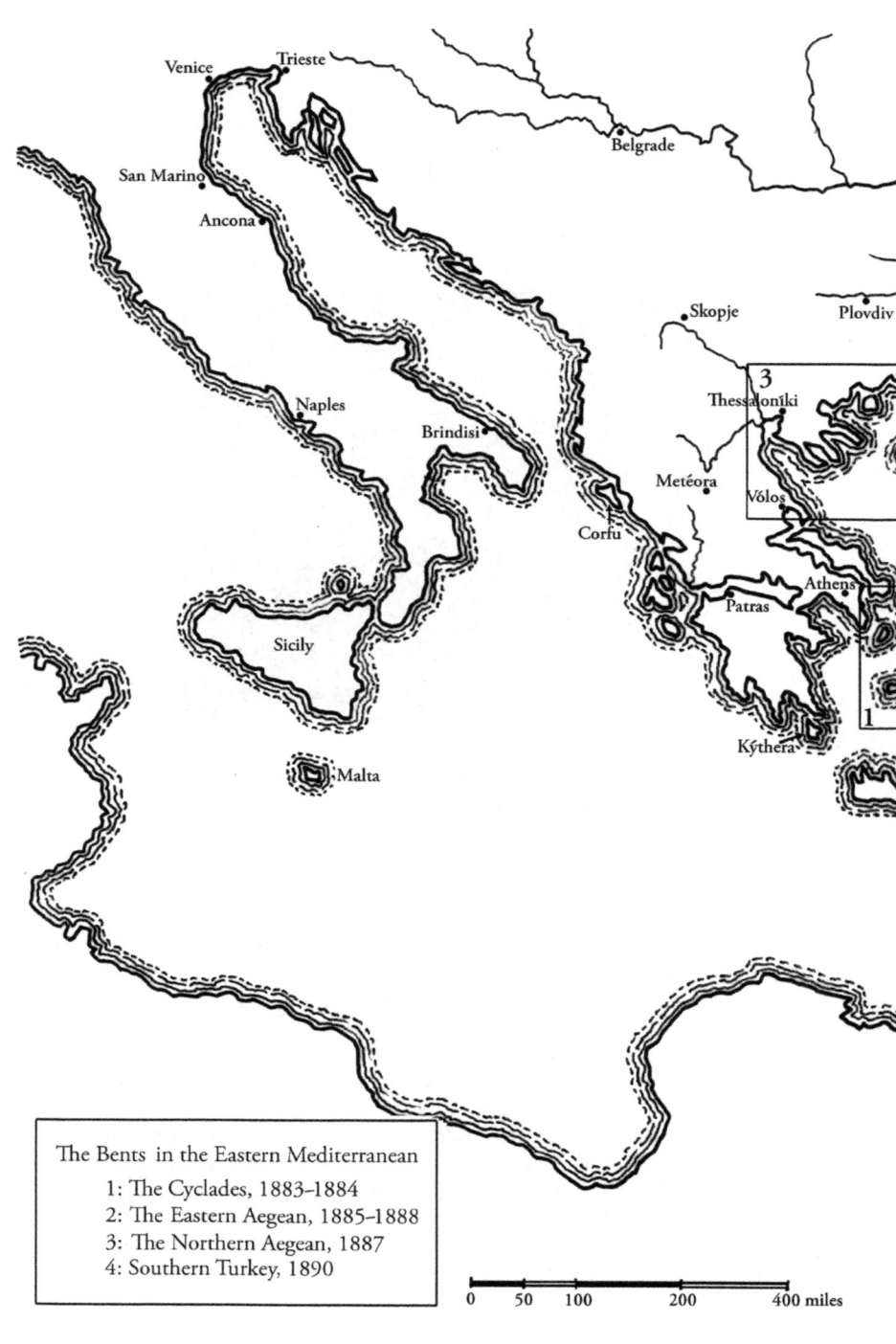

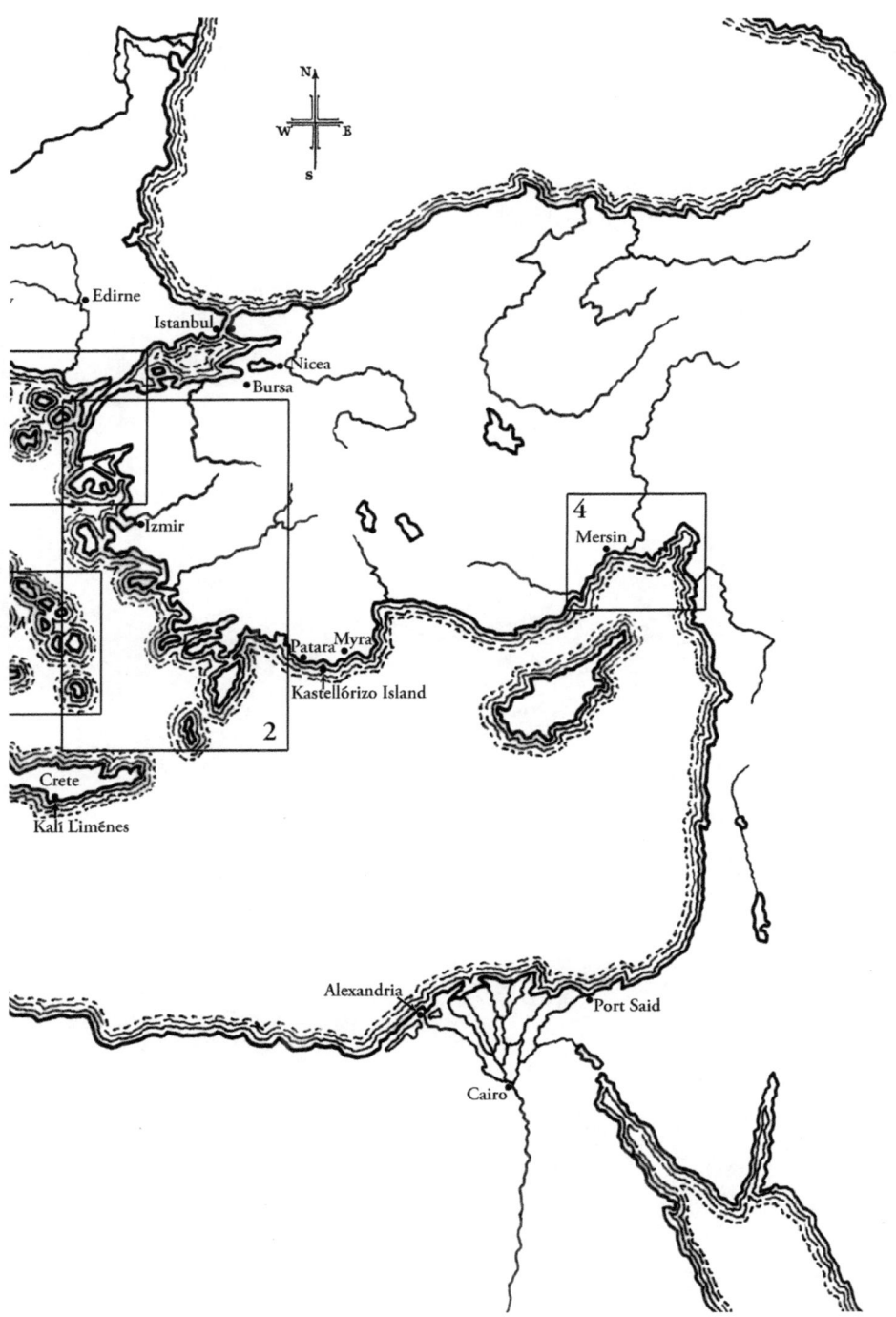

Contents

Preface by Marc Dubin	i
Introduction	v
Some notes to this edition	xii
Acknowledgements	xiii

J.T. Bent: Selected Writings on the Dodecanese

Rhodes	1
Níssiros	9
Tílos	10
Kárpathos	25
From Sými to Kastellórizo	68
Sýrna	72
Agathoníssi	73
Pátmos	75
Astypálea	94

The Travel Chronicles of Mabel Bent

Chronicle III – 1885	106
Chronicle IV – 1886	153
Chronicle VI – 1888	163

Sidetrack 1: *J.T. Bent: Related Writing*

'The Three Evils of Destiny'	174
'Parallels to Homeric Life Existing in Greece To-day'	176
'Personification of the Mysterious Amongst the Modern Greeks'	180
'The Carpathiote Dialect'	181
'Modern Life and Thought amongst the Greeks'	182

Sidetrack 2: *Mabel Bent: Related Writing*

On Insular Greek Costumes	184

Sidetrack 3: *The Itineraries in the Dodecanese*	186
Bibliography	188
Illustrations and maps	190
Index of Place Names	193

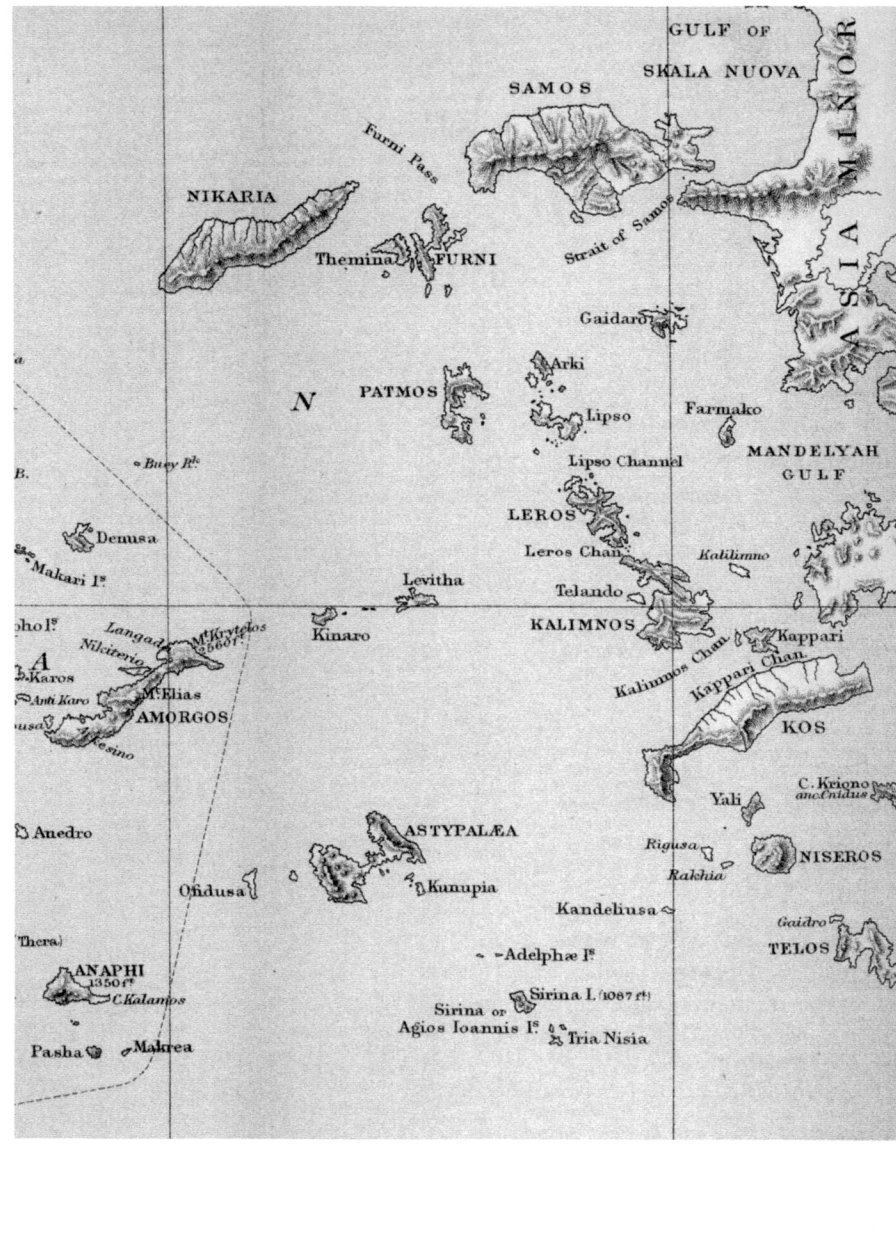

Preface by Marc Dubin

I have been writing about the Greek islands since 1981, and the Bents have accompanied me from the start. After graduating from UC Berkeley in 1977, I stayed around town for some years; I was fortunate in having a part-time job at the university library which was piecework-based and allowed me to work full-time for three months and then take equal time off to travel. It also gave me complete, unchallenged run of the book stacks, where I furthered my education through omnivorous reading. There was no security whatsoever at the employees' entrance, so books could be 'borrowed' indefinitely.

The pre-computerisation card catalogue listed no less than four copies of J. Theodore Bent's *Aegean Islands: The Cyclades, or Life Among the Insular Greeks*, published as a 1966 reprint by Argonaut in Chicago. I had just signed my first contract to write a guidebook on Greece. Why should the library keep four copies of this title, when my research needs were greater? Home it went, to stay, in 1980.

James Theodore and Mabel spent nearly a year travelling around the Aegean on their first trip, back when it took a year to visit all the islands given the vagaries of the wind – as he writes in the volume you are holding, 'those who go to Astypalæa must be people of a patient disposition'. They more (or less) cheerfully tolerated ferocious winter weather, leaking quarters, foul-smelling wooden boats, monotonous food ('pease porridge hot, pease porridge cold, pease porridge in the pot nine days old' was literally and repeatedly enacted), rapacious boatmen and voracious vermin. They took shelter in bare churches when necessary, something sadly unlikely now when so many rural chapels are locked against theft or desecration. It all puts today's island-traveller whinges about cancelled sailings, greasy food and wonky water heaters in stark perspective. To their immense credit, the Bents were keenly interested in the contemporary Greek islanders, not just in antiquities, unlike 18th-century Grand Tourists who disparaged the supposedly degenerated medieval Greeks and modern tourists who are only after sun, sea and sex.

The Cyclades, or Life Among the Insular Greeks, also available through Archaeopress, has the dubious honour of being the most plagiarized book ever written on the Greek islands – almost every 1960s to 1980s writer on the Aegean helped themselves to entire pages worth of Bent, verbatim. It was legally if not ethically okay to do so, since the text (as the Argonaut publisher told me when I asked him) had long since been in the public domain; the Bents had died without issue or any other heirs to extend the copyright. Copyright aside, it's easy to see why this happened: the intrepid Bents had been there, and done that, long before there were any t-shirts, and what they had observed and documented was far more compelling than anything actually visible on the islands from the 1960s onwards. Bent had also described their sojourns in brisk, to-the-point prose; it's hard not to warm to someone who could write 'on my remarking that I should prefer an inside place [on a raised communal family bed] for fear of a fall, they laughed and told stories of a sponge fisherman who dreamt that he was going to take a dive into the sea, and found himself on the floor instead; and of a priest, who rolled out of bed when drunk and broke his neck...in inferior establishments the space beneath the bed is used as a storeroom for all imaginable filth'.

On my extended 1981 trips to Greece, I had to quell lurking disappointment that the islanders were no longer as Bent described them. Or not quite anyway; on Sífnos my young hostess told me that there was still an old woman alive locally who could 'draw out the sun' from those afflicted with sunstroke-headache by sleight of handkerchief and incantations, exactly as described in Bent's Kímolos account from 1883. Later a much older friend told me how, serving as a British delegate to the United Nations Special Commission on the Balkans (UNSCOB), monitoring border violations during the Greek civil war, he had – despite his total disbelief in the rite – the effects of the Evil Eye exorcised, again through spells and fabric manipulations, by an old Sifnian man, Nikos, in 1948, in Macedonia.

But one can hardly expect such customs and costumes to have survived decades of emigration, electrification, radio and gramophones, public schooling whether Italian or Greek, meddling foreigners and government policy. Bent himself took a dim view of his own countrymen abroad: 'It is the Union Jack which scatters [quaint costumes and still quainter customs] to the winds: great though our love is for antiquity, we English have dealt more harshly than any other people with the fashions of the old world.' During the mid-1960s, even before the culturally destructive colonels' junta, Kevin Andrews observed how local police felt it necessary to ban the playing of bagpipes at Mykonos port lest 'foreigners...think us Mau-Mau'. You wonder what the Bents would make of today's mercenary anthropological zoo centred on the village of Ólymbos in northern Kárpathos, which I first decried in my own 1996 guide to the Dodecanese and North Aegean. Research for that first edition involved criss-crossing the archipelago for several consecutive seasons in just about every month of the year (barring February and March) and every conceivable seagoing conveyance. Perhaps my most Bent-ian experience was in that self-same Ólymbos, when a *nistísima* meal (compliant with the Lenten fast) turned out to be simply limpets and *myrouátana*, a delicious seaweed which I have never been served again despite asking repeatedly.

During the late 1980s, in Moe's – that Berkeley shrine of used books on Telegraph Avenue – I found another copy of the Argonaut Press edition of *Aegean Islands*, in mint condition, for the paltry price of $US7: a fair measure of the scant esteem then in the USA for the Bents and their writings. The same copy in Britain at that time fetched at least thirty quid. Even now, antiquarian bookselling websites do not much value this handsome original reprint.

Shortly afterwards – I had not yet left the US to settle in Britain and Greece – I retrieved the purloined copy from my own shelves and headed for my old haunt, the UC Berkeley library. Back then (and probably still now) you could return a book in perfect anonymity, which I did eight years after its initial 'check-out', using the large-mouthed chutes near the main doors. It is not a small book in any sense, especially the old cloth-cover edition which is by my desk as I write, and made a satisfying clunk as it hit the bottom. So there should be once again four copies of *Aegean Islands* in the library's holdings.

Marc Dubin
Áno Vathý, Sámos
December 2014

(For many years, Marc Dubin authored various Rough Guides *to the Greek islands, and still writes the* Insight Guide to the Greek Islands. *He also currently maintains webpages on many islands for* The Daily Telegraph. *Marc currently lives much of the time on the Greek island of Sámos.)*

Theodore and Mabel Bent

Introduction

What follows is a book of island travels never written, although it should have been. Its principal author is J. Theodore Bent (1852-1897), supported throughout by his wife Mabel Virginia Anna (1847-1929). Why it should have been will be clear by its conclusion, well meriting H.F. Tozer's opinion on its predecessor:

> The islands in themselves are an attractive study from the varied points of interest which they present: the beauty of their position, their history and antiquities, and numerous other features, besides the people themselves, whose life was the author's chief object of study. None of these have been neglected in this volume.[1]

Theodore met Mabel shortly after coming down from Oxford in 1875 and they wed two years later, in Staplestown Church, County Carlow, Ireland. They were both of independent means and devoted the too few years until Theodore's early death, in May 1897, to a breathless sequence of annual explorations of the Eastern Mediterranean, Africa, and Southern Arabia. The couple styled themselves 'archaeologists', but descriptions such as 'antiquaries' or amateur anthropologists/ethnographers, or even simply collectors, probably match their activities closer: they were quite happy to sell what they removed from sites as far south as Zimbabwe, as far to the east as the Persian Gulf, and as far north as the shores of Thrace.

Regardless of their results, without question the Bents can be grouped among the most recognized British husband-and-wife travelling partnerships of the second half of the 19th century, at the apogee of Empire. Theodore's ensuing monographs and hundreds of articles are referenced still by archaeologists and others publishing on sites or regions such as the ruins of 'Great Zimbabwe', Aksum, the Wadi Hadramaut, the Cilician littoral, and, of course, the Greek islands and the Eastern Mediterranean.

Theodore's first successful book was based on two winters they spent weaving in and out of the Greek Cycladic isles (1882/3 and 1883/4). This work, published in 1885, was *The Cyclades, or Life Among the Insular Greeks* and it has been rarely out of print since.[2] It is the elder sibling of this present volume and remains one of the breeziest accounts in English of the Cyclades: few serious travellers and tourists

---

[1] Review of 'The Cyclades; or, Life among the Insular Greeks. By J. Theodore Bent', by Henry Fanshawe Tozer, in *Academy* 27 (1885: Jan/June).
[2] Longmans, Green and Co., London 1885.

to these islands fail to discover it.

The temperate months the Bents spent sailing these waters were particularly happy and typically energetic ones. It was an inspired project:

> The islands of the Ægean Sea offer plenty of scope for the study of Hellenic archaeology, but they are more particularly rich in the preservation of manners and customs which have survived the lapse of years; and the result of a special study of both these points made during two winters passed by my wife and myself amongst the islanders in their distant hamlets, and in their towns by the sea-coast, I here place before the public.[3]

Extended biographical profiles on the couple are available elsewhere,[4] but some notes on their early interests in, and exposure to archaeological matters serve well here.

James Theodore Bent (he preferred Theodore to James) was born in Liverpool on 30th March 1852 (his uncle was for a short period Mayor); his parents were James and Margaret Eleanor, who married in April 1848. The Bent family could be traced back some generations in the north of England, related to the splendidly-named Hamlet Bent (1642-1728). Another branch of the family included the distinguished surgeon Sir James Justin Bent, who amputated Josiah Wedgewood's right leg in May 1768. The non-medical side of the family made their wealth collectively in the pottery and brewing trades – 'Bent's Brewery Co. Ltd.' only disappearing as a name in the 1960s. As well as their fine home in Baildon, not far from Leeds, James Bent also acquired Sutton Hall, near Macclesfield, which became a favourite residence for Theodore and Mabel on their return every early summer from abroad. Their main London property was a stone's throw from Marble Arch.

With a lively imagination and a predisposition to historical research there was no shortage of local antiquarian and archaeological activity to simulate the young Theodore. From 1866 to 1871 he studied at Repton School (Derbyshire), built on the site of a famous abbey: the crypt was opened there, and the school buildings developed, during his schooldays. The abbey's archaeological past revealed Bronze Age, Roman, and Anglo-Saxon remains – the crypt itself containing the burials of several Anglo-Saxon kings. Bent would have been able to observe the antiquarian research and architectural features of the abbey at first hand.[5] A little nearer to home, fine spear-heads were turning up around the Baildon boundary as late as 1882, and about which Theodore would have read in the newsletters of the Bradford Antiquarian Society.

Mabel Hall-Dare, five years Theodore's senior, was raised among the minor Anglo-Irish aristocracy.[6] There exists a rare autobiographical account of her earliest years,

---

[3] So begins J.T. Bent's 'Preface' to *The Cyclades*.

[4] See the 'Introductions' to Vols. I-III of *The Travel Chronicles of Mrs. J. Theodore Bent*.

[5] Fittingly, his old school remembered him at a ceremony there not long after his death (*Derby Mercury*, 30 June 1897).

[6] 'BENT, Mrs. Mabel Virginia Anna, of 13, Great Cumberland Place, W., and of the Ladies' Empire Club, is a daughter of Robert Westley Hall-Dare, D.L., of Theydon Bois, Wennington Hall, Essex, and Newtownbarry House, Co. Wexford. She was married Aug. 2, 1877, to the late Theodore Bent, of Baildon House, Yorks. Mrs. Bent accompanied her husband in all his explorations, and took part in the excavations with which he was associated in the Greek and Turkish Islands, Asia Minor, Abyssinia, the Great Zimbabye (Mashonaland), Persia, and elsewhere. She is the authoress of 'Southern Arabia, Soudan, and Sokotra,' compiled from her own and Mr.

'Beauparc – Lady Lambert's House'. Mabel Hall-Dare was born here, in County Meath, Ireland, in January 1847.

possibly never republished since its first appearance (1903), in the gossipy *Mainly about People*. A lengthy extract conjures her up:

> My baby eyes first looked out on an extremely beautiful bit of this world, for I was born at Beauparc, in the county of Meath, my grandfather Gustavus Lambart's place, which, being situated on a very high bank at a sharp curve of the River Boyne, seems as if it were upon an island looking straight down the river. The right bank is high and wooded, and the left has a narrow grassy flat between the water and a low craggy cliff, above which you see away over tree-studded fields to a ruined castle with woods beyond; and my eyes, which have since been so much exercised in seeking for archaeological sites where to make excavations, must also have fallen on the wonderful ancient tumulus of New Grange. So much did this view please me the first time I can remember seeing it, that, having arrived in the dark one night, the following morning about four or five o'clock my wretched mother was startled from her sleep by shrieks and shouts to find me jumping up and down as hard as I could at the window, a manifestation of my ecstasy of delight at the sight of the snow and icicles and all the wintry beauty spread before me. Although I certainly had no inkling of the fate that awaited me, being a 'Thursday's bairn who has far to go', no child was ever fonder of reading and poring over maps and lists and pictures of traveller's requisites than I was... I was also a most determined dweller in tents, for I used to pull my bed to pieces and hang up my top sheet by the nail of a picture,

Theodore Bent's notes.' (*Anglo-African Who's Who,* Wills and Barrett (eds.), 1905)

making a good hole that it should hold well, and then, arranging my bedding to suit my fancy, imagine I was sleeping on the ground. It was not comfortable, but there was something very nice about it. In one of my investigations of the library at home I came upon a book that I made up my mind to examine. It had a delightful title 'The Atlas of Undiscovered Countries'. It was firmly fixed, and to get at it I had to exert all my strength and become very hot, tugging out the great folios that were on each side, and then to my disgust I found my prize was only a false wooden book to support the upper shelf. Years after I exclaimed, 'Now I have really an atlas of undiscovered countries of my own', when I eagerly unpacked a map in eight sheets (that my husband had had made at Stanford's, of Southern Arabia, when we were first thinking of exploring that part of the world) and found two or three of the sheets blank save for latitude and longitude marks. I am glad to say that the blank is not so large now... Some very strange things have been written in the way of description of the dress I wore when travelling in outlandish places – just a shooting dress. The accounts are such that my friends refuse to believe in my photographs, as they in no way tally with what they have read. One paper had it that I wore a spiked helmet, whereas what goes by the name of my pith helmet is of rather a large mushroom shape. All this is very amusing to me. A statement which delighted the whole of my family[7] was one that 'Mrs. Theodore Bent is never tired of expatiating on the sagacity of the horse, and its superiority in this respect to the mule or the camel'. Against whose attacks have I had to defend the 'noble animal'. The first intimation of this came to me suddenly when I opened a magazine in a boatful of strangers in Aden Harbour. My husband, who had landed first to seek a dwelling on our return from Dhofar, had sent my mail (some months' accumulation) on board. I nearly went into hysterics, tears rolled down my cheeks, the various coloured fellow-passengers stared, but I could not control my mirth nor explain the cause of its sudden outburst. After all, in a residence of a week or ten days at Aden, which has been my unfortunate fate seven or eight times, one is glad of anything to cheer one up. On this occasion we were so lucky as to be able to hire an unlet shop, where we set up our camp in dust that never could be swept up, and by night slept in the surrounding dens, alive with bugs, and those horrid 'fish moths', which are rather like earwigs, and eat cloth, linen, paper, ivory – in fact, everything but metal. Our servants cooked at various fires in the inner yard according to their religion, and spread their beds on the floor of the shop at night. Neither window shutters nor doors could be kept open or shut for lack of fastening, and slammed and banged to and fro incessantly. What we could not help we tried not to heed, and only rejoiced that we were masters of our own kitchen and could feed as we pleased much better than in the hotels. I really was once taken for a man, and caused a terrible commotion as I entered a Turkish bath filled with ladies about whose costume there is nothing to tell. I had on a tight fitting ulster and a hat, and the waist and the hat and the long coat made me really look very like a Persian man... My youth was spent partly in England, but mostly in Ireland, my father having property in both countries, and we were often taken abroad for a summer or a winter. This is certainly the best way of learning languages, of which I was fortunately always very fond. It was a great help when it was necessary for me to look up references in various tongues and in old manuscripts. I have often been in places where I have heard

---

[7] The Bents left no children. Theodore's direct relations were few, but Mabel had several nieces and nephews in Ireland, and her descendants still live in her Wexford childhood home.

no English at all. It would have astonished me very much in the days of my youth if I had been told that I should ever abide for some time in the Republic of San Marino and become a citizen of it. The diploma was sent after my husband had written a history of the Republic ('A Freak of Freedom'), and he received a letter subsequently from a friend beginning, 'Dear Sir and Fellow Citizen,' congratulating him, and reminding him that 'no matter at what distance he might lie from the Republic, he would be under her protection.' It was lucky that I was so well used to riding, as I have had so much of it on horses, donkeys, mules, camels, and even elephants. I do not mind camel-riding at all, and really like it when I trot. However, no matter what I do abroad, when necessity compels, in the way of blacking boots, cobbling them, covering umbrellas, or mending their ribs, washing clothes, soldering cooking-pots, or 'washing up' (which last I hate), I try to live it down in after life, and when I am at home to enjoy the privileges of civilisation, to wear dresses of whatever length fashion desires of me, and hats that will pass in a crowd. I cannot understand the feeling which makes people wish to disguise themselves as travellers when at home. Certainly I have been granted some of the wishes that I made in the days of my youth! (Mabel Virginia Anna Bent)[8]

The 1880s, twenty years before the above musings, represented for the Bents their 'Greek' decade, and from the start of their journeys they both began a sequence of notebooks on which subsequently Theodore was to base all his lectures and publications for the years left to him (in addition he was a gifted sketcher and watercolourist, and Mabel trained herself into a pioneer travel photographer). All but one of Mabel's notebooks (*Chronicles* she called them) are in the archives of the Joint Library of the Hellenic and Roman Societies, London (where a few of Theodore's can also be studied).

In the year *The Cyclades* was published, 1885, the Bents decided to begin exploring the islands now commonly referred to as the Greek Dodecanese, looking for new material on which to lecture and publish. There is no reason to believe that Theodore was not planning a sequel for his well-reviewed travel account:

> Mr. Bent's book deserves all success, for it is the result of researches pursued in the most laudable manner. When an educated man selects for his field of observation an interesting and little-explored area of country, and, after learning the language, spends a considerable part of two winters there, living among all classes of people so as to familiarise himself with the details of their life, and to become intimately acquainted with their ideas and modes of thought, he deserves the title of an enthusiastic investigator. Any one who reads this book can see that the discomforts which the author – and his wife, who accompanied him – had to undergo, though they are comparatively little dwelt on, were often very severe…[9]

---

[8] Transcribed from: Mabel V.A. Bent, 'In the Days of My Youth: Chapters of Autobiography', *M.A.P.*, 10, Issue 240 (17 January 1903), pp. 72-3 (*M.A.P.* [*Mainly about People*]: *A Popular Penny Weekly of Pleasant Gossip, Personal Portraits, and Social News*, Editor: T.P. O'Connor).
[9] Review of '*The Cyclades; or, Life among the Insular Greeks*. By J. Theodore Bent', by Henry Fanshawe Tozer, in *Academy* 27 (1885: Jan/June).

Of course, when Theodore and Mabel were steering between this group of islands to the east of the Cyclades the region was still firmly under Turkish control, and any monograph Theodore might have compiled from their writings would probably have contained the term 'Sporades' in the title (both he and Mabel made general references to them as such). However, the islands were eventually returned to Greece after WWII, and as the Dodecanese we know them now.[10]

In the new Greece of the 1880s, whose sea-borders began only a few tens of nautical miles west of the Sporades/Dodecanese, when the Bents were at large, controls and restrictions on individuals wishing to undertake archaeological excavations made it increasingly difficult for freelancers such as Theodore and Mabel, and the easy option for the couple was to move east into Turkish waters. In an article (1885) for the *Journal of Hellenic Studies*[11] Bent reveals, 'Before going to Karpathos last winter a passage in Ludwig Ross's *Inselreisen* excited my curiosity...' His reference was to the little visited region on Kárpathos, west of Rhodes, and the couple accordingly made plans to visit the island, deciding to arrive there, with Turkish papers, via Egypt.

Mabel and Theodore arrived on Rhodes in February 1885, from Alexandria; they had been sightseeing in Egypt for the last few weeks. Theodore is anxious that the debate stirred up by his 1883 article criticizing Turkish rule on Chíos[12] could hamper his chances of excavating. His choice of entry from Alexandria, rather than Istanbul, reflects this. The Bents prefer to keep a low profile and they think it best to avoid asking for permission to excavate unless absolutely necessary.

Theodore's explorations on Kárpathos were of some significance and many of his finds are in the British Museum. He published his results (and those from Tílos) in a paper (1885) for the *Journal of Hellenic Studies*. It is on this tour that he and Mabel acquire the odd limestone statue that she describes as 'the most hideous thing ever made by human hands'. Their lengthy stay on the island, over most of which they travelled, was to provide Theodore with a wealth of material for a subsequent range of academic and general publications. A book (this one) may well have appeared by 1890, but by then the author was more or less *persona non grata* in the eyes of the Porte and Bent's focus had shifted generally further east still, and to the 'Phoenicians'. Instead the material that might have formed chapters on the Sporades/Dodecanese was transformed (with the aid of frequent, often verbatim, references to Mabel's notebooks, her *Chronicles*) into dozens of articles for periodicals (popular) and journals (academic).

For Rhodes, the Bents re-hire Manthaios Símos of Anáfi as their general assistant (*dragoman*), and he joins the couple on the island after several delays. This tour contains Mabel's first reference to her role as expedition photographer, a function she fulfilled enthusiastically, but with mixed results, for all the couple's subsequent travels. Very few of her plates or negatives have survived – the technical problems she had to deal with were considerable.

After the successes of their 1885 campaign, the Bents decide for their 1886 season to cruise south, down from the Turkish islands of Sámos and Chíos, which they

---

[10] There is no shortage to guides in most languages to the region. For a readable introduction (from an archaeological perspective), see J. L. Myers, 'The Dodecanese', in *The Geographical Journal*, Vol. 56, No. 5 (Nov., 1920), pp. 329-347.

[11] Vol. 6, pp. 233-242.

[12] 'Two Turkish Islands To-day', *Macmillan's Magazine*, Issue: 48 (1883: May/Oct.) pp. 299-309.

had first seen before their Cycladic voyage of 1882/3. The trip also took in visits to various islands in the Dodecanese, including a first stay on Pátmos.

But unlicensed exploration was now also becoming difficult on Turkish soil. Theodore, now a member of the council of the Hellenic Society, had obtained a grant of £50 to equip his next expedition. On Sámos he encountered problems with the authorities, and the Society's *Journal* of 1886 reports that '…owing to unexpected difficulty in obtaining permission to dig in the island, Mr. Bent has not been so successful as he had hoped. He has, however, spent only half the amount.' The £25 was returned to the Society and Mabel informs us that, 'Truly the balmy days of excavators are over'.

For their 1887 campaign, the Bents left the Dodecanese region to excavate in what is now northern Greece. On Thásos Theodore discovered Roman marbles of some importance but was refused permission to remove them to London. In January 1888 he received a further grant of £50 from the Hellenic Society to return to the same island and the couple duly left for Istanbul. Following their disagreements the prior season with the influential head of antiquities, Hamdi Bey, Theodore was expressly forbidden to carry out further investigations. Despite various appeals to the Ambassador, Sir William White, he and Mabel were forced to change their objectives.

Then, as now, it pays to have alternative travel plans in the region, and Theodore may well have been expecting this *impasse*. In a later article in the *Classical Review* (May 1889) he revealed that while he was first digging on Thásos in 1887 he had employed a local man 'to make some excavations in the neighbourhood of Syme' (the Turkish gulf north of Rhodes) on his behalf.[13] Obviously satisfied with the report, the couple, return to Sýros in the Cyclades and charter the yacht *Evangelistria*, under Greek papers made out for Cyprus. Forthwith they embark on Theodore's fallback plan to investigate the Turkish coast for a few months, taking in several of the Dodecanese islands *en route*. The investigations along the Asia Minor littoral (in particular the coastline opposite the island of Rhodes, and as far south as the present-day Greek island of Kastellórizo) were fruitful and finds from this expedition are now in London.[14]

1890 marked Theodore and Mabel's final major exploration to the Eastern Mediterranean, with their researches in 'Rough Celicia'. Impossible difficulties in obtaining digging licences, and Theodore's growing interests in early Arabian civilizations, shifted the couple's energies – first to Africa and then Southern Arabia. Ultimately the chills and fevers that Theodore was so susceptible to in the Greek islands in the early 1880s re-emerged more severely every year, culminating in fatal malarial complications east of Aden, in the spring of 1897. Three days after rushing back to London he succumbed to infections. Mabel never remarried. She died in their house near Marble Arch on 3rd July 1929.

Theodore and Mabel, therefore, never opened this book of islands that bears their names – a book never written, but should have been. And anyone who knows Bent's *Cyclades* will feel at home in his *Dodecanese*.

---

[13] In 'Inscriptions from Theangela', E. L. Hicks, *Classical Review*, Vol. 3, No. 5 (May, 1889), pp. 234-237.
[14] He briefly wrote up his discoveries of ancient 'Loryma, Lydæ, and Myra' for the *Journal of Hellenic Studies* (Vol. 9, 1888), but a lengthier account was provided by E. L. Hicks for the same publication (Vol. 10, 1889), including transcriptions of over 40 inscriptions and passages of text from Theodore's own notebooks.

Theodore and Mabel's grave and memorial (right) in the churchyard of St. Mary's, Theydon Bois, Essex.

Some notes to this edition

Theodore Bent's articles reproduced here are transcriptions from the original sources of the 1880s. They have never, to the current editor's knowledge, been previously assembled in the collection presented here.

The excerpts from Mabel Bent's *Chronicles* are transcribed from the original notebooks held in the archives of the Joint Library of the Hellenic and Roman Societies, Senate House, London. To protect these fragile notebooks they were not digitally processed; they are not presented as facsimile transcripts.

Our authors' language and attitudes reflect their times. There is some social and historical value in being able to assess such attitudes and so words and phrases that sit unhappily and unwelcome in modern texts have not been deleted.

A few abbreviations are used throughout, in particular *Chronicles* I-III for the three-volume transcription of Mabel Bent's notebooks in the archives of the Joint Library of the Hellenic and Roman Societies, London; 'Bent 1885b' for J.T. Bent *The Cyclades, or Life Among the Insular Greeks* (new edition, Oxford 2002).

In her notebooks Mabel Bent throughout refers to her husband as 'T' and their assistant Manthaios Símos as 'M'.

Acknowledgements

The Bents were early members of the Hellenic Society, founded in 1879, with Theodore being on the Council for several years. The present editor is indebted to the Officers and Council for their permission to publish transcriptions of these notebooks. The Society helps to maintain the Joint Library, in conjunction with the Roman Society, in whose archives Mabel's *Chronicles* are preserved. Sincere thanks are due to the Librarian, Colin Annis and his Deputy, Paul Jackson, and Senior Library Assistant, Susan Willetts.

Mabel and Theodore had no children, but several descendants of Mabel's siblings have been generous with their time in replying to questions and requests for family information. Mrs Clody Norton initially opened the door for me to the Hall-Dare family and their splendid home in Co. Wexford.

As well as acknowledging departmental staff at the British Museum, the Bodleian Library and the British Library, thanks must go to other British institutions with important collections of material relating to the Bents, including the Royal Botanic Gardens, Kew, the Royal Geographical Society, London, and the Pitt Rivers Museum, Oxford.

This volume begins with two quotations: The Edward Lear extract (May 1862 or 1863) is taken from *Edward Lear: A Biography* by Peter Levi (1995, p. 192). The Robert Byron quotation is from *Europe in the Looking-Glass* (2012, p. 212).

It is a great pleasure to include in this book a Preface by Marc Dubin, whose reference to the Bents, in a publication in the 1980s, engaged this editor's fascination with them.

Of the many fellow-travellers encountered on this project, the providers of serendipitous details and support along the way, singled out are David Davison and Rajka Makjanić, Glyn Griffiths and Revis Cruttenden, Michael, Mary and Iannis Nisiriou, Constance Rivemal and David Tomory, Ianna Bitha, Nikos Kasseris, Katerina Giannoula, Stephanie and Keith Ambridge, and Ourania Kostara.

This book is in fondest memory of Allan Millar Davidson (1941-2014) of Crete, islomane. XAIPE.

Gerald Brisch
Oxford – Megálo Horió, Tílos
January 2015

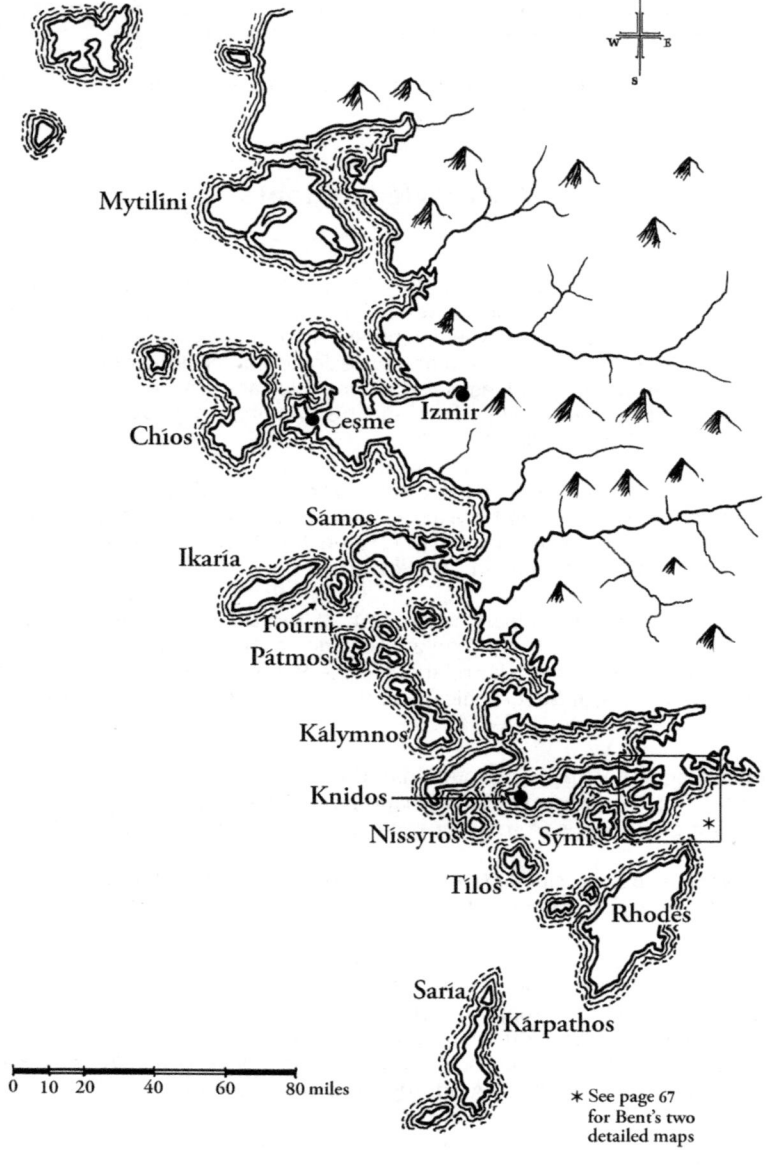

Rhodes[1]

If an invalid, that is to say an invalid whose malady merely necessitates his removal to an excellent climate, wishes to strike out a new line for himself, and to get rid of the conventionalities of popular health resorts, he could do no better than plunge into the Turkish Island of Rhodes. He will probably find that he is the only Englishman there; he will be as safe as anywhere in Europe; he will enjoy a climate where winter is unknown and summer heats are tempered by sea breezes; he will be made much of as the snug little inn; and he will be received with open arms by as conglomerate a society as the world can well produce.

In the bazaar of a morning he will be able to chat with exiled Turkish pashas, who are paying the penalty of their misfortunes in the Russian war; he will meet Italians and Greeks, Spanish Jews, Levantine English, and Asiatics – nay even Egyptian exiles will be in his visiting list, which will afford him a wonderful and diversified study of humanity. When tired of the town he can wander through mountain villages and study the simplicity of the Greek peasantry, whose homes have been undisturbed by the successive occupation of Italians, Knights of St. John, and Turks.

Rhodes is an open roadstead now, for the Turks have allowed the excellent harbour to become choked up with rubbish, so there is often some difficulty attending the landing there; not infrequently during stormy weather the steamers on their way north and south have to pass without touching. This is an obvious inconvenience in winter when storms are of frequent occurrence. A Smyrniote lady a few months ago had to pass her destination three times, and spend three weeks on the sea between Smyrna and Alexandria before she could be put ashore at the haven where she would be.

The portly hotel keeper, Nicholas, is sure to appropriate the stranger on the steamer and carry him to his hostelry in the Greek quarter, built on a sandy promontory about half a mile from the old walled town. It is as quaint an inn as one could possibly desire, with snug little rooms giving on to a balcony which overhangs a courtyard with pebbles. As he enters the dark archway he will be confronted with the larder, for here junks[2] of meat are hung from the rafters by pulleys so that they can be let down when a slice is required. Granny, Nicholas's mother, is the moving spirit of the inn. She toils from morning to night with her legs bare, and her head enveloped in a dirty black handkerchief. She cuts the wood; she tills the vegetable garden; she answers every clap of the hands, for there are no bells. She is the recognized slave of the establishment. It is always the same amongst these Greeks; old age is treated with no respect. It is to them a recognised law of nature that when the body is

---

[1] The Bents stayed on Rhodes from Friday 6 February to Friday 20 February 1885. This article appeared later that same year as 'Rhodian Society' (*Macmillan's Magazine* 52 (1885: May/Oct), pp. 297-303).
[2] 'Chunks'.

The D'Amboise Gate, one of the monumental entrances to the Old Town of Rhodes.

decaying it must give way to the rising generation. It is a common sight to see a gaily-dressed young married woman riding a mule, accompanied by her tottering old mother on foot as muleteer. This evil is in measure atoned for by the devotion which exists between brother and sister. No brother thinks of marrying until he sees each sister provided with a husband, and many romantic stories occur in this respect; perhaps it is the same with all primitive societies, that the useless aged are deemed of no account.

Everything is pebbled in Nicholas's hotel – the courtyard, the dining-room, the balcony, are all laid out in patterns of black and white. These pebbles are quite a trade in Rhodes; veiled Turkish women wander along the shore in search of them, and deposit their treasures in little heaps along the beach. In the good time of the Khedive Ismail in Egypt, very large quantities were exported to Cairo, and large fortunes were realized thereby. Even now the trade is a good one, and every Rhodian house is adorned with them. If you go out into society, you will find before long, to your cost, that you have to dance on a pebbled floor.

The Turkish element in Rhodes is larger than in most towns of the Turkish Empire; the whole of the old walled town which the Knights of St. John built and fortified is inhabited by Turks and Spanish Jews. No Christians are allowed within the gates after they are shut at sunset.[3] No beasts of burden are allowed inside the town at any time, for there

---

[3] Thus the Bents are obliged to lodge in a hotel in the narrow lanes of Neohóri (or 'Neo Marás' as Mabel refers to it), some of which remain, towards the tip of the modern town. This area seems to have provided accommodation regularly for 'Franks', as noted by H.F. Tozer and, in particular, C.T. Newton, the archaeologist.

is a current tradition amongst the Turks that the Christians will follow in their wake as conquerors. Very few Turks live outside in the villages, and when they do they can hardly be distinguished from the Greeks, whose dress, customs, and in many cases religion, they have adopted. It is a curious feature in these degenerate descendants of Mohammed, that they are not content to trust to their own prophet alone for succour. If they hear of a miracle-working Madonna, they are no above sending her a present, and worshipping at her shrine.

The Turk of Rhodes, curiously enough, is a more energetic individual than the Greek. Many of them are fishermen, and possess light sailing vessels for this purpose. Others are blacksmiths, tanners, painters and joiners. The bazaars are chiefly conducted by their industry, and they may be seen plying their various trades all day long in tiny boxes along the streets. The Greek is an idle vagabond for the most part, whose great ambition is to become proprietor of a sweet shop, to which is added, as time goes on, a bar for spirits and sometimes a café. They pass their days in complete inactivity in the midst of tobacco fumes, listening to the shrill sound of a lyre, and singing bacchic songs. In these establishments the oft-recurring feast days are observed with rigorous fidelity, and from morning till night drunken revelry is conducted therein. As for the Greek women, they never seem to have anything to do; they sit on their doorsteps and gossip from morning to night. They are a degraded lot; and the ease with which a husband can get a divorce on the merest caprice cannot tend to elevate them.

It is not difficult to make your way into the society of Rhodes. If you stroll down the bazaars of a morning, enter the druggists' shops and talk to the first person you meet, you will immediately be welcomed as an addition to the circle. You are sure to come across the stout florid ex-minister of war, Rigdoff Pasha, who was sent off here after the Russian affair, and has not yet succeeded in obtaining leave to return to Constantinople; he will taking a cup of coffee in the principal druggist's shop, and will be complaining in bitter terms of the narrow limits of his present society as compared to what he was accustomed to in 'the city'.

Mohammed Pasha has been more fortunate; he was recalled from this exile a short time ago to the sphere of his former labours. When in Rhodes he bought for 250l. a most charming residence, with lovely grounds and views over the mountains of Caria, and sheltered from every wind by Mount Smith, which rises just behind the town, and still retains the name and memories of Sidney Smith, who lived there for a short time.

But the aged Suleiman Pasha is perhaps the most fortunate of all these Turkish exiles. After being known as the Victorious, the Invincible, he belied his epithets at the Shipka Pass, and was banished for life to Rhodes. This life came to a close at the advanced age of ninety-six, when we were in Rhodes, and we attended his simple but impressive funeral.

Khamel Bey is governor of Rhodes. He is an invalid, and does not often appear in the bazaars or at the bath, and he now lives in Mohammed Pasha's charming house. He is a man of extraordinary literary attainments for a Turk, and is considered the best poet they have; but his writings are too liberal and European to suit the Sultan, who pays him 50l. a year to keep his pen quiet – quite a novel and oriental way of making the profession of literature pay. He has one son, Khem Bey, a youth of twenty, who affects most oppressively dilettante manners. We asked him why he had not seen him at any of the social gatherings, and if he liked dancing. 'No,' he replied, 'I always remember what Napoleon the Great said of dancing

The latter records a stay on Rhodes in the summer of 1853, and his later account is still of the greatest interest and enjoyment as an early guide (*Travels and Discoveries in the Levant*, 1865, pp. 146-214).

Turkish cemetery, Rhodes Town.

– that it was too trivial for a soldier. But,' continued he, 'for some years I gave way to a life of pleasure, the chase, riding, &c., but now my papa has impressed me with the necessity of work, and my only diversion is a little walk.' He is not a pleasant youth to look upon, being fat and pasty, and as he talks to you he cracks his knuckle joints in a most irritating fashion.

Many of the Turks are the proprietors of gardens and houses on the slopes behind the town, just outside the dismal belt of Turkish tombs which entirely hems in the town on the land side. These gardens they cultivate with truly oriental laziness. We were surprised occasionally to see their wives assisting in the garden, hewing wood, drawing water, and making themselves generally useful. Turkish women are not so strict about veiling themselves as they used to be; some indeed affect very thin gauze veils, whilst others do not mind showing their faces to a Frank, and only cover themselves when they see a red fez coming along. Owing to the poverty which reigns in Turkey, harem life is not what it used to be; most men can only afford one wife, and she must be useful as well as ornamental. All the lovely embroideries which travellers see in the show harems of Constantinople or Smyrna have long since disappeared from ordinary homes, and have found their way to European markets.

As a rule the Greeks and Turks of the upper class do not amalgamate so well as those of the lower. The better-class Greek is aware of the state of politics in Europe, and looks ardently for the day when he will cease to be a Turkish subject; such matters do not trouble the peasant population, who live like beasts in the darkest ignorance. But the upper-class Greek is essentially an astute time-server. He knows well how to make himself indispensable to the Konak, and treats the governor with flattery and respect, reserving his remarks on freedom for the bosom of his own family or the ears of an Englishman. He is the personification of the traditional old Greek woman, who always in church lit one candle before the picture of St. George and another before a picture of the devil, and, in reply to inquiries, stated it as her principle always to be well in with both parties.

Sometimes as a Greek party you may meet a few Turks, but they sit together in the smoking-room, growling away at their narghiles. They never join in the dance, and if one may judge from their faces, one would say that they are internally laughing at what they see; and well they may, for a Turkish gentleman is always a man of refined manners and good breeding, and that cannot be said of the Greeks of Rhodes. A ball in a Greek house is a thing for ever to be remembered. The dresses of the ladies would provoke a smile from even the most indifferent beholder. Round dances are not much appreciated; but what they really love is a species of romping quadrille with most complicated figures, through which a master of the ceremonies puts you in vile French. On one occasion this official insisted on directing us to dance a variety of the Lady's Chain,[4] which he called *Chaîne de Chevaliers*, and which my partner naïvely remarked was excusable in a place which is everywhere haunted by reminiscences of the Knights of Rhodes.

When the romp was over we conducted our partners to the smoking-room, where the chaperones were sitting, smoking cigarettes, and where the air was dense with fumes of tobacco. I noticed that the younger ladies did not venture on the entire control of a cigarette themselves, but pressed their partners to do so, with a view to enjoying an occasional pull. Supper was provided on the most primitive principles. A large dish of tinned lobster salad was put on a table, round which everyone crowded; those who were not lucky enough to secure a knife did not hesitate to plunge their fingers into the tempting dish. Glasses of wine circulated freely, and after the repast was over the ball degenerated into a scene worthy of a Parisian music-hall. No wonder the Turks smiled a little as they watched this scene, and retired as soon as politeness would permit.

Another easy method of studying this conglomerate society is afforded by the bath. Every Rhodian, of whatever nationality, indulges in the Turkish bath on some day or another in the week, from the lowest menial to the exiled pashas, and everyone pays according to his rank. The common soldiers – of whom there are plenty in Rhodes – only pay a penny a piece; they go to the bath in companies, and they shampoo and rub each other. Anybody who has travelled in the Turkish dominions will have been struck with the wretchedness of the soldiers' uniform, but this is nothing to their underclothing, any portion of which a London beggar would reject with scorn. When a pasha is coming to take a bath they clear the place of all such objectionable people, and the pasha is then supposed to leave a pound after he has bathed. This must be a great tax on their limited incomes, and if Khamel Bey were to be regular in his ablutions he would more than exhaust all the income that he derives from not writing, in this way. This Turkish method of making the rich pay for washing the

---

[4] In which the ladies advance, extending their right hands to each other and pulling by. The men step forward and then right, turning left to face in the same direction as the lady beside him; she offers her left hand to the man and turns with a token courtesy. The couples complete the move facing each other.

poor certainly has decided merits, worthy of the consideration of reformers, who might enlarge upon it. For instance, if every time we bought a new pair of trousers we had to supply a pauper with a pair of corduroys, our poor-rate might be so elegantly disguised in tailors' and other bills that we should cease to grumble.

The Spanish Jews are not a pleasing element in Rhodian society. With the usual astuteness of their race they have managed to secure for themselves the best quarter of the walled town, and they are as far as possible removed from the Greeks, for there is always enmity between Greek and Jew. In Greece, properly so called, a Jew is rarely seen; and a Greek, if he mentions a Jew in conversation, always apologises for alluding to so despicable a personage. These Jews, however, have interesting costumes, and a most astonishing *patois*, being quite the most polyglot I ever struggled with; and the Jewish children in Rhodes are far more inquisitive than those of other nationalities. If you venture into the Jewish quarter you are sure to be mobbed by them; and this you must do, for these Israelites have secured for themselves the best houses in the old town, containing wood carving and decorations dating from the days of the Knights.

The Jewish 'Sunday' is the recognized beggars' day in Rhodes. Beggars from the country villages invade the town on Saturday afternoon, and they do not disguise their expectations, for they all carry on their shoulders many-coloured mule bags in which to deposit the alms which they collect from door to door; and to judge by what one sees, the Rhodians appear to be very generous: a beggar is never refused. On Saturday morning the housewife collects in the corner of the yard scraps of food which she doles out to each beggar as he comes; and most of the peasants when they come into the town with their market produce deposit a gift of fruit or vegetables by what is commonly known as the lepers' well.

As spring comes on – and spring comes on early in Rhodes – the invalid will doubtless feel anxious to see what the Rhodian peasants are like in their mountain villages. The lovely slopes around the town, the old walls and fortifications around the harbour, the gay scenes in the bazaar will pall in time; he may try his strength by hiring one of the tiny Rhodian donkeys, no bigger than a large Newfoundland dog, which will take him to Mount Philerimo, from which he will enjoy one of nature's most lovely views, and whet his appetite for a more extended tour. If he would see the peasant in his full simplicity, he must go some days' journey inland to the village of Embona, on the slopes of Mount Atabyros, the ancient hill of Jupiter, where two temples stood in olden times, and where was the bronze ox which bellowed whenever any evil was in store for Rhodes – a story of antiquity which has lately been in a measure substantiated by the discovery of numerous little bronze votive figures of bulls. Doubtless the bellowing bull was something like the oracle of Delphi, over the utterings of which the priests had entire control.[5]

The country folk of Rhodes cannot be said to be either rich or poor. Everyone has a house which he has probably built for himself, and a plot of land, containing olives, figs, and vegetables. The ordinary peasant's house consists of one square room; the roof is made by placing rough branches of cypress trees on the walls, on which are spread reeds and oleander branches, with the leaves left on. Upon this foundation is deposited a certain kind of earth, which they press with rollers and with the foot until it attains the firm consistency of cement, and is usually impervious to rain. The interior of this house is humble enough: the floor is of pressed manure, and the furniture of the simplest. A sort of platform, supported by four stakes fixed in the ground, and surrounded by planks, answers two purposes; within is the family store-room, above is the family bed – not that the family

---

[5] There is no indication in Mabel's diary that the couple ever travelled on the island further than Triánda.

Lindos, Rhodes.

trouble the bed much, except on the three important occasions of birth, marriage, and death. They chiefly lie down to sleep wherever night overtakes them – in winter on their home-spun cloaks, and in summer on the grass. Against the bed is placed a great chest, which also serves for two purposes, firstly, as a step by which to climb on to the platform, and secondly, as a wardrobe for the family clothes, the gay costumes which are only brought out on feast days and marriages. Along the wall runs a long sort of settee, the top of which is covered with many-coloured cushions, and inside which is the granary, and the receptacle for all sorts of horrible luxuries, in which the frugal Rhodians indulge when their lengthy fasts do not compel them to abstain – rancid lard, which they dignify with the name of 'pig's butter,' to distinguish it from 'milk butter;' red caviare and old twisted rolls of bread, which have developed more or less of green mould, according to the lapse of time they were made for the last festival.

Then there is a hole in the wall in which the water-jug is leaning, for these primitive mountaineers still adhere to the same shape of jars, made on the principle of soda-water bottles with no foot, in which their forefathers rejoiced. The inconvenience of these is great, and why the Greeks should have been so conservative in this respect for so many centuries is unaccountable. The walls are surrounded by plates and jugs for household use. Once upon a time these utensils consisted of Lindos ware, but now these have all found their way to the museums and drawing-rooms of Europe. The greatest feature of a peasant's house is the decoration of the wall opposite the door as you enter. In the middle of this wall is a large painting in numerous compartments, the work of some local artist, the subject of which it is often very difficult to discover; they are always devotional, illustrating some quaint legend in a highly grotesque fashion.

For example, on one wall we saw the legend of St. Gregory Thaumatourgos (the miracle worker) represented in the following fashion: The saint in one portion of the picture was followed by two individuals dressed in Phrygian caps; they entered a forest which was represented by three trees, like those of a child's farmyard, reaching up to the waists of the men. Another portion of the picture represented them as cutting off a branch, which act is for the benefit of the uninitiated described in writing. Again the branch is next represented as having grown too big for the men to carry, so they dig a hole, plant it, and watch it growing to an enormous size. Next we saw St. Gregory and his friends filling gourds at a stream so as to water their new plant, and on their return they found to their surprise that a church had sprung up where the branch had been planted, and the holy men were so amazed at this phenomenon that they did not perceive the devil sneaking up behind and drinking the water in the gourds so that they might not be able to water the newly-planted church; but in this extremity the final portion of the picture depicted St. Gregory's horse as appearing on the scene, and before the devil had time to empty the gourds he was kicked back into hell.

This picture is always painted in startling colours, and rejoices in surprising contrasts, and it is the special property of the master of the house; all the rest, the house, the furniture, and the plate, are the wife's property, and will go to her eldest daughter. No Rhodian peasant girl is eligible for the marriage market until her parents or next of kin have provided her with a house and furniture. Under the great picture are hung the wedding crown, a profusion of plates, bottles, images of saints, scraps of illustrated European papers – anything in short that is deemed to possess decorative merit. An oil lamp, suspended from the roof, hangs before this picture, and is lighted every night in honour of the saint represented thereon. Chairs and tables are deemed superfluous in these houses; they sit on the ground, and eat of a big bowl placed in their midst.

If the hardships of a few days in this mountain village are not too much for our invalid he will revel in the simplicity of these people. He will be treated with that primeval hospitality which teaches that to place before the guest the best of everything is a duty imposed by the gods. Before he has partaken of food he will not be asked whence he has come or whither he is going. From all the cottages round the peasants will bring gifts to assist the host in entertaining; one will bring a fat sucking pig, another wine, another fruit, eggs, and milk; the best embroideries will be spread over his bed, and in that hyperbole, which finds such favour amongst Greeks, he will be pressed to stay a thousand years under the hospitable roof. If this lengthy invitation be commuted by promising to stay a few days the guest will see much to amuse him. He will assuredly be asked to stand as godfather to any unbaptised infant that the place may produce – a doubtful compliment indeed when it is considered that the godfather has to provide quite a *trousseau* for the child; but in this delicate way he will be able to repay the hospitality with which he has been received, for a direct offer of money would be considered rather an insult than otherwise.

Then again the guest is sure to develop a hitherto unknown talent – he will find that he has quite an extensive knowledge of medicine as compared to these poor peasants. In a remote corner of the world where doctors do not exist, and where the people are too poor to send for one from the town, it is extraordinary to find how the inhabitants live and die without the most rudimentary knowledge of physic. Charms and incantations abound, to be sire; traditional remedies for both external and internal use, in which garlic and onions are the chief ingredients, are numerous; and there will always be found an old crone who visits the invalids with a sickle in he hand, and executes certain passes around them as she mutters her incantations in an awe-inspiring voice; but of the use of the simple remedies with which the country abounds, the aromatic herbs, chamomile, rue, &c. – this old crone is profoundly ignorant. And the stranger who comes amongst them with quinine, pills, vaseline, and the ordinary stock of a traveller's medicine chest, will be embarrassed not only by the multiplicity of his patients, but also by the nature of his fees – hard boiled, coloured Easter eggs, stale bread, snails, and kindred luxuries will be showered upon him by his grateful patients.

The village priest will soon be discovered to be the ringleader of all superstitious practices he, of course, is only a peasant himself, and he has no income except what he gets from reading liturgies, consequently it is only natural that he should seek to multiply the occasions for these liturgies by every means in his power, even though his bishop has given strict orders to the contrary.

Many of these liturgies are performed under cover of night, and at the dark of the moon. A mother may be seen secretly carrying a sickly child to church, that the priest may read an exorcism over it to drive away the demon which she thinks possesses it; for this he receives twice as much as for a liturgy during the day. The priest again will be summoned by a farmer whose shed is infested by rats and mice, to exorcise the same. Under an ancient olive with gnarled stem and creeping branches he will read the liturgy to St. Tryphon; the farmer will say the following words: –

> 'Rats and mice, and vermin vile,
> Hurry away full many a mile;
> That I may gather in my seed
> Free from such a hurtful breed.'

The priest has a cure for fever, too; he writes on a scrap of paper 'Mother of God, divine miracle;' this he ties round the sufferer's neck with a red thread, and goes away with a fee in his pocket, or with a basket of bread and figs on his arm. No wonder the priests support superstitions which pay so well, and that they and the old crone are great allies, and throw work into one another's hands. Perhaps they will look suspiciously at the traveller's quinine and pills as commodities likely to interfere with their practice; but I don't think they need be afraid as long as the Turks rule in Rhodes, and education is at a discount.

Níssiros [6]

We will now proceed to take examples of the educational work that is in progress from various points of the Turkish Empire. Where the monastic resources are sufficient, and where help is not urgently required, matters are allowed to pursue their old course. On the island of Nisyros, for instance, we found the Archimandrite Cyril, of the monastery of the Holy Virgin of the Cave, the chief mover in the diminutive society on this island; besides acting as banker for the peasants and issuing cardboard notes, an inch and a half square and of the value of one penny each, signed by his name, as a medium for exchange,[7] and, besides paying for a doctor, who attends the poor people free of charge, he has likewise, with the income of the monastic property, established a boys' school and a girls' school at Mandraki,

---

[6] From Rhodes, by way of Sými and Hálki, the Bents reached Níssiros late on 21 February 1885 and left on the 24th for Tílos. This extract is from 'Modern Life and Thought amongst the Greeks', published in *National Life and Thought of the Various Nations Throughout the World: A Series of Addresses* (London 1891, pp. 287-302).

[7] Mabel exhibited one in her display for the Royal Anthropological Institute in 1886. She describes it as: 'A banknote, a card 1¼ inches square, covered with paper with the name of the Monastery of Spiliane and the signature of Kyrillos, the Prior, who issues them – legal tender in the Turkish island of Niseros.' (*Journal of Royal Anthropological Institute*, Vol. XV (4), 1886, pp. 391-403)

the chief village on the island, which are presided over by efficient teachers, who have been sent out thither through the agency of the Society;[8] the books of instruction have likewise been provided from the same source. But all this has been done at the expense of the monastery, which is a prosperous one; and to realise the real benefit of religious institutions on mankind, and the readiness with which even effete monastic institutions work for the advancement of the Greek race, one ought to travel in the out-of-the-way corners of the Turkish Empire.

In Greece proper, the work of the monasteries is practically over, since the Government has taken upon itself the sole superintendence of education, and is alone responsible for the improvement of the people. What monasteries once were, and what good they have done, can now only be realised in Turkey; the smaller ones, as the one in Nisyros, for example, have provided education for the masses; the larger ones, as Mount Athos, have provided instruction in the higher branches of learning, and act as universities; and it is a question open to much doubt, as to whether the Greeks have benefited by the transfer of education from the priests, who have acted for ages as their protectors from annihilation and barbarism, to the Government schools; in Turkey, as we have seen, they provide for the better education of the clergy, and, if this can be effected, the priesthood will continue as the natural instructors of their flocks.

On the neighbouring island of Telos, which is inhabited by semi-barbarous Greeks, living in a state of shocking ignorance and superstition, the monastery, in a similar fashion, has of late years commenced to work for the good of the people. Five years ago, the monks decided to expend £25 per annum on the maintenance of a schoolmaster, who gave us a lamentable account of the ignorance he found there, and which still exists among the elder inhabitants; but when we visited the school, each boy had in his hands the books which the Society has printed for educational purposes, and the elder ones could read Xenophon quite fluently, and translate it into modern Greek. The monastery of Telos is far from being as rich as that of Nisyros, so the inhabitants have to die without physic, and the girls have to grow up without instruction; but doubtless, in good time, the Society will step in and see to the rectification of the latter deficiency, for such ground as this is the field on which the Society has done such admirable work elsewhere. But the island of Telos is only thinly populated, and as remote a spot as well could be found from any centre of civilisation.

Tílos[9]

I do not think anything but a wedding of magnificent proportions, and the festivities attendant thereon, will ever take anybody to Telos, an insignificant island off the coast of Asia Minor, unapproached by steamer, rarely visited even by sailing boats, and possessing only two small villages, one of which is known as 'the town' and the other as 'the other place,' no more elaborate nomenclature being thought necessary.

---

[8] Theodore refers to the Greek Philological Association (Hellenic Philological Syllogos/Ellinikos Philologikos Syllogos) founded in March 1861 in Constantinople. For its patriotic aims and history, see http://constantinople.ehw.gr/Forms/fLemmaBodyExtended.aspx?lemmaID=11575.

[9] Arriving from Níssiros, the Bents stayed on Tílos from Wednesday, 25 February to Thursday, 5 March 1885. Theodore's article 'A Protracted Wedding' appeared in *The Gentleman's Magazine* in October 1888 (pp. 330-341). Oddly, a slightly reworked version with the same title was published by him in 1891 for the *English Illustrated Magazine* (93: June, pp. 672-676) but with a slightly less sour ending.

Acropolis above Megálo Horió, Tílos.

These villages offer absolutely no attractions, and are, as my friend in Rhodes told me, who excited my curiosity by accounts of weddings, full of lepers, 'there is not a clean house on the island,' he added, wishing to dissuade me from my desire to go. But we went, my wife and I, and our servant Matthew,[10] and with us we carried our beds, our frying-pan, and numerous little comforts, determined to brave the dangers of leprosy and starvation, with the sole object of seeing two foolish young Teliotes joined together in holy matrimony.

On the eve of a fine February day we reached Telos in a small sailing craft, thankful enough to have escaped the treacheries of a winter's sail in these dangerous waters, and, as we approached, some few inhabitants came down to stare at us, prior to beating a hasty retreat, and for some time after we landed we could not induce them to approach. 'They take you for pirates,' said our sailors, and, to assure them that our intentions were anything but hostile, we despatched Matthew to open negotiations. Very soon we were surrounded by a jabbering crowd, to whom it conveyed nothing when we stated that England was our native place; their only tangible geographical idea was Constantinople, and England they supposed must be some neighbouring village.

These first acquaintances of ours on Telos were all women, dressed oddly enough; on their heads they wore a red-peaked cap, like those Phrygian helmets one sees on old vases, tied on with a red handkerchief round the forehead; from their ears hung down immense silver rings or bangles, five or six in each ear, until the lobe of their poor ears was distorted in a truly revolting

---

[10] A first reference by Theodore to Matthew (Manthaios, and other spelling variants) Símos from Anáfi. Manthaios travelled as far as Yemen and the Sudan with the Bents during the term of his employment with them. Just twelve years later (1897) he helped the couple, desperately ill from malaria, return home from Aden. Theodore lived a few days more.

The Bents' Greek friend and dragomános, Manthaios Símos, in old age and among his family.

manner. They had on dark-brown coats of course home-spun material, which came below the knee, and they were girt with a red girdle; beneath this coat peeped their white shirt, rich at the edge with many-coloured embroidery; as for their feet, they were bare just now, and their long yellow leather shoes, with pointed ends, were cast on one side, for the women down here were washerwomen, engaged in treading flannel clothes and other things on boards; for the Teliote women wash in this fashion with their feet, like Nausicaa and her maidens, who 'bore the clothes to the black water, and briskly trod them down in the trenches in busy rivalry.'

We were soon excellent friends, and, as the shades of evening were coming on, the quaint females offered to carry our luggage for us up to 'the town'; they led the way with an agile bounding step, making nothing of the weights they carried, and when we reached 'the town' after half an hour's walk we were almost breathless. Not all the inhabitants of Telos were so wanting in education as our first acquaintances. Mr. Kammas, to whom we had a letter from Rhodes, knew all about England, and what an important place it was; but still neither he, nor the Superior of the convent, nor the schoolmaster, appeared to be conversant with the topics of the day. The Russo-Turkish war was our chief theme of conversation, and was treated as if it was quite the latest piece of news on record. During the winter months there is no communication with the outer world, and only on great occasions, when Mr. Kammas goes to Rhodes to sell a cargo of grain, and buy with the proceeds European wonders with which to dazzle the Teliote eyes, does news penetrate thus far.

Late in the evening the Superior conducted us to his convent, which was to be our home during our stay on Telos,[11] and after making minute and satisfactory inquiries with regard to leprosy and its relation to monks, we retired to a cell which was set apart for us. This was a fair-sized airy room, for the windows had no glass in them, only shutters: nevertheless, when these were shut, our abode was haunted by several smells, for each of which we subsequently discovered a sufficient reason. Smell number one arose from the fact that the Superior was by trade a maker of those long yellow shoes we had seen the women wear, and the cell adjoining ours was the depot for his indifferently cured hides. Smell number two arose from the fact that the Superior kept and fattened snails for his own table in a cupboard beneath the settee which ran along on side of the cell. Many of these dainties lay dead at the bottom of their prison, and the survivors did not look at all inviting. Numerous minor smells arose from the harbouring of horrible 'tit-bits' in the various cupboards, all of which we unceremoniously expelled.

---

[11] The little monastery where they lodged below Megálo Horió can still be entered.

The small monastery, just below Megálo Horió, where the Bents roomed on Tílos.

Weddings in Telos usually take place before the great feast,[12] but the Superior informed us that weddings in Telos are by no means of annual occurrence; but, as we manifested such extreme anxiety on this point, he promised to send a messenger at once to know whether a certain Peter and a certain Catharine would be married this year or not, and during the absence of this messenger we remained in great suspense, for on this depended whether our journey to Telos would be a futile one or not.

It was greatly to our contentment when we learnt that the parent of Peter and Catherine had definitely decided that their children should commit matrimony this year, and that the crowning ceremony would be on the following Sunday fortnight, and although we disliked the long detention among the lepers of Telos, we decided to remain and see it all to the bitter end.[13]

Never shall I forget our first walk through 'the town' under the guidance of our host. I tried to sketch some of the women as they sat spinning on their roofs, but they either flew

---

[12] The 'great feast' on the island is that of Ayíou Pandelímona, 25-27 July every year.

[13] Mabel makes no mention at all of this wedding in her diary (and efforts to trace the island's records have failed). The couple's stay on the island was only some 10 days, not long enough to attend the various celebrations to which Theodore refers. Everything points to him having made up this particular ceremony, but the ritual components are genuine.

Megálo Horió, Tílos: 'I tried to sketch some of the women... but they either flew into a passion, threatening dire revenge, or ran hurriedly away. No bribe whatsoever would induce any of them to stand for a photograph.'

into a passion, threatening dire revenge, or ran hurriedly away. No bribe whatsoever would induce any of them to stand for a photograph; they believed that we intended to work magic on them, and that, if their image appeared on paper, they would pine away and die.

We entered with trepidation some of the dark houses, which crept like the steps of a giant's ladder up the mountain side. Some of the inmates were crouching on the floor, taking their midday meal, which they eat, like swine, out of a large round trough called a *skaphos*, which is placed in the midst; on a festival day the meal consists of rice, onions, and oil, all boiled together, poured into this trough, and eaten with a wooden spoon; on ordinary days they eat nothing but bread and olives. This trough, too, serves for other purposes; on the seventh day after birth they choose the child's name saint after this fashion: the trough is put in the middle room, and the infant, according to its sex, is placed naked on a bundle of its father's or mother's clothes in the trough; around it burn seven candles of equal length, each dedicated to a saint; in solemn silence the family sit around, singing and praying, until one candle goes out and determines the patron saint and name of the infant.

The invalids of Telos soon found us out, and came to us with all manner of strange sores and diseases to be healed. No doctor lives on this remote island; they have no drugs, and they live and die as birds of the air. Our limited pharmacopœia, which chiefly consisted of pills, quinine, and Vaseline, was taxed to the utmost; this latter remedy was the only one we had to offer to the 'decayed men,' as they call the lepers, who lurk in the dark corners of the houses, dreading to show their faces to strangers, for the Bishop of Rhodes is in treaty with the Government for the removal of these smitten creatures to the proper hospitals, and the ties of home and friendship are strong, and banishment to the island rock, where lepers are sent, is for them banishment for ever.[14]

It was on a Monday, nearly a fortnight before the appointed day for 'the crowning,' that the festivities for the wedding of Peter and Catherine began. The several families and friends of the bride and bridegroom, dressed in their best, came to the house of Catherine's parents. The bride elect was a somewhat wild defiant-looking young person, with her bright red cap and long yellow shoes: around her neck she wore rings of glass beads, and no less than fourteen bangles were suspended from her poor ears, through the holes in the lobes of which one could easily have passed a sixpence. She would have made an excellent model for a gypsy queen with her raven locks wandering over her rich mahogany-coloured cheeks tanned with exposure to the sun; her eyes were jet-black, her eyebrows deeply pencilled, her nose aquiline, and her teeth snow-white. On several occasions I tried to draw her, but she always darted away, until one day she fell into a great rage with me and I was warned to desist. When we left Telos, Catherine the bride carried some of our luggage to the boat, and when we pushed off from the shore I took out my book and pretended to draw, whereat she and the other women shook their fists at me and darted behind a rock.

Peter, the bridegroom, was just a clodhopping yokel unaccustomed to fine clothes, so he sat very erect in his embroidered waistcoat with red back and sleeves, looking anything but the happy man who was about to wed an heiress. Here, in Telos, the laws of succession are curious: a first-born daughter inherits all her mother's property, clothes and jewellery – even the stone slab in the woman's quarter in church, on which her maternal ancestors have stood and knelt for generations. The eldest son inherits his father's property, whereas younger daughters and younger sons inherit nothing, the result being that Teliote society is flooded with old maids, and younger sons go away to seek their fortunes elsewhere. Love matches and romance are unknown, and marriages are settled by the parents before the younger people know anything about it. No wonder Peter had a scared look on his face, for he was being driven into matrimony much as we should send a boy to school; and, furthermore, he was to receive with Catherine a goodly dower of lands, and this is a serious consideration to a Teliote, for in Telos everybody tills his own lands, and consequently the richest man is the greatest slave; so the position of a man about to wed an heiress appears under quite a different aspect in this primitive society.

Presently Papa Nicolaos walked in to give his blessing on the auspicious occasion, which we might designate a sort of public betrothal; but the Teliotes call it 'the lesser flour,' from the fact that a small portion of flour is ground in a handmill, blessed by the priest, and distributed to the guests; it is called the 'lesser,' to distinguish it from 'the greater flour,' a wedding ceremony which took place on the following Wednesday. With the lesser flour the festivities are thoroughly inaugurated; henceforth the bride's house presented a scene of perpetual bustle, for here were gathered together all her female relatives day by day, to assist in the preparation of the trousseau, which in Telos is not very elaborate.

---

[14] Spinalónga, off Crete, is the major example, the leper colony there expanding from the early 20th century.

It must be understood that the bride always provides the house and it is the first care of a Teliote parent to obtain a house for his marriageable daughter, to which she may bring home her man, on which occasion they throw stones into it with lichen attached expressing a wish, as they do so, that the man may cleave to his new home like the lichen to the stone. Catharine's house consisted of one large windowless room, as yet unfurnished, except for the raised platform at one end, where the beds would be spread, approached from the mud floor by two steep steps; beneath this was the cupboard where Catharine would keep her stores; all round the room were shelves on which would be placed the crockery, and from the ceiling hung a sort of net on a round stick, in which would be kept the bread. From another nail hung the branch of a tree, on which the wedding macaroni would be hung, and on the mud floor sat the women, stitching and sewing, and singing snatches of songs as they worked.

Papa Nicolaos was a constant visitor in our monastic cell, and he had many interesting things to tell us, which illustrated the superstitions and ignorance of out Teliote friends; amongst other things, he told us anecdotes about the devil and his influence over certain classes of diseases; epilepsy, nightmare, anything wrong with the stomach, are all attributed to the direct influence of his Satanic majesty.

I questioned him much on this subject, and to my utter confusion, at the conclusion of our conversation – for I did not think that my thirst for knowledge would be thus interpreted – he solemnly stated: ' If you are afraid you have a devil, burn incense at your door, light a candle to St. Basil, and all will go well.'

Our wedding festivities were renewed on Wednesday, when many guests wended their way to Catharine's house, bearing baskets of grain. In Telos wedding presents are exceedingly practical, and partake chiefly of the nature of food to be consumed at the wedding festivities; and towards evening on this day, when all the baskets of grain had been gathered together, the young men of the village distributed it to be ground in the hand-mills, and for the space of two hours nothing was to be heard in the town save the monotonous grinding of the two stones and the equally monotonous songs of the women engaged in this occupation. It was nearly dark when Peter, the bridegroom elect, was informed that all the flour was ground; whereupon certain young men of his acquaintance, with flutes, bagpipes, and lyres,[15] escorted him from house to house to collect this flour in large sacks. At each house they tarried for a little time, the instruments played, and the young men and maidens danced a curious little dance, in which one man and one maid alone take part, at the same time singing little love songs as they move to and fro.

From house to house they wandered, singing and dancing all the evening, and when the flour was collected they took it to Catharine's house, where a table was spread, at which the women who had ground the grain and the young men who had accompanied the bridegroom were entertained. After this meal, and when all were merry with wine, the dancing began again, and continued well into the night; it was very interesting and pretty to watch the interlaced Cretan dance, the quiet, stately, singing dances, and the brilliant acrobatic feats of the leader of the circular dance. Thus ended the great prenuptial ceremony of 'the greater

---

[15] This primitive bagpipe is the *tsamboúna* (see also page 32). A regional speciality is the fixing of small bells on the *lýra* bow. This originates from the times when the *lýra* (a sort of violin, placed upright on the knee) was played unaccompanied by the *laoúto* (guitar) and the bells would add interest. Theodore was a keen collector of musical instruments and brought back a *tsamboúna* and *lýra* and bow from Kárpathos to England. The *tsamboúna* was exhibited by the Bents at a meeting of the Anthropological Institute in 1886 and both instruments are now in the Pitt Rivers Museum, Oxford (1903.130.23) and 1903.131.18). He also acquired a reed 'trumpet' from the island, also at the Pitt Rivers (1888.37.5).

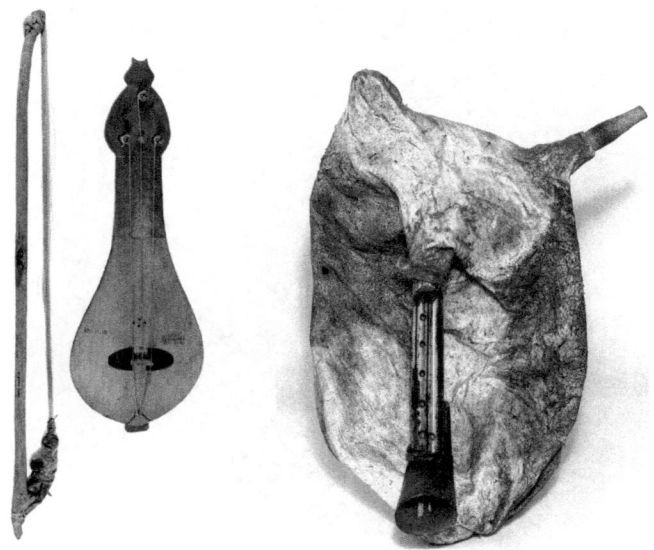

Theodore Bent's lýra *and* samboúna *acquired in the Dodecanese in 1885.*

flour.' Now the flour was all ready for the making of the macaroni and the bread, and Peter's shyness was beginning to wear off, and he accepted his position of hero of the occasion with a certain amount of grace, for which, at our first acquaintance, we had not given him credit.

We will hurry over the events of a few days passed by in our cell as best we could in endeavouring, for the most part in vain, to contend with our surrounding discomforts; we visited the cottages, wandered over the hills, made an expedition to 'the other place,' and killed time as those only can do whose interests are diversified.

The Sunday before 'the crowning' is the day on which the wedding festivities begin in real earnest. On the morning of that day, after the early service in the church, all Catharine's female friends assembled at her house to assist in making the macaroni for the succeeding feasts; each woman brought with her gifts – baskets of almonds, figs, and other produce of their gardens – and very hard they worked all that day, kneeling round the low wooden table, on which they the long strings of macaroni are rolled and then put out in the sun to dry. As the shades of evening draw on another festive gathering of men and maidens assembles; they collect the macaroni, bring it into the house with music and with song, and then hang it up on the tree branch from the ceiling to which we have already alluded.

Then again a table is spread, groaning with the presents of food and jugs of wine, and after all are satisfied and sufficiently hilarious they fall to dancing again. The capacity of a modern Greek for dancing is perfectly extraordinary; at weddings, at Eastertide, at pilgrimages, they will dance for whole days and nights with only sufficient interludes for the consumption of food and wine; it is the height of a young Greek's bliss to wave round perpetually in the enchanting circle like the Nereid goddesses which, they still tell you, haunt their glens, and whose passions for dancing can never be satiated.

Local produce for sale, Tílos.

Monday and Tuesday were again busy days of preparation – sewing, singing, and talking – but on the Wednesday before 'the crowning' the festivities commenced in uninterrupted succession. On the morning of this day Peter, the bridegroom, sent out his young male friends to the mountains to collect firewood for cooking the wedding meals, and towards evening, accompanied by all the youth and gaiety of Telos, he set forth to meet them on their return at a certain point, where they tarried to play, sing, and let off guns. It was a curious and pretty sight to see this cavalcade return home – the young men with their huge bundles of brushwood on their backs, others playing bagpipes and lyres, others singing, all excessively hilarious, and Peter heading the procession, gun in hand, which he constantly let off to indicate the exuberance of his feelings; and again the evening was closed with a feast and a dance.

The Thursday preceding the wedding is always devoted to catching fish for the wedding feast, if the sea be calm and the weather propitious. The day was everything that could be desired, and, as soon as the first rays of the sun appeared over the hills which encircle 'the town,' Peter was astir, collecting his friends, and despatching them with their nets down to the shore. During the course of the day we went down ourselves to watch them; the method of fishing in vogue in Telos is called *grypos*, and consists of throwing a very long net with corks attached out of a boat in a semicircle, at each end of which were long ropes, which the men pulled to draw in their spoil. It was a very picturesque sight indeed to see these simple-minded islanders at their work, cheering one another on with many a quaint saying and snatch of song; their legs were bare; their blue baggy trowsers [*sic*] were tucked up behind, and on each head was a weather-stained cap, which had once been red. As the day drew to a close Peter came down to see how his companions had fared, bringing with him the musicians and guns to fire off; and the procession homewards was again formed, baskets full of fish and dripping nets being this time the trophies. These were all deposited on the threshing-floor adjoining Catharine's house, and as soon as a portion of the fish had been fried they fell to their evening meal with hearty goodwill, and again the evening was passed in revelry and dancing.

Friday, too, had its special ceremony, and this time the young men were despatched by Peter to the shepherds on the mountain sides to purchase lambs and kids for the wedding feast, and in the afternoon he went forth again with the same retinue to meet them on their return. The victims were slaughtered on the bride's threshing-floor, and were skinned according to a process of their own, namely, by blowing under the skin with a tube. Many of the mountain shepherds had come down to join in the fun – wild, unkempt-looking men, who appeared to enjoy the evening meal immensely, and added to the riotous character of the ensuing dance by their wild laughter and curious antics.

Saturday was a very busy day indeed, for on the afternoon of this day Peter was to move; that is to say, all his clothes and personal effects were carried with music and much pomp from his father's house to that of his bride. They sang quaint little distichs as they carried his things, and Peter himself, whose voice was none of the sweetest, on leaving his father's roof, had to sing what I was told every Teliote bridegroom sings on a like occasion – some verses alluding in a poetical fashion to the bark which was about to set sail on the matrimonial ocean, and which began in this fashion: 'Rig the bulwarks, cast in ballast, this evening we must see that the ship is secure.'

On reaching the bride's house they deposited all the bundles on the floor, and dancing began; but this night it was only for a limited time, for at nine o'clock the music was peremptorily stopped, and the more solemn duties of the evening began. The fathers and mothers of the happy pair then proceeded to publicly announce what previously had only been arranged in private – the portions which they were prepared to bestow on their children. In this primitive society it is astonishing to see what sacrifices parents will make occasionally to secure what they think is a good match for their children. An old mother will give up everything to a daughter, and she will live as a menial in her daughter's house for the pleasure of speaking of her son-in-law the captain, or the schoolmaster. Old age is in no way respected, and at a certain time of life it would seem that they think that the declining generation ought to give place to others who are robust and in their prime.

The parents of Peter and Catharine no doubt did their duty on this point, but, not being intimately acquainted with their circumstances, I could not gauge the extent of their sacrifice. As soon as the business of the settlements was over, the clothes of the bride and bridegroom were spread out on the floor to receive the blessing of the priest. We admired the richly embroidered dresses which the mother was handing over to the sole and separate use of Catharine; the bright red Phrygian cap, decked with gold, for the coming wedding; the coarse silver jewellery, the weighty earrings, and the yellow shoes. All the guest assembled stood devoutly in a row as the priest pronounced his benediction, and after the clothes were properly blessed Papa Nicolaos turned round and blessed us all, in return for which attention everyone produced a coin and put it on a plate which was handed round. Papa Nicolaos himself handed round the dish with honey and sesame seeds on it, after he muttered a prayer over it, and, in the absence of spoons, each guest helped himself to some of this with his fingers; and, as he ate it, addressed the young couple with these, 'May your union be as sweet as honey, and as fruitful as the seeds of sesame.'

The most curious ceremony of all came next, namely, the hanging up the clothes (κρεμμαστρά as they call it). First of all, above the nuptial couch, the priest hung up with his own hands over a pole a piece of rich embroidery which is known as the *sperveri*, which, I imagine, corresponds to the *aski* or canopy which is hung over a Turkish bride; but I have no clue to the origin of the custom. Every family has a *sperveri* in its possession. Some of them are old and tattered, but they are regarded with especial veneration.[16]

From a pole suspended over the entrance into the house the young men next proceeded to suspend the clothes of both bride and bridegroom; and as each article was hung up eight young girls, four arm-in-arm at each side of the door, sang distichs as follows: First came an embroidered robe of Catharine's, and the maidens sang: 'The bride, the lovely bride, is like a well-freighted vessel, laden with golden apparel.' Then came a pair of blue baggy trowsers [*sic*] appertaining to Peter, and they sang: 'To-day the handsome Pallicari[17] has gained the queen, to-day they have read the firman from the city.'*[18] And so on until all the clothes were hanging from the pole, and each garment had been greeted by a song. These are not the clothes for the wedding, it must be understood, but the wardrobe which will last the young couple for their lives and be handed down to their children; and here they will be left to hang for forty days, after the expiration of which time the priest comes to bless them again, and they are taken down and put into chests.

For some time after this the young men and maidens continued their singing and their work, adorning the walls of the cottage with pieces of rich embroidery; and, having hung up the family pitchers to nails on the wall, and having arranged the family plates along the shelf, they then contemplated their work with satisfaction, as, indeed, they might, for they had converted the miserable hovel into a handsomely decorated drawing-room, such as no æsthetic lady of our refined age would have despised; and when it was all over every one retired for the night – all, indeed, except poor Peter, who was left to pass the last night of his bachelor life in solitude in his new home. The door was locked upon him by his best man, who carried off the key, and Catharine, the bride, was conducted to the house of her future mother-in-law, there to sleep her last maiden sleep.

Peter was released at an early hour by his best man, and came forth shy and diffident, though radiant in his new clothes; the bridesmaids were busy decking Catharine in her bridal attire; the crowns were made amidst singing, drinking, and general mirth; 'the town' was a lively scene of bustle and excitement, and towards midday the ceremony of 'crowning' took place in the church according to the usual rites of the Greek Church, which do not require to be described here, and Peter and Catharine came forth man and wife, to be embraced by an excited crowd in the courtyard of the church, and to have cotton seeds, almonds, and grain showered on their heads.

They were forthwith conducted to the bride's house, and, as the newly-married pair crossed the threshold, Peter threw in a rose and bruised it with his heel, symbolising thereby love and concord, and days to be passed as sweetly as the scent of the rose. His mother-in-law was there to meet him, holding in her hand the share of a plough, in which she had put some burning charcoal ashes; this she waved before the newly-married couple after the

---

[16] There are two *spervería*, embroidered bed canopies, in the Decorative Arts Collection (Folk Museum) in the Old Town, Rhodes.

[17] From 'palikar', warrior, but with the added meaning of 'gallant', or even 'pal'.

[18] * 'A relic of some old custom of getting a permit from Constantinople.' [Theodore's own footnote]

Easter goats at Ag. Andónios, Tílos. The Bents also landed here.

fashion of incense, and I was afterwards told that this ceremony is called the incensing of the share (τὸ θυμίαμα τοῦ ὑννίου): by this she is supposed to augur for them both strength, like the iron of the share, and success in agriculture.

Peter and Catharine entered their home, and were placed on a settee, to be stared at by their friends: she sat upright and defiant, as if quite accustomed to be married every day; he lolled awkwardly by her side, and played with his red silk sash in a nervous fashion. Trays of sweets and rakki[19] were handed round, bits of Turkish delight and honey cake, and, after the priestly blessing, the wedding party repaired to the bride's threshing-floor, where they danced until the shades of evening and the pangs of hunger obliged them to retire for the bridal banquet, at which a marvellous amount of fish and lamb was consumed.

Thus they cook their lambs in Telos: the flesh is cut into square lumps, and these are thrown into a huge cauldron which simmers for hours over a slow charcoal fire outside the door, casting its fragrance around to hungry nostrils. Each guest had a plateful of this savoury stew, besides much fish, much macaroni, and very much wine, so that when they returned again to the threshing-floor to resume the dance many steps were unsteady and many voices husky. They did not remain long here, for the rain came on and put out the torches which illuminated the scene, but they repaired to the bride's house, there to continue the orgy, whilst we, sickened by the stifling smell, preferred to bid adieu to the revellers and return to our monastic cell; and long after we were in our beds we heard the uproarious shouts of drunken men as they returned home from the nuptial feast.

Monday morning betimes Peter came forth from his new home in answer to the summons of his friends, who, having slept off their potations of the previous night, were anxious to plunge again into further dissipations. After partaking of a light repast of bread and olives the young men proceeded round 'the town' and issued invitations to what is called

---

[19] The ubiquitous grape spirit, rakí.

'the false wedding.' 'To-day is my wedding-day,' jocularly says the best man; 'let us celebrate it with more dancing and more drinking,' and the entertainment and food provided for that day is generally paid for by the best man. In short, it was an exact repetition of the previous day's festivities – more dancing, more singing, more drinking. Though these Greek islanders on similar occasions eat, drink, and make merry to excess, they are by no means drunkards; as a rule they drink nothing but water, and eat nothing but bread and olives; but at Easter time, pilgrimages, and weddings it is almost part of their creed to get drunk.

On Tuesday the same festivities occurred, but this time they took place on the threshing-floor and at the expense of a near relation. On the Wednesday we had planned to depart, but the winds were unfavourable. So we had to be present at what they called 'the cooks' day,' on which all who have cooked, or otherwise exerted themselves in making the wedding festivities pass off well, are regaled. That evening we took a last farewell of our Teliote friends, who warmly pressed us to stay for other festivities – 'the return wedding' on the following Sunday, the ceremony of taking down the clothes and hangings from the walls of the bride's house on the fortieth day. Nay, even they pressed us with their unbounded hospitality to stay till the anniversary of the wedding, when we should see the priest with his own hands take down the *sperveri* from over the nuptial couch, and Catharine would promise to take charge of it until the marriage of her eldest daughter. But we had had enough of such ceremonies, and felt that we could very well imagine the rest; so next morning we set sail from Telos and left behind us the lepers and the smells.

Excavations on Tílos[20]

Having visited these two outlying islands of the Sporadic group last winter, and having spent in them over two months, I propose to put together a few notes on the antiquities to be found in each. They are islands which are very difficult of access and rarely visited by foreigners, and are consequently peculiarly retentive of customs and myths which bear the stamp of extreme antiquity. Both these islands appear to have had a much more considerable population in ancient time than they have now, though much behind their neighbours on Rhodes and Kos in the arts and civilisation.

The principal feature of the small island of Telos is a precipitous mountain which rises directly behind the chief of the two modern villages of the island, on the summit of which is a fortress covering a triangular plateau about three quarters of a mile in circumference; the foundation of the walls of this fortress are Hellenic, on which during the Middle Ages more modern walls have been constructed. In the centre of this fortress there stands an Hellenic temple now converted into a church, and almost buried on two sides by the *débris* of Hellenic masonry covered with brushwood. From the gateway which enters the walls on the south side, a broad approach with steps flanked on either side by huge blocks of stone leads straight to the temple; the form of the temple is almost intact and built of neatly fitting stones without mortar of a course bluish marble.

---

[20] Despite Theodore's inference in his previous article that the success or not of their visit to Tílos lay in their witnessing an island wedding, the main purpose of their visit here, as to all the islands, was to excavate and remove items of archaeological and ethnographic interest – often for sale back in Britain. Once home in London that summer, Theodore wrote up and published his Tílos finds for the academic *Journal of Hellenic Studies* ('The Islands of Telos and Karpathos', 1885, No. 6, pp. 233-242). Bent was an early member, and then official, of the Society; his widow's *Chronicles* ended up in their archives.

Tílos landscape.

From a stone on the outer edge of the proaulion I took an impression which I afterwards found to be published in the *Bulletin de Corr. Hell.* iv. p. 43. Also I took rubbings of some other inscriptions on the walls of the pronaos, doubtless ψηφίσματα which were too much obliterated to be of any value.[21] The entrance to the *cella*, which is now used as a modern church, is also preserved, and is thirty-five inches across; the cella itself is covered with plaster in most places, which was fortunately sufficiently destroyed to enable me to see that the walls are Hellenic; it is five yards thirteen inches in length, by three yards thirty-four inches wide.

The triangular plateau is covered with the ruins of Byzantine houses, but at the northern apex there still stands an old Hellenic tower of the nature usually found in the islands. From the wall which runs along the northern side of the fortress, another Hellenic wall seems to have started off at right angles, which apparently divided the plateau across the centre, and which seems to have run in the direction of the temple, but is now lost in the *débris* of the houses. On this side the Byzantine fortifications run much below the Hellenic wall, and in what is left of the latter, the existence of a small postern gate is easily distinguishable.

---

[21] Psephísma/ Psephísmata (ψήφισμα/ψηφίσματα) are local decrees/proclamations on stone. Theodore's '*Bulletin de Corr. Hell.*' (*Bulletin de Correspondance Hellénique*) reference is incorrect, echoing Tozer's earlier criticism: '[His] notices, especially of inscriptions, often fail us at the point where exactness is most needed, and his references are extremely vague...' (*Academy*, 27 (1885: Jan/June) Rather than Vol. IV, Vol. III (1879), pp. 42-45) refers to two stones, one found in the small monastery where the Bents were staying in 1885, and noted by Ross, who '[au] printemps de 1844 passa deux jours dans l'île de Télos', and the second from 'le mur de l'église des Saints Apôtres, dans la plaine au-dessous du village.' (http://www.persee.fr/web/revues/home/prescript/revue/bch) Theodore is describing a stone in the temple/church within the Knights' castle *above* the village.

Antique altars in a ruined chapel, Tílos.

On the fertile plain below the fortress there are many traces of antiquity with marble bases of columns, some of which have as yet escaped the lime-kilns, marking the sites of several small temples; these have been converted into churches during the Byzantine occupation, but have since fallen into ruins. In one of these I found the following altar-shaped tomb inscribed ΚΑΛΛΙΡΟΑ (?) ΧΑΙΡΕ, and this memorial tablet:

The Hellenic graves of Telos are curious and uniform, and constructed doubtless as the nature of the ground suggested. In two cemeteries where I excavated, I found that deep clefts in the rock had been chosen for the graves, and at about ten feet below the soil which filled these clefts, we came upon holes chiselled in the rock in rows along the clefts. Each grave contained pottery of a rude description pointing to a backward state of art, numberless course plates were found in each, from which traces of the feast laid out for the dead were not altogether obliterated, fish bones, remnants of eggs and figs being still preserved in some of them.

Kárpathos[22]

We arrived at Karpathos a wreck – that is to say, a gust of wind from the mountains struck us when sailing on an almost glassy sea, carried away our sail and our mast, and reduced us to our oars. Where is Karpathos? and why did we go there? are always questions put to us; and we reply that it is one of the most lost islands of the Ægean Sea, lying between Crete and Rhodes, where no steamer touches, and that my wife and I spent some months on it last winter with a view to studying the customs of the 9000 Greeks who inhabit it, and who in their mountain villages have preserved through long ages many of the customs of the Greeks of old.

Our island delighted us immensely for its own exceeding loveliness: sharp-peaked mountain rise 4000 feet out of the sea, deep clefts lined with fir-trees run down to the water's edge. Near one of these, where nestled a tiny fishing hamlet to the north of the island, we deserted our wreck, and hired a boat manned by four wild-looking Karpathiote oarsmen to row us along the coast for seven hours to the chief village. The oars were like great branches, and with each stroke they pulled they rose from their seat, and kept time by repeating in a shrill voice little rhyming distiches, commenced by stroke and carried on by the others. These sailors know hundreds of these rhymes, which have been handed down from father to son. As a specimen I will give this one: Stroke commences by shouting, 'Everything from God;' number two, 'assistance;' number three, 'and supervision,' bow concludes the couplet by, 'and our bark shall proceed well.' When not singing, the sailors were chiding and chaffing one another, so that for the whole of the seven hours they were scarcely silent for a moment – not even stroke, a grey-haired man, who will not see sixty again.

Diafáni, the small harbour for Ólymbos, Kárpathos.

---

[22] Kárpathos was the main focus of the Bents' 1885 tour, staying several weeks and covering much of the island. They arrived from Tílos on Friday 6 March, departing late on Monday 20 April 1885. The visit inspired several articles on several themes. This first one is 'On a far-off island' for *Blackwood's Magazine* (Vol. 139, Feb 1886, pp. 233-244).

The Governor of Karpathos is a Turk, his treasurer is a Turk, the custom-house officer is a Turk, and there are five Turkish soldiers on Karpathos to uphold the Government of the Porte. Except these, all the inhabitants are Greek, and the villages up in the mountains are allowed almost complete self-government, provided their annual tribute is paid. It is absurd to see how keen party spirit is in these tiny village communities over the election of the *demarch*, or mayor of the place. We attended one of their annual Parliaments, at which the election takes place. Eighty members of the village were assembled and seated cross-legged in the church, wild unkempt shepherds, with rough goatskin cloaks, and priests with long hair flowing loosely over their shoulders. Suddenly would arise a perfect pandemonium of voices in eager dispute, and as quickly would it be hushed, when the oldest man of the village arose, Deacon Saint George as he is called – Deacon, because he can read and write, and Saint, because his grandfather once had been a pilgrim to the Holy Tomb. 'He is the most honourable man of all Karpathiotes,' they whispered to me in mute admiration; but a few days after this I had an opportunity of testing his honour, for he always tottered after us with a stick, with his long tasselled fez and long blue coat. One day my wife dropped a trifling ornament, value sixpence, which our old friend saw fall. He picked it up, looked at it, looked to see if my wife noticed her loss, held it in his hand for some time, and eventually consigned it to his pocket. Thus for this trifling loss we gauged the standard of honour of the most honourable councillor, the Nestor of Karpathos, at the sound of whose voice the hubbub of the village Parliament was for the moment lulled, though only to break forth again with redoubled vigour when Deacon Saint George sat down, until weary of dispute another lull ensued, during which the village schoolmaster was called upon, as the only decent scribe of the place, to write down the minutes of the meeting. A psalter was fetched from a stand in the church, pen and ink were produced, and, amidst a torrent of the advice from all sides, the schoolmaster wrote down – well, I expect, pretty nearly what he pleased. Such is home rule amongst the mountains of Karpathos.

After our long and lovely row, we landed in the most popular corner of the island, where a group of villages run up a fertile gorge far into the mountains, down which a stream dashes, called the Chaos, leaping and boiling through chasms scarcely two yards wide.[23] It is considered a most uncanny stream, which no man durst approach at night for fear of Nereids and other water-sprites. In the chief village the Turkish governor lives, – the Kaimakam, 'the superior lord' – *kaimak* being the word for anything superior. Cream, of which we got an endless supply in Karpathos, is called *kaimak*; so for the sake of simplicity, we soon took to calling the governor 'the cream.'

With a view to a prolonged stay in one of these villages, we tried to secure for ourselves a house, but experienced much difficulty; for we had three introductions with us, and soon we discovered that three families were quarrelling amongst themselves for our possession. Old Koubìs was a very talkative, desponding member of society, who came to visit us later than the others, apologising for his delay by saying that his 'bride' was ill. We could not imagine what so old a man could be doing with a bride, until we learned that his son had lately taken a wife, who was for the time being the family bride.

We spent the two first nights in the house of the Greek interpreter to the governor; and here we might have continued to dwell had not our third friend made us feel uncomfortable by privately insinuating that we were making ourselves inconvenient to 'the interpreter,' and that he could secure for us an empty house up in the village of Volà. By this plan he got us

---

[23] Mabel confirms that the river was called 'Chaos', along the track up from the coast at Vróndi *en route* for Apéri.

out of the interpreter's house. Not till later did we discover that our third friend had lately been studying Turkish hard, and aspired to the post of interpreter himself; so that a few weeks later he actually attempted the life of our first host.

Housekeeping at Volà was difficult. We had to send to the mountains for meat and milk whenever we wanted it; for the good Karpathiotes are most abstemious, rarely eating anything but bread and olives. As for groceries, save coffee and sugar, they were not to be had for love or money; and no vegetables, except onions, existed in the island. Our house consisted of one large room. Half of it had a mud floor; half was a raised wooden platform for our beds, below which were store cupboards for oil and wine. The windows had no glass in them; and some days, when the mountain mist came down upon us, we crouched over our charcoal brazier and shivered again. Our servant[24] dwelt in a tiny kitchen adjoining, where his struggles to light a fire with damp wood, and to cook without utensils, used to call for our keenest pity. Every evening a party of old women would come to keep us company, with their faces enveloped in handkerchiefs. They told us local customs and beliefs of an extraordinary nature. One evening I tried to sketch these old crones, and was discovered so doing. I thought my eyes would have been scratched out and my handiwork destroyed for my impudence, so infuriated were they; for they believe that if their portraits are taken they will waste and die.

Six months before our arrival, the owner of our house had died, and her sister, Sebastà by name, had inherited it; but she had kept it closed ever since, until our third friend, a relative of hers, had persuaded her to open it for us, on the condition that we should not sing or hold festival therein. We were not informed on taking possession of the delicate nature of our tenure, and in an unlucky moment we invited 'the Cream,' his interpreter, his treasurer, and our two other friends to a meal, and were prepared to put forth all our limited resources to do credit to our nation on the occasion.

The evening before our party Sebastà rushed in, in great distress. 'You are going to give a table in this house of mourning,' she cried. 'You will sing, you will get drunk, and the neighbours will sneer and say how soon has the memory of the dead been forgotten.' Our position was an awkward one, for it was too late to make other arrangements. In our extremity we protested that we would not sing, nor would we get drunk, though I felt inward misgivings on this latter point with regard to one or two of our guests. Sebastà wept and stamped with rage alternately. The old grandmother expostulated, and our third friend, who came in to our assistance, argued. The point was not settled when we retired to rest that night, nor did we obtain leave to hold our party until a short time before the guests were due. Then arose another difficulty. Our kid and our milk, for which we had despatched a special messenger to the mountains, did not reach us until two hours before the time appointed for 'the table,' and an agonising two hours we spent, literally tearing our kid limb from limb to prepare it for the pot. Of course the milk got smoked, and our English pudding was a disgrace to the nation. And then, to our horror, an hour before they were invited our guests arrived, bringing with them two others for whom we were not prepared. No party that we shall ever be called upon to give in civilised regions will appear formidable after this, and it really passed off remarkably well, with the assistance of a bottle of brandy for the Turks, who get over their vow not to drink wine by this subterfuge, and plenty of wine for the Greeks. We did not sing, and I don't think any one got drunk: at all events, Sebastà came in afterwards to thank us for having thus far respected the memory of her departed sister.

---

[24] Manthaios Símos.

The east coast of Kárpathos.

Only a few weeks later our third friend attempted the life of the interpreter; but when sitting at our table, no one would have guessed their animosity. They related how once they had together, at one sitting, eaten seventeen new-born lambs, so plentiful are they in Karpathos, after which they had consumed forty sardines apiece, and got drunk by going round from house to house asking for wine. When they came to the doctor's house, he gave them some wine, but placed in it a drug which was very beneficial to them after their debauch. Our third friend, the would-be interpreter, is very poor, and glories in his poverty, for it has come to pass as follows: he gave his eldest daughter so large a dower, that she was enabled to marry the schoolmaster of a neighbouring island. It is a curious feature in Karpathos, where romance is unknown, and, as our friend the interpreter said, 'All our marriages are for substance.' Firstborn sons inherit their father's property, firstborn daughters their mother's, and no girl can marry without she can provide her husband with a house. The result is excellent in checking the population, and in producing old maids; but we could not help thinking it was a little hard in the second daughter of our third friend, a plain girl, who went about without shoes and stockings, and was ready to earn a trifle by carrying our luggage on her head.

As a return for our 'table,' 'the Cream' and our other friends arranged a sort of picnic for us, to a lovely spot called 'Mrs Madonna' (Kera Panagía), where a church contains a miraculous picture, and is looked after by a well-known old hermit-monk called Vasili. The church is at the foot of a narrow gorge down by the sea, amidst tree-clad heights, which culminate in Mount Lastos, the highest peak in Karpathos, 4000 feet above sea-level. Close to this church there is a water source, which springs right out of a rock: it is icy cold and clear, and all around its egress the rock is garlanded with maidenhair; mastic, myrtle, and daphne almost conceal it from view. To this spot, the most favoured one in the island, our friends took us. In 1821 a Cretan refugee whose flocks had been destroyed by the Turks, vowed a church to the Panagià if she would lead him to a place of safety. So, says the legend, she conducted his boat here, where he found water, fertility, and seclusion, and here he built the church he had vowed. Once a year, on the day of the Assumption, the Karpathiotes make a pilgrimage to this spot; for the rest of the year it is left to the charge of poor old Vasili, who told us the very sad story which had driven him to adopt this hermit life. A few years ago he lived in the village, with his two sons and one daughter. She married a sea-captain, a well-to-do sponge-fisher, who owned a boat and much money he said. On one of his voyages, the sponge-fisher took with him Vasili's two sons, and on their way they fell across a boat manned by pirates from Amorgos. The pirates shot the captain, boarded the caïque, and strapped the two brothers to the mast. After they had cleared the boat of all they could find, they sank it, and shortly afterwards some other sponge-fishers found the two brothers fastened to the mast at the bottom of the sea. They gave notice to the Government, and a steamer was despatched from Chios in pursuit of the pirates, and the bodies were brought home and buried. It was but poor satisfaction to old Vasili to hear of the capture of the murderers. His daughter shortly afterwards married again, and left Karpathos, and he, with his broken heart and tottering step, donned the garb of a monk, and came to end his days at Kera Panagía, where he lives in a little stone hut alongside the church, and tills the ground, lights the lamps before the sacred pictures, and rings the church bell.

Our picnic meal was the greatest possible success, for 'the Cream' brought with him one of his soldiers, an Albanian, who spoke no language but his own. This man was despatched to the mountain for a lamb, which he cooked for after the fashion of the Albanian 'klephtes.' A wooden skewer was passed through the body, and it was roasted whole before a smouldering fire of brushwood, and basted with cream and salt. When ready, it was served on a table of sweet-smelling herbs – mastic, rosemary, etc. We all squatted around on the ground, and the lamb was rent in pieces, and to each guest was handed a bone, which we picked with more or less dexterity, according as we were accustomed to such procedure. We were very jovial over our meal, and our friends foretold pleasant things for us from the shoulder-bone of the lamb, according to their custom; and then we drank a large bowl of cream, 'the flower of milk,' as they call it, which, with native honey, is truly delicious, and afforded us the opportunity we wished of making a complimentary pun, by comparing the governor to the beverage before us. After our meal, we smoked cigarettes under the shade of a carob-tree – the tree which the peasants tell you was the only one which the devil forgot to spoil, for all the others shed their leaves and fruit, but the carob-tree is for ever green and fructifying. It is better known to us as the locust-tree, the pods of which are sweet and like honey to eat, and made us not pity St John the Baptist so much for his desert fare. Late in the evening we returned to our home at Volà, on excellent terms with our friends.

A young married woman of our acquaintance died when we were at Volà, and the melancholy ceremony attending her death will remain fixed in our memories until our turn comes to die. A few hours after her death the corpse had been washed in wine and water, when it was dressed in a richly embroidered robe, and placed on a bier like a low table, with handles for carrying, in the one-roomed house. Around stood the family groaning and screaming and lacerating themselves in their demonstrative grief, awaiting the arrival of the hired mourner, a woman of commanding but repulsive mien. Her first action was to fall upon the corpse and weep; then she stood erect at the foot of the bier and lifted up her voice to sing her dirge in a shrill, heartrending key. 'How can the sun dare to shine on a scene of grief like this?' she began, 'where the children are deprived of their mother's care, where the hearth is left desolate for the husband on his return from toiling in the fields. Would that I could descend to Hades, and see my darling once more, to give her a parting kiss from her dear ones, whose minds are troubled like the sea, when it rolls in after a mighty storm on to the shore.'

The pathetic strains drove the relatives into an agony of grief, which continued with more or less vehemence for two hours, until the priest and his acolytes came to convey the corpse to the tomb. Before the procession left the house, a jug full of water was broken on the threshold: it is customary here to spill water at the door when any one starts on a journey, as an earnest of success. To-day the traveller had gone on her last long journey, so the jug was broken. The family tomb was at some little distance from the village, and on their way thither the priests chanted offices, interrupted frequently by hideous wails from the lamenters who headed the procession; and as the mournful company passed, women came forth from their houses to howl in concert.

Every Karpathiote family has its tomb on the hillside, with a tiny chapel attached, in which the corpse is placed before interment. Here the final offices for the dead were chanted, and the mourners ceased to wail, until the very solemn *stichera* of the last kiss came, which begins, 'Blessed is the way thou shalt go to-day,' whereat each in turn advanced to give their last kiss to the cold face of the corpse, and then, with one accord, they burst forth again into loud and uncontrolled grief.

They never put the body into a coffin in Karpathos, for there is a poplar impression that a spirit enclosed in wood cannot escape. One year after the death the bones are taken out, placed in an embroidered bag, and thrown into a charnel-house below the chapel. They believe that if the flesh is not decayed altogether off the bones, the spirit does not rest in peace; consequently this ceremony of opening the grave is a very anxious one for the survivors, who consider that they can thereby tell the destination of their lost friend's soul. When there is any suspicion that the defunct is not at peace in Hades, the name is without delay entered on the 'soul paper,' or priest's memorandum-list of the souls for which he has to pray during the divine mystery.

Many superstitious practices are carried on in connection with the inquietude of souls. Sometimes the ashes are removed to an island rock, for ghosts cannot cross water; sometimes they are burnt and scattered to the winds; and a dying man must never be covered with any material made of goats' hair, for it will detain the spirit, neither must anything be handed across a corpse for the same reason; and they never button the clothes they put on after death: finally, they remove all rings, for the spirit, they say, can even be detained in the little finger, and cannot rest.

The tomb was a plain square building of stone: into it the corpse was laid, a few handfuls of earth were thrown on by the relatives, and here the body was left to decay, and to pollute the vicinity with a terrible stench during the summer heat. When closed, they placed on the grave the axe and spade which had been used in opening it, in the shape of a cross, for twenty-four hours.

It was truly heartrending to hear the wails of the relatives all that evening by the grave. The old mother of the deceased, with dishevelled grey locks, knelt there for hours with her other daughters, working themselves from one paroxysm to another, with short intervals to gain breath; and then next day, and on stated days afterwards, they brought the boiled wheat adorned with raisins to place on the tomb, and each time their wailings were renewed. Yet with all this excessive grief, it is surprising to see how evanescent is the respect paid to properly denuded bones. Many of the family charnel-houses have fallen into ruins through neglect, and the embroidered bags, which I was almost to steal, were scattered about, with the bones peeping out. One particular instance struck us forcibly: it was the charnel-house belonging to the chief priest of the village, which had been almost washed away by the winter's rain. All around lay the skulls and bones, in hideous confusion, of his deceased relatives, amongst which of an evening old witch-like crones would wander to collect such bones as they deemed of use for incantations. For example, a skull set upon a post facing the direction they wish the wind to blow from, is considered efficacious in producing the desired current of air, and it does not strike them as a hideous notion that the skull of some dear departed one should be used for this purpose.

The Karpathiotes live in the depths of superstition, with their soothsayings and incantations. A doctor does exist in the chief village; but he told me that his practice was almost entirely confined to the Turks and a few of the more enlightened Greeks. In the mountain villages they never think of calling in anybody to the sick but the old witches, who mutter incantations and wave a mysterious sickle with weird gestures over their patient; or sometimes a priest is called in, for they profess to be able to bind diseases, especially fevers, to trees by writing on a scrap of paper the mystic words. 'Divinity of God, divine mystery.' This they tie with a red thread round the neck of the sufferer; next morning they remove it, and go out on the hillside, where they tie it to a tree, and imagine that they thus transfer the fever from the patient to the branch.

At Volà we witnessed several of those curious customs by which the priests manage to extract money from these benighted people. They exorcise rats and mice by sprinkling holy water and by saying a prayer under the tree or barn which the vermin frequent. At Easter they sell candles from the church, by burning which and saying some mystic words in their houses, they think they will drive away beetles from their dwellings.

At the neighbouring village of Othos there lives a portly and well-to-do prophet, who has grown rich and very sleek on his soothsayings, for seldom do marriages or voyages take place without consulting him, and he does not give his advice for nothing. We visited him one day, and heard him prophesy as he lay in bed with a many-coloured coverlet over his inspired limbs. It was a cheery little house, the walls of which were hung with holy pictures, sacred olive twigs to keep off the evil eye, a vial of sacred oil from Easter, and scraps of meat preserved from the last Easter lamb, now nearly one year old. There were crowds of people in the room, including a priest, who joined devoutly in the prayer to the Father, the Son, and the Holy Ghost, before the soothsaying began. From beneath the pillow the prophet produced his books of magic art, out of which he professes to expound the future: one of these is an ordinary psalter, which he opens, and from the first line on which the eye falls he reads his divination. Again, he has a list of numbers, one of which you select at haphazard with a pointed bit of wood: this number corresponds to a prophecy in his book of magic, which he reads to you as the decree of fate. People come from all parts of Karpathos to consult this strange man, and, said the priest, 'the utterings of this oracle are seldom at fault.' We clearly ascertained by experience that the priests, the prophet, and the old crones who cure diseases have it all their own way, and play into one another's hands in the game of extortion.

I think the time we enjoyed most during our stay in Karpathos was Easter, and the opportunity it afforded us of seeing the amusements of these primitive islanders. By that

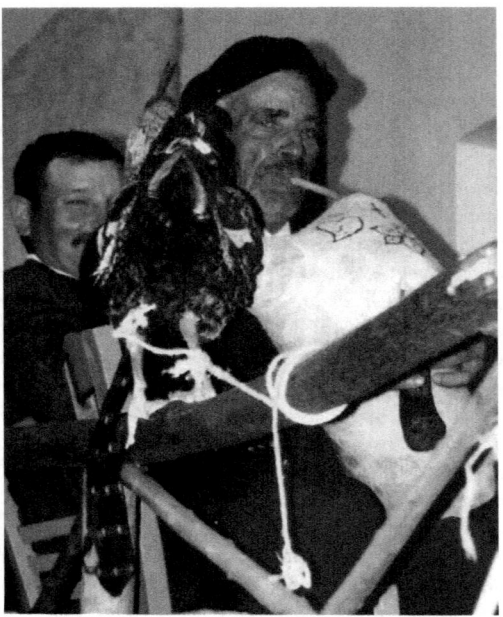

A tsamboúna player at Easter. The cockerel is eaten when the music stops.

time we felt quite at home amongst them, and were welcome visitors in most houses. Furthermore, the uncertain spring had settled down into delicious summer weather, and the slopes at a stone's throw from our house were carpeted with lovely flowers.

Amusements in Karpathos certainly are not numerous, and may be summed up as consisting of music and dancing in a variety of forms. In every occupation they sing; the very washerwoman, as she kneels at the brook, is practising death-wails for the next funeral. It is a curious sight to see women treading their homespun flannel to get out of it the long hairs. Two of them sit at either end of a sort of trough, with their legs bare, and leaning their backs against the wall: here they tread wearily away from sunrise to sunset, singing as they do so little idyls, the poetry of which is peculiarly quaint and pretty – *mantinada* they call these idylls in Karpathos; and sometimes to assist them in their drudgery, a man will come and play the lyre, – just one of those lyres which their ancestors played, a pretty little instrument about half a yard long, with silver beads which jangle attached to the bow. Besides this they have the *syravlion*, a sort of pan-pipe made of two reeds hollowed out, with blow-holes and straws up the middle, and placed side by side in a larger reed.

A third instrument is the *sabouna*, a species of bagpipe, being a goatskin with the hairs left on, which palpitates like a living body when filled with air. These instruments are romantic enough when played by shepherds on the hillside or in the village square as an accompaniment to the dance, but they are intolerable in the tiny cottages where women tread their flannel.[25]

---

[25] See page 16.

Singing is the accompaniment and conclusion to every feast, for the feasts in Karpathos are merely the symposia of ancient days, in which men only take part, and are attended upon by women. Co-operation in labour is customary here. If a man plants a vineyard, builds a house, or ploughs a field, he has but to call upon his friends and relatives to assist him, and the only payment expected is a handsome meal, after which the men sing *mantinada* with their arms around each other's necks, and reel home dead-drunk at night. Many of these took place during our stay at Volà; and when we learned that the giver of the feast looks upon it as a positive insult if his guests do not get drunk, we ceased to feel shocked when our slumbers were disturbed by the shouts of revellers on their homeward way. Our third friend gave one to the men who had assisted him in tilling his fields, and he invited me to it. I fear I insulted him by leaving before the entertainment had reached its height, for we saw little of him after that; and we did not regret this when we learned about the desperate attempt that had been made on the life of our friend the 'interpreter.' All Volà affirmed that our third friend had hired the assassin, for was he not a relative of his, and was it not to his interest to remove the object of his dislike? At all events, the wrong man got killed in the fray, and our third friend was present at the funeral; the murderer escaped, and the interpreter never went

Ólymbos, among the clouds.

out without a soldier with a crazy old musket to attend upon him. Such was the 'murder at Volà,' in which we shall always feel that we were more or less implicated.

During the Sundays of Lent at Volà the people got very much excited over the game of swing, which took place in the afternoon in a narrow street. Damsels hung from one wall to the other a rope, and on this they put rugs to form a swing. Two of them generally sat together, and sang *mantinada*, and took a toll from each man who passed by, the fine being a penny, a swing, and a song. Some of the young men came primed with ditties, which looked as if romance was not so wholly unknown to them as the 'interpreter' had told us.

> 'Your figure is a lemon-tree,
> Its branches are your hair;
> Joy to the youth who climbs
> To pluck the fruit so fair.'[26]

Whilst another favourite ditty is, 'Your lips are honey, mine are wine; come let us eat honey and drink wine.' But here the flirtation ended; the young men kept together, and the young women kept together. We never saw a case of 'keeping company' whilst we were there.

Before Easter we went up to a mountain village called Olympus,[27] whether from its exalted position or not I cannot say, where customs of an exceedingly quaint nature existed, and where we tarried in the house of the schoolmaster. They began their preparations on Palm Sunday; and at four o'clock on that morning our slumbers were disturbed by a herald, who went round to summon everyone to church. In his hand he carried a reed called a *nartheka*,[28] and in this he had a light, for the morning was windy; and, like Prometheus of old, who thus brought down fire from heaven, he went to the houses of all the priests to light their candles, they having for this purpose left their doors open the night before. Then he lighted the candles of the chief inhabitants, after which he shouted from a commanding height his summons to worship; and as a reward for his services he was presented with a loaf of holy bread. The church was very crowded at this early service, the women remaining outside in the *proavlion*, where they could get a glimpse at the performance through the door. They have no pews to sit in, but each mother of a family possesses one of the stone slabs which form the pavement: on this she performs her devotions, and brooks no encroachment. This slab she leaves, together with her jewellery and her embroidered dresses, to her eldest daughter.

That afternoon every household was busy making 'the candles of the resurrection;' and very quaint they looked, squatting on the floor close to a fire of embers, with lumps of honeycomb, which they were moulding into candles on the low wooden tables used for making macaroni. During the next few days everybody went about with exceeding gay fingers, as each household had been dyeing their Easter eggs, some purple, some golden, some green; for eggs have been forbidden by the Lenten fast, and every egg that has been laid during Lent in Olympus has been hard boiled for Easter, and was now being coloured with dyes made from their mountain herbs.

Every house and church had to be whitewashed, inside and out; and every evening the labourers returned from their work groaning under bundles of brushwood, for Thursday

---

[26] Curiously an identical refrain to that recorded by Bent on Anáfi in the Cyclades some years earlier (Bent 1885b, 49). The swing game, on the other hand, Theodore is remembering from Sériphos, where again the streets are 'narrow' (Bent 1885b, 3).

[27] Ólymbos, in the north.

[28] Genus *Ferula*.

was the great baking-day, when every oven was heated, and nothing was seen at Olympus but women running about with long boards on their heads, carrying twisted cakes covered with sesame seed and a coloured egg in each; also pasties of green herbs – horrible things, which we were frequently offered, and had a difficulty disposing of. The baking day was a very gay scene. When the ovens were sufficiently heated with burning brushwood, and the embers had been swept out, these boards were shoved in; and after seeing a baking such as this, it was easy to realise the popular enigma which asks you what a black-faced heifer is which consumes brushwood, and without hesitation you answer, an oven.

On Saturday before Easter all the shepherds come into Olympus from their mountain dairies – in most cases mere caves in the rocks – where many of them pass the entire year. On their backs they carry goatskins full of cheese and milk and cream, which they distribute as presents to each householder, receiving in return a sufficiency of bread to last them many a month, – for most of this Easter bread is not consumed till it has acquired the consistency of biscuit. On Easter eve we looked out upon householders rushing hither and thither with bowls of cream and milk, whilst we poor strangers could buy none at all, so intent was everybody in providing for the morrow's feast.

We did not attend the Easter-night service at Olympus, nor did we receive kisses of peace which are distributed broadcast on such occasions, for having experienced the sensation before, we did not wish to repeat it; but we arose early enough to see the women roasting their lambs in their ovens. In one oven we counted as many as twelve lambs roasting and stuffed with rice, – unpalatable things enough, with distorted limbs, looking as if they had been thrust in alive and died in agony; and at each house we visited that day, we were presented with a most embarrassing limb of lamb.

We did attend the afternoon service, and got our clothes well covered with wax for so doing. Every worshipper carried a lighted candle, and ignored the angle at which it was held. We assisted at the merriment in the churchyard after service was over, when the young men shoot a Guy Fawkes erected on the wall, popularly believed to resemble Judas Iscariot.[29]

On Monday the good folks of Olympus danced in the space before the church, resplendent with barbarous jewellery and quaint costumes. These dances interested us much, as being genuinely archaic in character. A circle was formed, in the midst of which we and the sober-minded who did not dance sat like sardines in a box, everybody eating something, and everybody asking his neighbour to have a bite at the delicacy which he was consuming. Mothers had their babies strung like bundles on their backs. Every child had a gorgeous Easter egg, with which it was dyeing its cheeks and lips; and here was sat, whilst the dancers never ceased to revolve in the weary circle of alternate men and women with arms intertwined, so that each alternate dancer held the hand of the next but one. Sometimes it was fast, and the leader performed feats of agility; sometimes it was slow, when the men smoked cigarettes, and the women sang ditties; but the dancing never stopped for a single moment, nor did the grinding of the lyre, or the gurgle of the bagpipe, till darkness drove them to drink and to dance in their stifling houses.

Early on Tuesday morning the head of each family solemnly repaired to his tomb with his offering of bread for the dead: this he placed on the stone pedestal in the midst of every chapel, and about nine o'clock the priests went round with acolytes and large baskets to collect the same for their own consumption. At eleven commenced the annual procession to the tombs, which wended its way up and down rugged paths along the mountain side, and was composed of the most energetic inhabitants, carrying the sacred pictures from the

---

[29] See page 137.

Above Diafáni.

Church and the banners: at each tomb they passed on their route guns were let off, and prayers were said. We were content to watch them from a distance, as they wended their way like a gigantic caterpillar along the hills for many a mile. Finally they descended to the stream, into which was put the most revered of their pictures, that the Madonna might bless the waters. In the afternoon they returned to Olympus, where the priests blessed the multitude before the church, and the bearers of the pictures and banners grew exceedingly wroth with the priests for not giving them as much money as they considered their labour deserved.

On Thursday we went down to the tiny port of Diaphane, where the men of Olympus own a few cottages and a few crafts, and where a church is built, containing a miracle-working picture, to worship which the Olympites make a private pilgrimage once a year on the evening of the Thursday after Easter. I have attended pilgrimages before in Greece, but none so quaint and simple as this.

We started before the pilgrims down a lovely gorge clad with fir-trees,[30] down a road which was a succession of tiny waterfalls, the worst of the many bad roads of Karpathos, and we found the few inhabitants of Diaphane busily engaged in preparing for the feast, cutting up lambs and kids into hunks, decorating the church floor with myrtle, and opening barrels of wine for the night's debauch. We found quarters with the priest, and from his roof had an excellent view of the proceedings. Towards evening the pilgrims, with their mules

---

[30] Still existing, this is the ancient trail that falls from high up in Ólymbos to Dhiafáni.

and their baggage, came down, letting off guns to announce their arrival, and greeting every one they met with 'Christ is risen!' which they continue to do in Karpathos for forty days after Easter is past; and at sundown they tinkled a goat's bell as a summons to the evening liturgy.

It was a pretty sight to see the pilgrims squatted in merry little groups along the shore, 'breaking their bread,' and refreshing themselves for the dance, which commenced at ten. Such a night of revelry I have seldom heard: dancing and singing went on without cessation out in the courtyards, and sometimes inside, so that whatever rest we got was haunted by the heavy tramp of the dancers and the piercing voices of the singers. The sun was high in the heavens before the sound of the lyre and the bagpipe ceased, and the goat's bell once more tinkled to summon the revellers to their devotions. I went to the liturgy, and found but few inside the church, for the male pilgrims, wearied with their nocturnal orgies, were either washing in the sea or stretched on the shore to secure a few moments of repose; and the women have no place allotted to them inside this edifice, so that they have to crowd at the door and hear what they can of the sacred mystery.

Meanwhile the hunks of lambs and kids were boiling in a huge caldron outside a house where planks on boxes had been improvised as tables for the pilgrims' meal, and the savoury smell of the stew must have been keenly appetising to their nostrils. When the liturgy was over, an old man with a large wooden ladle took up his position by the caldron, ready to fill the bowl each pilgrim had brought with him and to receive the coppers; and as each was supplied, he retired into the house to consume his portion, and washed it down with wine, which now flowed freely. Seldom have I seen a merrier company or a nastier meal more thoroughly enjoyed; and then they fell to dancing again in an open space by the sea, not a few by their antics demonstrating the potency of the beverage they had imbibed. It was a curious scene, – the women in their gay festival garb, the men in their embroidered waistcoats, red fezes, blue baggy trousers, and gaudy stockings. The steps of the women were now more active; and as for the male leader of the circle, his acrobatic feats were of an extraordinary vigour: and as they danced their local dances and sang their local songs by the side of the waves, under the shadow of the mountains, accompanied by a blind old bard who played the lyre in their midst and sang songs to infuse them with merriment, I thought that dancing like this could not have altered much since Homeric days.

The last act in this pilgrimage was to us an interesting one. The chief priest of Olympus had just built a large caïque down at Diaphane, which he had settled to launch this afternoon, and to christen her the Madonna of Diaphane. He was wise in thus doing, for the crowd of pilgrims assisted nobly in the weary process of dragging her to the sea; and as she glided into the water, all stood eagerly to watch the manner in which she righted herself, for in this they see an omen as to the future of the craft's career. Then came the benediction by the chief priest and his colleagues: with the blood of a slaughtered lamb a cross was made on the deck, and the chanting of the service sounded quaintly over the waves. We looked to obtaining a passage for ourselves on the Madonna of Diaphane, so we joined heartily in the wishes for success; and when all was over the captain-elect jumped off the bows into the sea, with all his clothes on, and came dripping to shore amidst the laughter of the lookers-on. The priest gave the pilgrims a farewell repast after the ceremony was concluded; and ere the day was very old, we were left in quiet enjoyment of Diaphane, a very paradise, for a few days of repose amongst the pine-trees and craggy heights overhanging the azure sea.

'A Christening on Karpathos'[31]

I do not suppose any one who reads this will have been to Karpathos; and perhaps not many will be able to say off hand that it is one of the Sporades, lying between Crete and Rhodes. There is absolutely nothing to take an ordinary traveller or a merchant there, and the two seas on either side of this long riband-shaped island are, moreover, exceedingly dangerous. No steamers cross them, and rarely sailing boats; consequently no happier hunting ground could exist for the study of unadulterated Greek peasant life. The island is certainly very lovely, being particularly rich in mountains covered with rare plants; in fact the only European who had visited the villages before ourselves within the memory of the present generation was a German botanist.[32] In parts it is densely wooded with low straggling fir trees, which on the slopes exposed to the north winds crawl along the ground with their stems as if supplicating the angry blast for mercy. The mountainous backbone of Karpathos is curiously knife-shaped, and as you travel from one end of the island to the other you go along the summit of this backbone, with the sea on either side of you three thousand feet below, while behind you and before you rise a surprising conglomeration of angular many-coloured peaks.

In these mountains there are villages, the inhabitants of which, and there are not nine thousand souls in the whole of Karpathos, are buried in the depths of ignorance. Amongst them we passed several moths last winter, and many amusing incidents we witnessed during our stay. We were lodged with the schoolmaster of Mesochorion in a one-roomed house, which was abandoned to our sole and separate use. One day, shortly after our arrival, we were made aware that a very near neighbour of ours had had a baby, by the sudden breaking upon us of unmistakable sounds of infantile distress. The schoolmaster was promptly summoned and questioned on the subject, and he promised without delay to obtain for us an introduction to the happy mother, that our desire to study the folk-lore of Greek babyhood might be satisfied.

Undoubtedly the schoolmaster might be termed 'a superior man' in Karpathos, for he could both read and write. I should not like to answer for his possession of any further accomplishments, seeing that one day he asked us if we were acquainted with the great European traveller, Captain Hatteras. The name struck me as familiar, so I said we had often heard of him, but had not the pleasure of his acquaintance. 'I have an account of his travels which I will lend you,' said he, and that evening put us in possession of a Greek translation of Jules Verne's work, which our friend believed to contain nothing but the truth. Nevertheless he was a superior man, and a great assistance to us in collecting local beliefs. Furthermore, he bore the title of 'deacon,' which is given in Karpathos to all who can read or write, to distinguish them from the common herd. As a proof of the Karpathiote conservatism in customs, it is only necessary to state that still they observe the first of September as New Year's Day, washing out their houses and wishing each other a happy new year on the day which the Byzantine calendar recognised as the first of the year.

Yet even here there are instances of civilisation having crept in. The better class of inhabitants are weary of the monotony of calling themselves John, the son of Nicholas, and Nicholas, the son of John, for alternate generations. We became acquainted with a person called Mr. Palamedes Black Seagoer, who once penetrated as far as Odessa; and our

---

[31] 'A Christening in Karpathos', *Macmillan's Magazine*, 54 (1886: May/Oct), pp. 199-205.
[32] Perhaps a reference to the German botanist and philhellene Theodor Heinrich Hermann von Heldreich (1822-1902). He travelled widely in the Aegean and some species from Kárpathos bear his name, along with his Swiss colleague Pierre Edmond Boissier (1810-1885). Their plants are commonly cited as Boiss. & Heldr.

Rhodian baptism.

muleteer, Nicholas, proudly told us that he had inherited the surname of Hare from his father, who had been thus dubbed for the fleetness of foot he had displayed in the days of the revolution.

A few years ago in Karpathos the extent of a boy's education was to be able to read, after a parrot-like fashion, a page in the Greek prayer-book, beginning 'Cross, help me;' after which they were hurried through the Psalter and the Apostles, and then sent out into the world to dig and delve, and to forget the very form of letters. As a rare instance of ability, a boy was allowed to read in church the canons and the Apostles, and the proud parents on this occasion prepared a feast in honour of their son's success, and brought presents of fruit and bread to the erudite preceptor. This was the education of the generation now grown up, and it is a question if their successors will be more deeply learned.

The mother lay in state on her upper floor when we visited her, for all Karpathiote houses are built after one fashion. Each consists of one long single room, which is divided into two parts down the middle. That nearest the entrance is paved usually with manure, and is used for receiving guests. The inner part is constructed like a stage; below are the storerooms, above are the beds, approached by steps. The walls are gay with plates and cups and household utensils, and in the homes of the better class there is much carving, which pleases the eye; quaint griffin heads and intricate labyrinthine patterns, testifying to the skill of the self-taught Karpathiote carpenters.

Never, as long as I live,[33] shall I forget the shock I received on being introduced to the attendant physician. These villagers have no belief in the efficacy of drugs, and their only medical attendants are old women who can mutter incantations, and priests who can bind diseases to a tree, and exorcise the devil. They have not even any practical knowledge of the many herbs which cover the mountain sides to help them in the combat with disease. At Mesochorion almost the only practitioner is a witch-like creature called Marigo, of whose sex no one seemed quite certain, for we heard our old school-friend the article ὁ, ἡ, τὸ, gone through in all its subtle variations when addressing this individual, who for the sake of simplicity we will call 'her'.[34]

Marigo had lost one leg long years ago, by the fall of a mast when at sea. She had supplied the missing member by what looked uncommonly like the stump of a tree. Assisted by this and by a crutch she was daily to be seen going her medical rounds within the precincts of the village; but if called to a distant hamlet, a mule had to be sent. She was always dressed in rags and tatters; her nose is Wellingtonian in shape. Her hair clotted and straggling. She will tell you your fortune with a greasy pack of cards, and few of the inhabitants of Mesochorion get married or go on a voyage without consulting Marigo's sooth-sayings. She is seldom sober, for her medical fees are generally invested in *raki* or rum. Such is the physician of Mesochorion. I have seen her perform her incantations for fevers and headaches. I have seen her whilst muttering mystic words wave a sickle, the point of which had been dipped in honey, over the head of a dying man. I have seen her amongst the bones in the charnel-house looking for a skull to stick upon a post, which she thinks will attract the wind from the quarter from whence she wishes it to blow. But I think I never saw her look so repulsively awe-inspiring as when contrasted with the tiny speck of human life, at whose entrance into the world she had presided.

Primitive societies are not, as a rule, gallant in their reception of female babies; in fact some Karpathiote parents are so very benighted as to consider the advent of a daughter as a distinct curse to their house. There is, however, an exception to this rule, made for the first daughter, for a first daughter succeeds to all her mother's property. Consequently they fire off guns on her appearance, to indicate that an heiress has been born into the world. The arrival of subsequent daughters is passed over in silence, whilst every son is greeted with a flourish.

Marigo was very busy as we went in, for the public washing of the infant was about to take place, and at such an occasion she always presides. A huge wooden bowl was placed in the middle of a table, into which warm water was poured; a few lemon leaves were then dropped in, and the relatives who were near cast in salt and sugar. In this concoction Marigo washed her young charge, frequently calling it a little dragon as she did so, one of those pet names by which Greek children are known before their christening, and which are thought to indicate its future strength. After this exertion she had to be supplied with a glass of *raki*, to prepare her for the mighty effort of saying the 'Kyrie Eleison' forty times, which she did with remarkable velocity. It is done always in this occasion, as a thanksgiving to God for allowing another male child to be born into the world.

---

[33] Which was not to be long. Theodore died of malarial complications in London on 5 May 1897.

[34] This unpleasant description is not repeated in Mabel's notebook. She refers to Marigó as being from Spiliés, but not to the baptism at all. As with the Tílos wedding above, it is hard not to conclude that Theodore used the two locations as settings for the details of ceremonies he had encountered, or learned of, elsewhere in the Aegean, e.g. Síkinos (Bent 1885b, p. 89) for the christening and Santoríni (Bent 1885b, p. 66) for the wedding.

Picking olives, Diafáni.

Before the priestly blessing, after the washing and swaddling has been done to Marigo's satisfaction, no one is allowed to come in or go out of the house; but as soon as Papa Manoulas has delivered this blessing the doors are thrown open, for now they say there is no fear of a Nereid or uncanny hobgoblin seizing upon the child and making it waste away. Before our departure we were given glasses of *raki* and sweets, and we wished the mother a happy forty days; for, according to custom, for forty days after the birth the mother does not go to church. Before the birth the mother is very seldom seen abroad; this is not inculcated by any feelings of modesty, for they have none, but from the belief that if she should see an ugly person the child would be unsightly. On the same principle, the handsomest man ought to embrace the child after birth, so as to impart to it a portion of his beauty; and the soberest and most moderate woman, that the child may grow up temperate in all its ways. At Mesochorion Marigo is always sent for secretly when the birth is imminent, for fear that at this critical moment an enemy may hear of it and curse the child. No one in the house, for the same reason, is allowed to utter a harsh word, for it would damage the infant.

Our schoolmaster told us much about the superstitions connected with births that evening. At sunset, for many days, the doors of the house are kept scrupulously closed to whomsoever may arrive. Even if it is the father who has returned from a long journey he has to seek repose elsewhere, for from sunset until cockcrow the demons of the air are roving about, and they may come in and hurt the child. The clothes of the child must not be exposed to the stars, and if by accident they have been, they must be fumigated with a censer; if this is omitted the child will have thrush. There is some sense in this in a climate where the atmosphere is so often impregnated with sea moisture.

St. Eleutherios is the protector of new-born babes, and is usually called upon by the mother in her distress, as anciently was the goddess Eileithyia; and when summoned to the bedside of her patient Marigo always takes with her an olive branch, which is called from its shape, 'the virgin's hand,' which the patient holds with a view to expediting the event.

But on the seventh day after the birth there takes place the most interesting ceremony of all Karpathos. It is usually performed the day before the christening, and is looked upon as of the greatest importance, for on this day the Fates are called upon to decide who is to be the child's patron saint. It was on the seventh day, Apollodorus tells us, that the Fates told the horologe of Meleager and the torch was lighted on the hearth. This ceremony of fate-telling is still, as in ancient days, called ἑφτὰ, and is an interesting thing to witness, so we were obliged to stay longer at Mesochorion than we originally intended; we never regretted the delay as it gave us an opportunity of becoming better acquainted with a deliciously primitive and hospitably-inclined people.

In these remote villages there are always one or more women, who once in their lives have left their native island. These are wonderfully overbearing, and during the day time, when the men are absent in the fields, they maintain the importance of royalty. Mrs. Chrysanthemum was the ruling spirit in Mesochorion; she had once been with her husband to Alexandria, and looked upon us as her special property, being always at hand to conduct us in our walks, and to apologize for the ignorance of her fellows. 'I know civilization,' she would boast proudly, and her listeners would nod their heads in assent; 'these people are animals, burnt people, no men at all;' and by their silence the other women would acknowledge the truth of Mrs. Chrysanthemum's definition of them.

Perhaps our life was a little monotonous at Mesochorion; at all events the delicacies of our table were; for daily we discussed the boiled limbs of kid or lamb; we had no vegetables save onions. Our only real delight was boiled sheep's cream mixed with native honey, and now and then a pilaff of snails. Snails boiled in rice, with oil poured over them, and served up with hairpins, are a welcome luxury in these parts. Then we had numerous patients with every imaginable disease, who came to consult us, regardless of Marigo's sneers; and though we did not stay long enough to hear if our remedies were successful in the most interesting cases, yet I have my doubts if the Vaseline we gave to lepers would ever do more than bring a ray of hope for a time to those stricken outcasts of society.

Last winter the inhabitants of Karpathos suffered a dire calamity, traces of which we saw in every village. An account of this disaster never appeared in the European papers; no subscription list was ever opened at the Mansion House[35] on their behalf; yet I question if these islanders did not suffer more than others whose catastrophe has been better known. The island was visited by a cyclone or rain which never ceased for a fortnight; their houses were washed away; their vineyards were destroyed; their fields, which are built in terraces on the mountain slopes, subsided. Some of the villages represented the appearance of those in Chios after the earthquake, and the greatest distress prevails, for there is no government to lend a helping hand; their taxes have to be paid as usual, and they have nothing to assist them in their adversity save their habitual abstinence, which enables a Greek peasant to subsist on what to others would be sheer starvation. At Mesochorion they were busily engaged in repairing the damages when we were there; but they do not know how to guard against a recurrence of this catastrophe; their stone walls have only mud for cement; their roofs are of mud, and their floors of manure. The flat roof of one house serves as the courtyard and

---

[35] As there was, for example, for the 1881 quake that devastated Chíos (Chios Earthquake fund. Corporation of London Records Office, Mansion House Funds, COL/MH/AD/06 [n.d.]).

approach to another on a higher level, and it is of common occurrence for the family to be awakened at night by a stray mule which has got on to the roof, and whose leg has gone through the ceiling.

The seventh day arrived at last, and we were all in readiness for the fate-telling ceremony which was to be performed on behalf of baby dragon. People in their best were seen hurrying to the mother's house carrying baskets of figs and other delicacies as a present for the 'table' which would afterwards be laid. Our friend Papa Manoulas, the chief priest, was there as a matter of course, in his long blue greasy cassock and tall hat and straggling hair, which well regulated Papas usually fasten up with hairpins, but which Papa Manoulas generally so contrived to tuck into his hat that it stood out behind like the handle of a teapot. He is a mason by trade, and just now, owing to the quantity of house repairing that is going on, he is driving an unusually food trade.

Marigo we saw hobbling along towards the house looking more tattered and witch-like than ever; most of the relatives of the parents were directing their course thither, besides numerous guests, and amongst these ourselves. In the middle of the floor was placed a thing which might easily have passed for a wooden pig-trough, but it really was a bowl into which the family put their boiled rice on feast days, and out of which they eat, squatted on the floor around, without the assistance of forks or spoons. To-day this bowl was to serve another purpose: it was carefully covered first of all with a suit of the father's clothes, for the child was a boy; if it had been a girl, one of the mother's embroidered dresses would have been used for this purpose. Then baby dragon was brought from his cradle, which in these parts consists of a swing attached to the beams of the roof. He was tightly swaddled[36] like a malefactor about to be hung, but these bandages Marigo proceeded to unloose, and placed him naked as he was born on a pile of his father's clothes on the bowl in the middle of the room. Around the bowl were placed seven jars; each jar contained honey, and into the honey were stuck seven candles. Now these candles form the chief factor in the ceremony of fate-telling. When a child is born a neighbour comes in to make 'the candle' as it is called. She gets a very long wick, and around this she rolls seven coats of wax; this long candle she cuts into seven pieces, and they are ready for the ceremony.

When all the relatives and guests were seated around the naked body of baby dragon, the seven candles were blessed by Papa Manoulas; one was to be the candle of St. Athanasius, another of St. Mammas, and so on; generally the patron saints of neighbouring churches are chosen for the sake of convenience. When blessed the candles were lighted, and for the space of twenty minutes we all sat around in solemn silence, broken only by the periodical cries from baby dragon, and the groaning of some prayer. At length a candle went out – If I remember right it was the candle of St. Panteleomon; thus the indication of the Fates was made plain, St. Panteleomon was to be the patron saint for life of the youthful Karpathiote. To this saint he would have to offer up his prayers when in danger; before his picture he would have to light his candle in church; on his day baby dragon would have to entertain his friends. St. Panteleomon would act as his intercessor for favour with God; for according to the idea of the Greek Church no man can make his prayers direct to so sublime a being as the Creator of mankind; some mediation is necessary.

At this juncture the other candles were extinguished; the mother on one side and Marigo on the other held the swaddling clothes over baby dragon's head; one said as she did so 'You have crossed the river,' and the other replied 'Therefore be not afraid.' The bay was

---

[36] The Bents donated a 'swaddling band' from Kárpathos to the Pitt Rivers Museum, Oxford in 1888 (1888.37.7). It featured in Mabel's select exhibition to the Royal Anthropological Institute in 1886 (see page 185).

Beekeeper's store, Diafáni.

thereupon dressed again and restored to his swing; the honey was distributed amongst the guests, together with presents of figs and wheat, and as each went away he wished for the infant some great good fortune.

But the fate-telling ceremony was not over yet. That evening the bowl was again put in the middle of the room and in it they cast this time flour and water, which was stirred until it had assumed the consistency of dough; in the midst of this honey and butter were put, and the men and women squatted around to eat and talk. The last thing at night when all the guests had disperses, old Marigo filled the bowl once more, put it again in the middle of the room, shut the door, and went round to sprinkle the walls with sacred oil; as she did so she said, 'Come, Fate of Fates, come to bless this child; may he have ships, and mules, and diamonds; may he become a prince.

The bowl was left all night thus filled with food, that the Fates might partake thereof, and be willing in their consequent good humour richly to endow the child. This was the conclusion of the ceremony – a conclusion, said the schoolmaster, which puts much money into old Marigo's pocket, for they think no one can do it so well as she, and her charges are made accordingly. A year after birth they go through another fate-telling ceremony of a similar nature, only that this time a tray is set in the middle of the room, filled with various articles; the first of these the baby touches is held to indicate the calling in life which the Fates wish him to pursue.

'[A] plough such as Homer would have seen if he had not been blind.'

Eight days after birth baby dragon was received into the bosom of the Orthodox Church, and we could not leave Mesochorion till the day after, for we wished to be present at the ceremony – and furthermore our Greek servant was to be godfather. Marigo on this occasion was again very busy, and Papa Manoulas too, who looked considerably more respectable in his robes of office than in his every-day garb. It interested us greatly to see our little friend dragon immersed bodily in warm water, and the ceremony of dancing round the font, as performed by the priest and godparents, made us think of the *amphidromia* of antiquity; but these things were not new to us – they happen in Karpathos, as they do elsewhere.

But when they took the child home, and presented him to his mother, we saw what we had never seen before – for the good woman met them on the threshold, and performed what they term the incense of the ploughshare; that is to say, she waved the family share with embers in it, after the fashion of the priests in church, in front of the child, supposing that thereby she would secure for her offspring strength like the iron of the share, and skill in agriculture such as former owners of the share had possessed. They do this also on the return of a bride and bridegroom from the church; and though the better-class Karpathiotes, with Mrs. Chrysanthemum at their head, affect to scoff at this custom, nevertheless the poor adhere to it still, and it will do for many a year.

The mother then received them into her house; as a mark of reverence to Papa Manoulas, who entered first, she touched the ground with her fingers, and then raised his hand to her lips to kiss. The god-parents came next, bearing the child, now known as Matthew, which name he received from our servant, his god-father. He, poor man, was not accustomed to this ceremony, and looked bewildered when called upon to give the words expected of the god-father on the delivery of the child; so Papa Manoulas stepped forward, and said them for him: 'I deliver up to you the child, baptised, incensed, anointed – in fact made a Christian;' and then, specially addressing the mother, he continued, 'that you may protect it carefully from fire, precipices, and all evil; that you may deliver it up again to us at the second coming spotless and undefiled.'

The grateful mother took her infant from Matthew's arms and placed it in its swing, whilst the father handed us all once more sweets and *raki* to conclude the entertainment. I should like to have been at Mesochorion forty days after the birth, the day on which the mother was again received into the church and into the houses of her neighbours – for it is not considered proper for a mother to visit in any house before the forty days have expired. But not even the pressing invitation of Marigo to enter ourselves as medical students under her guidance could tempt us to remain. If we would stay, she promised, by ocular demonstration, to prove the superiority of her system to our own; nevertheless we contented ourselves with hearing what they were going to do on the fortieth day.

The mother and child first go to church with a jug of water; after the service is performed, and the water blessed, they visit their neighbours, and the mother sprinkles each house she visits with water out of the jug, saying as she does so, ' that your jugs may not break.' As she crosses the threshold it is expected of her to put the handle of the door-key into her mouth, to make the plates as strong as the iron of the key, as the saying goes.

The perils that surround babyhood from the uncanny demons of the air are numerous at Mesochorion. Nereids love nothing better than to strike children with a mysterious wasting; greedy Lamiæ will suck their blood. The evil eye affects them more than it does grown-up people, and to counteract these perils mothers will subject their children to tortures innumerable. If the child is weakly, and Nereid-struck, it must be left naked on the cold marble altar in church for some hours;[37] if a child is in any way distorted, it has been struck by a Nereid's laugh, they say, and the only remedy is priestly exorcism – secret offices performed frequently by Papa Manoulas at the dead of night in church, for which he gets a loaf and a cheese.

Children's necks are one mass of amulets and charms to protect them from the unseen dangers, like those in antiquity they wore to avert the glance of the god Fascinus. Old Marigo is especially skilled in making these articles. Whenever there is a new oven built, the first loaf baked is stamped with the church's seal, I.X.N.[38] Marigo secures this, and sells it afterwards to a parent who is rich enough to invest in so valuable a phylactery for his child. She has her charms to ward off erysipelas and warts. On the first day of May she binds round he patients' waists branches of mallow, that their stomachs may not ache; and on the first of March she sees that every inhabitant binds round an arm or a finger a bit of red string, as a charm against fevers; these they cut off on Easter Sunday, and burn in the churchyard, saying, as they do so, that they are sending the fevers to the Jews.

Marigo's remedies, we discovered, were especially based on the theory that 'prevention is better than cure,' and then there are so many chances against individuals suffering from the complaints that she professes to ward off that she is generally sure of success. When we left Mesochorion, we did so with Marigo's curses ringing in our ears. She had been exceedingly kind to us, she said, and she had taught us valuable secrets unknown in our land, the only

---

[37] A practice Theodore will recall from Sérifos (Bent 1885b, p. 7).
[38] 'ΙΗΣΟΥΣ ΧΡΙΣΤΟΣ ΝΙΚΑ', popularly 'Jesus Christ Conquers'.

equivalent for which was a far larger sum of money than we thought fit to offer. In spite of her curses we reached the village of Olympus in safety, with only one mishap – our baggage-mule took to kicking, and scattered the mountain side with dearly-treasured provender.

Shepherds on Kárpathos[39]

Then again, I spent some time in a shepherds' village on the island of Karpathos, high up amongst the mountains. Karpathos is perhaps the most isolated of the larger islands, being situated betwixt Crete and Rhodes, from which it is divided by two dangerous seas only to be crossed in small sailing-boats. The shepherds' village we visited is in the most remote corner of this island, with lovely views around and panoramas on all sides over the island-dotted sea. The shepherds speak a dialect rich in old classical words which have survived here alone. Their mules they call their 'possessions,' and they are ignorant of the word usually made use of by the modern Greeks; their goats they call their 'thousands,' a word suggestive at once of patriarchal life, and flocks which could not be counted for multitude. These goats are classified according to their distinctive marks, and in the names used to distinguish these classes we found words which appear now only in Liddell and Scott. The shepherds and their families for the greater part of the year dwell in caves high up in the mountains, and die in them like their goats, with this difference only, that their friends do not allow their bones to bleach in the sun, though they inter them without any religious ceremony; they wail over them a great deal and wait for the religious part of the business until a priest chances to pass that way. For the three months of winter they reside in the village, which is composed of small homesteads or *mandras*, probably like that in which the herd of Ulysses dwelt in Ithaca. Each house is a low cabin, to enter which you have to stoop, and consists of one room only, where cattle and people live together. It is built of large stones without cement, and through the cracks the north wind whistles horribly. Across the roof is a beam, the top of which serves as the cupboard. There is a place for a fire, but no outlet for smoke; some brushwood laid on stones is the family bed, and the floor in wet weather is inches deep in slush and filth. The summer spent in the caves and in the open air must be a delightful change from this. Sometimes you may see a serpent in these cottages, which is never disturbed, but deemed the *genius loci*, just as in ancient days if a serpent was found in a house an altar was erected to it, and it was esteemed a symbol of happiness, and there are invisible serpents too they say, which bring good when blessed, but when driven away by neglect cause the destruction of the houses, and thus they account for the Greek ruins in their midst. They look upon green lizards which run over their walls with a very different eye. The idea prevails that it is from eating these that serpents derive their venom, so they kill lizards whenever they can, and it is thought that whoever succeeds in killing forty of them is sure to go to heaven, having saved so many men from poison.

I visited many families in their mountain caves, which are deliciously cool in the summer heats, and the mud floors are scarcely ever dry. Stone benches are put along the sides covered with dairy produce; in one corner is the oven, where the new milk is simmering all day. When the family goes out to attend the flocks, a lot of prickly brushwood is placed at the cave's mouth; no other door is needed. The mountains of Karpathos are exceedingly high, rivalling those of the neighbouring Crete, and a story of a golden treasure on the slopes of Mount

---

[39] The extract is from a longer article in the *Fortnightly Review* (1886, 40:236 (1886: Aug.) pp. 214-224), called 'Greek Peasant Life'.

Lastos curiously reminds one of a similar legend told in ancient times in Crete. It is now said there must be gold up there, because the teeth of their flocks are often tinged with gold after browsing on this mountain. The shepherds wear sandals of untanned ox hide – just a flat piece of leather fastened by thongs to the feet; these are most comfortable for long mountain journeys, and exactly the same that Homer describes. The peasant's wife is but a chattel, to be hounded and worked like a slave. She waits upon her husband, but never eats with him. She is a pitiable object, much as she must have been in the time of Hesiod, who considered it the worst feature of a bad wife to sit at meals with her lord. Hesiod's advice to a young man starting in life would be apply to a Karpathiote to-day: 'You must begin with a house, a wife, an ox, and a plough.'[40] The women almost invariably have their faces covered all but the eyes. This, I am inclined to believe, is not a Turkish, but an ancient Greek custom, for an island like Karpathos, which has only been two hundred years under Turkish rule,[41] and on which a Turkish woman has doubtless never stepped, it is not likely that the fashion has been borrowed from them. An Italian traveller in the Middle Ages tells how Greek women never went out of doors in broad daylight, and were never seen in public. Michael Psellos, the best authority on Byzantine customs in the eleventh century, tells us how his mother wore a veil to hide her face from the gaze of men, and how the officials in attendance on the Empress Zoe and Theodora never raised their eyes from the ground, out of respect to the sex of their rulers. Thus did Penelope walk, followed by two women, and her face covered with a magnificent veil.

In the village each house has its threshing-floor attached, and close to each threshing-floor are curious round holes in the ground, called lakkoi, in which the farmer stores his grain.[42] When dug, they cover the inside of these holes with straw, and on this they pile up the grain so as to form a cone-shaped mound; this they cover with straw, and on the top put some brushwood, and then pad the whole down with earth, so that the rain never penetrates. This is a very ancient method of storing grain, and is peculiar now to this spot. Ancient Greek husbandmen called these holes σιροὶ.

Not far from the threshing-floor reposes their primitive plough, a plough such as Homer would have seen if he had not been blind. The chief requisite for a Karpathiote plough is a tree with a trunk and two branches: one branch serves as a tail, whilst the other, tipped with the share, penetrates the ground, and the trunk serves as the pole. Sometimes there are slight improvements on this primitive instrument, but not often; its chief merit is that it is so light that the farmer can carry it over his shoulder as he drives his bullocks before him to their work. They never care about making deep furrows, and they never make straight ones. The ploughman begins his day by a ploughing a circle, over which he goes, round and round and across, in a careless fashion, till his task is done. The share is a pointed cylindrical bit of iron in no way altered from those that are found in ancient days. A Karpathiote peasant has a great veneration for his share; it is handed down from father to son, and from plough to plough. When a marriage takes place, the mother of the bridegroom meets the happy pair on the threshold of their new home on their return from church, and there she gives them what is called the 'incense of the share;' that is to say, she puts into the iron some ashes from the hearth and waves them about in front of the young couple, after the fashion of the priest in church. This is supposed to insure for them strength like the iron of the share,

---

[40] *Works and Days*, line 405.
[41] The Ottomans captured Rhodes in 1522 and by 1540 had taken control of the neighbouring islands, including Kárpathos.
[42] Common to the wider region, Theodore had already seen these on Kéa in the Cyclades (Bent 1885b, 220).

and industrious habits such as former owners of the share have displayed. There is usually a sort of shed against the cottage, where rude tools are kept – wooden spades, a pickaxe, and perhaps a saw. On the wall of the shed hangs what the owner calls his φλὰκι, that is to say his φυλὰκι, or skin in which the grain they want for household consumption is kept. You find in Aristotle exactly the same name for exactly the same article.

The peasants do not often go to the neighbouring village of Olympus from their mountain hamlet. This village, which contains about a thousand inhabitants, and is itself replete with old-world customs, is to them the centre of the world and dissipation; but they generally contrive to go on the 11th of September, the day of the raising of the cross, and then they take with them a bundle tied up in a white handkerchief. This they hang on the tripod on which the tray for holding the cross is put, and they do not remove it until the cross is elevated. The handkerchief contains corn, barley, beans, two roses, figs, garlic, and a little beeswax. When the time for sowing seed has come, they rub a little of the garlic on the foreheads of their oxen, and say as they do so, 'May you, my oxen, and may you, my family, be strong! May the fruits of the earth be blessed!' The roses are broken up and scattered about the first field which is sown that year, as an emblem of abundance and success, and all the rest of the contents of the handkerchief are thrown into the earth. A strict fast is maintained all day, and in doing this undoubtedly they perpetuate the old sacrifices (Πρηρόσιαι) before the sowing of seed to ensure a productive harvest.

In the village of Olympus much of the primitive old life is left. The men carry the thick hair garments which their wives weave at home, they wear their hair long and shaggy, and they govern themselves by a sort of parliament, which meets once a year in the village church. We were present at one of these meetings, and were struck by the deference shown to the elders and the attention which the younger men paid to the words which fell from their mouths. At their feasts the same deference to old age is manifest; the elders sing first those idylls which are only found on Karpathos, and are of a genuine archaic type. Very few of them can write or read, and any one that does so is honoured at once with the title of Diakos, or deacon, and is a person of great importance at the assemblies, for he it is who keeps the minutes, and can write down pretty nearly what he pleases, sitting cross-legged, with the inkstand on the ground before him. By the stream which flows down a narrow valley from Olympus to the sea, great reeds grow which are often used for the ceilings of their flat-roofed houses and for hedges. This they call νάρθηκα (ναρθηξ), a survival of the old word for the reed by which Prometheus brought down fire from heaven. And one can easily imagine the origin of this myth by watching the customs of to-day. A peasant housewife of Olympus, who wishes to carry a light from one house to another, will put the embers into one of these reeds to prevent it being extinguished…

In Karpathos houses are built on this principle: wood is carried up from the shore, stones are brought, and when the house is finished the relatives bring presents of food for the table which is to be spread for those who have taken part in its erection. Some of the islands, especially Eubœa[43] and those contiguous to the mainland, indulge in the abominable luxury of resinated wine; that is to say, the wine is put into barrels with resin in it, with a view to preserve it, and this gives a very strong flavour of varnish to the beverage. The Greeks love this wine, and it acts as a strong and refreshing tonic in hot weather. Foreigners, as a rule, are rather doubtful about its excellence, though I do not think the flavour is worse than that which beer must present when drunk for the first time. The custom is by no means

---

[43] The Bents spent a few days on Évia, in the early 1880s, as part of a trip to the Argolid and major tourist sites. Mabel did not start her *Chronicles* until the expedition to the Cyclades in 1882/3.

modern. Plutarch (Quest, Nat. x.) tells us how the ancients put sea-water into their wine to give it a flavour, and that the Euboeans actually did put resin into their wine to flavour it...

A curious instance of the tenacity of ...old customs in remote places is to be found in Karpathos, where the inhabitants celebrate New Year's Day twice, once on the 1st of September, and once on the ordinary first of the year. The 1st of September was the first of the old Byzantine year, and on this day Karpathiote women at dawn wash the streets with water, which is brought from a certain sacred well; they likewise wash their houses, and no one may enter the houses until after the ceremony except the person who has been sent for the jug of sacred water, and who receives in return a present of figs and bread. They spread the leaves of a rose, which has been blessed in church, on the floor, and wish each other many years, as the master of the house says, 'May you, my family, be healthy, and may money be showered into my house like the leaves of this rose.' On the usual New Year's Day, they go through the same ceremony of washing and wishing prosperity, only if the day is wet the street cleansing is omitted.

On their many festivals and saint's days, the Greek islanders are the most enthusiastic players of games. Some of these are wild, some of them are amusing, and some can be distinctly traced to antiquity, as probably all could if we had ample records to go upon. At Easter-time the maidens of the islands have the game of swing (κουνιά). They hang a rope from one wall of the narrow village street to the other; on this they put some clothes to form a seat, and two maidens seated side by side, facing in opposite directions, swing, and as they swing the sing local ditties, plaintive for the most part, and in a high shrill voice. Aware of this, the young men try to pass by, and are called upon for a toll of a copper apiece, a song, and a swing. They generally sing such words as these, 'The gold is swung, the silver is swung, and swung too is my love with the golden hair,' to which the maiden replies, 'Who is it that swings me, that I may gild him with my favour, that I may work him a fez all covered with pearls?' Having paid this copper, the youth is allowed to pass, and another comes by and does likewise. These games at Volatha, in Karpathos, take place on the Sundays in Lent, when the young men who are at home from their work on this day can be present. We are strangely reminded of the game of swing which the maidens of Athens played in remembrance of the death of Erigone, who hung herself from a tree, when they sang plaintive ditties in honour of her name, and garlanded themselves with flowers, whereas now they sing solemn ditties about the passion and resurrection of our Lord.

'Idylls of Karpathos'[44]

A long thin island stretches like a riband in the sea between Rhodes and Crete; this is Karpathos. It is visited by no one, no steamer touches there, and all communication with the outer world is carried on by sailing boats at uncertain intervals. Before going there I could get but little information about the place, only the records of a hurried visit which a German paid it some fifty years ago, and one passage in his book*[45] struck me forcibly. It ran as follows:- 'The village of Olympos or Elympos has about 250 houses; the dialect of Elympites is said to be in the highest degree Hellenic, and their ballads so poetical that they

---

[44] From 'Idyls of Karpathos' (*Gentleman's Magazine*, 260:1862 (1886: Feb), pp. 185-190). (Theodore's preferred spelling is with one 'l'.)

[45] * Ludwig Ross, *Inselreissen* [Theodore's note; more fully: *Reisen auf den griechischen Inseln des ägäischen Meeres* (Band 3), Tübingen, 1845, p. 63.]

Easter and the windmills of Ólymbos.

often move the listeners to tears. I have heard such wonderful things related of both, that it was with great grief that I had to abandon my intention of visiting the place.'

A remote island such as Karpathos is, affords the best possible study of Hellenism as it exists to-day, and the remotest village of this remote island is Elympos, lost away amongst precipitous mountains, a village of shepherds who speak a dialect which even their nearest neighbours can hardly understand, and which contains old classical words and idioms which have disappeared from amongst other Greek-speaking communities.

I now propose to give a few of their ballads as we heard them during a stay of some weeks in this village – ballads, which these shepherds sing on their feast-days and at their weddings as they dance, which the women sing as they ply their looms and spin, for there is something poetical in the air of this place; nothing can be done without singing, and every vocation in life is illustrated by its own peculiar idyl. Even the oarsmen who rowed us away from a tiny harbour about two hours distant from the village kept time as they rowed by the repetition of certain rhymes, of which every sailor knows a large store.

The stroke of the boat rises from his seat at each pull, and as he does so screams the first word of the rhyme, for example, 'assistance', number two continues, 'and protection'; number three says, 'and God'; and bow rapidly repeats the last line of the rhyme, 'the boat shall go onwards.'*[46]

The pastoral idyls of Elympos recall to one's mind passages from Theocritus and hi odes, full of touches of social life, and they are unique in their simplicity. None but a simple-minded peasant could have conceived such ideas as those contained in a ballad called 'The Queen and the Shepherd,' a very favourite one at all their feasts. The moral, of course, is contentment, and no one is more contented in the world than a Karpathiote shepherd in his mountain *mandra*, where he and his family live for months. It is perhaps only a cave in the rock; nothing is heard but the bleating of the goats around them; they live on milk and that delicious white curd called 'mysethra,' which, when eaten with honey, is, as they term it, 'food for the gods.' Their only bed is brushwood spread on the bare ground, and their only diversion is a tedious journey once a week to the village with skins full of cheese, butter, and milk. In this translation I have endeavoured to adhere to the original as much as possible, I fear to the detriment of the rhythm.

The Queen and the Shepherd

The king and the herd each a wage made
That the heart of the queen was his –
  The queen with the golden hair.

'Come, prithee, my lord, what's your stake to be?'
Quoth the shepherd with bantering voice –
  The shepherd with long wild hair.

'My crown, my realm, mine all I'll stake;
What have you to offer like this?' said the king,
  With a royal, disdainful air.

'A thousand sheep with their silvery bells,
And a black-eyed, yellow-cheeked lamb
  With flowing silken hair.

'Such as gives you wool for your royal robes,
And the queen for her mantles gay –
  The queen with the golden hair.'

Down from the crags for the shepherd came,
With his sheep, his goats, and his lamb –
  The lamb with the silvery hair.

The king was amazed, and the queen she yearned

---

[46] * **The words of this distych are** – Βοηθὸς καὶ σκεπὸς Θεός / Ἡ Βάρκα πάει ἐμπρός. [Theodore's note]

> To possess such treasures as these,
> Such sheep and such goats so fair.
>
> 'Make me your shepherdess,' she cried
> 'Your maid for your *mandra*, your slave;
> > Give me every care;
> That I may eat 'mysethra' white
> Out of its basket of reeds;
> That I may drink of the freshest milk;
> May hold in my hand the shepherd's crook;
> That I may have from morn till night
> > My shepherd with shaggy hair.'

Another idyl requires a little prefatory explanation. When a man contemplates matrimony in Karpathos he does not propose himself, but sends his mother or some elderly female relative to do so, which is called προξενία. In some parts this old lady wears stockings of two colours. 'I see her coming with stockings of two colours, I think we shall have an offer,' writes a modern Greek poet. If the proposal is refused the man is said to 'eat gruel.' In this idyl a prince is supposed to have fallen in love with a girl, and he has applied to his mother with a view to the proposal. The prudential sentiments of a Karpathiote parent, who never allows a son or daughter to marry unless the marriage is financially advantageous, is very true to life; also the love of excessive numbers as indicating grandeur, a feature common to many of their songs.

Prince.	Mother! I yearn for a fair-haired girl
	    Whom I saw the other day;
	Amongst the vines she was wandering,
	    And she washed in the brooklet's spray.

Mother.	If she's poor and needy, harkee, my son, My consent to your marriage will never be won.
Prince.	Nay, mother, her feet were in golden shoes; Mother, her shoes were of gold; She's clad in velvet of different hues. Her wealth must be untold.
Mother.	Truly, my son, if it is as you say, Believe me, your mother will never say nay.

Here there is a pause, during which time the mother is supposed to send the *proxenia*, and an offer of marriage is made. This is the reply: –

Mother.	Ten learned men and eight-and-twenty priests
	    I have sent to the damsel's home;
	And sixty-two scribes, her dower to write,
	    Have thither also gone.
	Full forty days they ascended her stairs,
	For forty more they delayed;

But the girl gave cautious answer to them,
    And prudently she said:
'Why come ye scribes and learned men?
    Why come ye priests to me?'
The prince has sent us, my lady,' they said,
    'To ask you his wife to be.'

'If the prince can sow the waves with corn,
    And build his threshing-floor right in the main,
So that neither the seed nor the straw be spoiled –
    then may you return to me again.'

So many of the idyls are melancholy, even those that they sing as they revolve in the dance on a feast-day in the village square. To suit these songs they dance what they call the *siganos*, in which men and women form a semicircle with arms interlaced, so that the leader holds the hand of number three, number two holds the hand of number four, and so on. This dance is looked upon as an occasion for rest and singing after the more violent steps of other dances, and in the *siganos* they will sing such a song as this:-

In her virgin couch a damsel slept
    Alone on Good Friday night;
And as she slept she dreamt a dream,
    Which she sought to divine aright.

A palace she saw, with windows all
    Of silvery, sparkling glass;
Whilst fountains sprinkled far and wide
    Their spray o'er the mossy grass.

When told, her mother joyfully said,
    'The meaning to me is clear:
The palace is your husband's love,
    The windows are babies dear;
And all the relatives of your lord
    Will be fountains bright and clear.'

'Hush, mother dear!' the girl replied;
    'you do not explain it well.
The palace means my cold, dark tomb,
    The windows are Charon's knell;
The fountains of water are your two eyes
    Which with weeping soon will swell.'

Another of these plaintive ditties runs as follows: –

Its lonely life a tiny bird
    Bewailed by the river-side.
With loving notes another bird

Thus tenderly replied:
> 'Bewail not, little one, your fate,
> Cease to pour out your grief;
> To-morrow's dawn shall see us wed,
> And together we will live
> Down by the stream where the daphnes grow,
> The daphnes so green and so fair,
> Where the red ones*[47] scatter their blossoms around,
> And the white ones their perfume rare.'

Many of their songs turn on a curious feature in Karpathiote life, namely, that the men go away for the summer months to seek employment in Asia Minor or elsewhere, leaving the women behind to gather in the harvest and make the wine; consequently many men, attracted by the life and gaiety of the world, never return to their homes. This is constantly the cause of grief and lamentation to the women who are thus deserted. As they are baking bread at the ovens you may hear them sing of their absent friends. A mother will every Saturday bake biscuits for her absent son, who will never return to eat them. This feature in their life gives rise to much that is melancholy in the women, their songs more often resemble dirges. And then there are women who develop a knowledge of the black art, and pretend to mix horrible portions, which if a damsel can introduce into her lover's food unawares he is sure to return, and if a wife can give to her husband before he leaves he will remain faithful to her during his absence. One of the favourite songs on this subject runs as follows:-

> For fourteen years away from me
> My love has made his home
> It is in Armenia he lives,
> And no news from him has come.

A short pause here ensues.

> And thus he writes to me at last,
> To drown my memories of the past.

Another pause, to give weight to the climax of woe which the message brings.

> Go marry now, if not wed yet,
> For the truth I thus must tell:
> An Armenian girl has won from you
> Your love by magic spell.
>
> She has charmed the stars of heaven,
> She has charmed the winds and the sea,
> She has charmed the ship that it cannot sail,
> And she, too, has charmed me.

---

[47] * *Oleanders*, which grow in wonderful profusion in a valley near Elympos. [Theodore's note]

> Go marry now, if not wed yet,
>   Or bury yourself in a cell;
> For never again will you look upon
>   The boy whom you loved so well.

Poetry pervades every branch of life in Elympos. Charms are said in poetry, blasphemous, many of them, according to our notions, but warranted to cure diseases, drive away vultures from the flocks, vermin from the grain; and in these rude charms are hidden many beautiful ideas. A mother has pretty lullabies for the baby who swings in its primitive cradle tied from the rafters of the house, one of which thus runs:-

> Mrs. Mary Magdalene,
>   Sleepest thou alone?
> No, my Lord, my master Christ,
>   I am not all alone.
> Peter guards me, so does Paul,
>   The twelve Apostles, one and all.
> My door is locked, I've turned the key,
>   So no one can frighten me.

Everywhere in out-of-the-way corners of Greece the laments over the dead are extremely poetical. Women sing them as a rule, and as they work in the fields you may hear them composing verses, which will be sung as improvised wails over the corpse at the next funeral. These death-wails they call *mœrologia*, and those of Elympos are wonderfully quaint. Charon[48] is the hero of them all, the mysterious giant, who wanders about naked and girt with three swords. 'One is for the archons, another for the rich, and the third, the poisoned one, is for us, the herds.'

One of the prettiest ideas is that which represents Charon as planting a garden with the bones of the dead for plants. It is as follows:-

> Charon wished to make a garden.
> The aged he planted as lemon trees,
> And the young as cypresses;
> But the little children he put as flowers in his vases.

'Karpathiote Dialect'[49]

As a field for the study of modern Greek manners and customs, with a view to comparing them with antiquity, I consider Karpathos almost unique; at their ceremonies connected with religious worship, deaths, marriages, and births, medical cures, exorcisms, incantations,

---

[48] Theodore echoes these musings on Charon and Kárpathos for *The National Review* in 'Personification of the Mysterious Amongst the Modern Greeks' (Vol. 9, April 1887, 224-233).

[49] From 'The Islands of Telos and Karpathos', *Journal of Hellenic Studies*, 6, 1885, pp. 233-242. Theodore was always interested in dialects – only a few weeks before his death in May 1897 he was sitting outside his tent on Socotra, quizzing a local assistant on words and phrases and making notes. Theodore expanded this essay from his short article (see page 181) for *Athenæum* ('The Carpathiote Dialect' (No. 3011 (1885, July), p. 48), written, and apparently sent to London, from Sýros, on the couple's way home in April 1885.

and so forth, we came across things, by entering into the routine of daily life, which can have changed little during many centuries.

Before going to Karpathos last winter a passage in Ludwig Ross's *Inselreisen* (which book contains the only reliable information we have on this remote island)[50] excited my curiosity. It ran as follows: 'The village of Olympos, or Elymbos, has about 250 houses, the dialect of the Elympites must be in the highest degree Hellenic, their ballads and songs so poetical that they often move the listeners to tears, I have heard such wonderful things related of them, that it was with great grief that I was not able to visit this place.'

Added to this, former experience in the Cyclades had taught me that the existence of an almost classical Greek-speaking population in the remote islands was quite possible, so it was with keen interest that we took up our residence for a few weeks there. Glossaries of words in use in out-of-the-way corners of Greece have appeared, but none, as yet, from Elympos, so I here say a few words about the dialect, hoping thereby to induce others more competent than myself to collect a glossary of these words and expressions, and to confer a boon on philology and Hellenic studies alike.

For the most part the inhabitants of this village are a wild, uncultured race of shepherds, and their customs of great value to the student of folk lore and comparative mythology, and it was in the pastoral life of the place that we found most to interest us; about an hour from Elympos is a hamlet, or rather a collection of small homesteads where the shepherds from the mountains pass the three winter months with their flocks and their families. Each homestead is constructed on the same principle as on the accompanying plan.

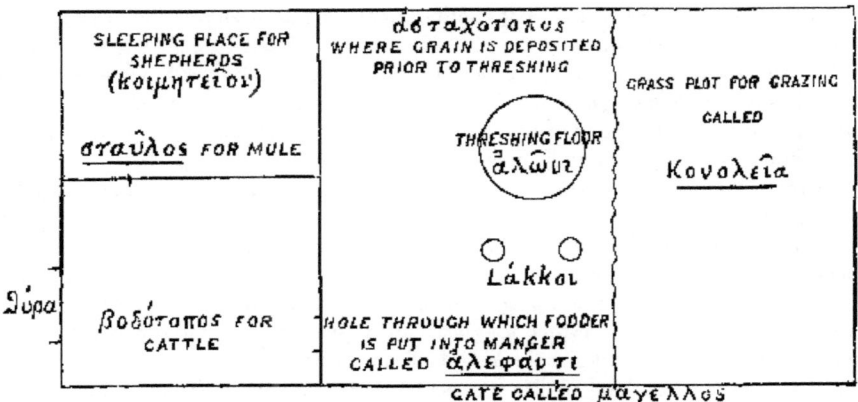

The hamlet is called Stavlalonia, from the fact that each house has its σταῦλος and its ἀλῶνι, and in connection with this homestead there are several curious words. In the first place you enter a θύρα, not a πόρτα, the usual word in Greek *patois* for a door. Then there is the ἀλεφάντι, a hole in the wall through which fodder is introduced into the manger, the κονολεῖα, a grass plot where the mule is tethered, and the λάκκοι, or holes in the ground where the grain is buried when threshed; this, I fancy, is the same custom which they practised in antiquity when the holes were called σιροί.

---

[50] See page x, note 11.

These shepherds call their mules κτήματα, or possessions, and do not understand the use of any such word as ζῶα or μουλάρια, common elsewhere in Greece; this use of the word κτήματα is, I take it, of distinctly classical origin. Their goats they called χίλια, or thousands, a word suggestive of patriarchal life and flocks which could not be counted for number; and in their distinctive words for goats they have many curious words, for example πολιομούρια is used for goats with grey faces and ears, retaining the classical use of the word πολιός, which in the vulgar is always ψαρὸς.

Κόρνοψ is used to express a goat which is black behind and white in front. Is this word the same as the word Κόρνοψ, used by Strabo, instead of πάρνοψ, to signify a locust? Again, they use words to distinguish goats, which must have crept in through a Latin-Byzantine agency; for example μαξιλλάτος, for a goat with reddish cheeks, the word μαξιλλάρια being now only used in the modern language for pillow. ρουσσόμερτος, too, expresses the same class of goat – the word ρούσσιος being unknown in modern Greek, but common amongst Byzantine authors, who adopted the Latin word *russeus* for red.

They use the expression ἀπ' εἰκασμοῦ ὁμιλῶ, instead of the usual μὲ συμπερασμὸν, to express 'I speak from conjecture.' I don't think the form of the word εἰκασμὸς occurs in modern Greek; εἰκασία does, but I never heard it used in this idiomatic way which we find in Strabo and Byzantine writers. For an apron they use the New Testament word λέντιον, instead of the vulgar ποδιὰ or 'μπροσθελλα, and the narrow alleys of Elympos are called ῥύμαι. Now this again is a New Testament word, being used in the Acts for the street which is called 'straight,' and suggests a comparison with the celebrated oracle ἔσται μὲν 'Ρώμη ῥύμη καὶ Δῆλος ἄδηλος.

A *young* man they speak of as ἄωρος, 'unripe,' reminding us of Herodotus, ἄωρος θανεῖν, and Plutarch, ἄωρος πρὸς γάμον.

Κανάχια is a word in use for caresses, kisses, which strikes one as a possible survival of the classical words κανάχη, κανάσσω, to make a sharp noise; though this meaning was originally confined to the sound of water, there is no apparent reason why, after the lapse of ages, it should not be applied to the noise produced by the lips.[51]

There is a place near Elympos where labourers are accustomed to meet together morning and evening, so that they may go to and from their work in company. The spot is situated at the summit of a beetling cliff, and they call it ἀποθόκτρια, which appears as if connected with the classical word ἀποθρώσκω, which was used to express the abrupt rising of a cliff. Να μεθάρομεν, 'let us change places,' appears as if connected with the classical word μεθάρμοσις. Words like νικαδὸ for πρωΐ, early in the morning, and others of curious, and in many cases inexplicable, origin are to be found at Elympos.

But the most curious thing of all in connection with the Elympitan dialect is the existence of a gamma which is introduced under circumstances which are at once suggestive of the digamma and its existence in real life. This gamma is especially remarkable in a dialect which drops the ordinary gamma on every possible occasion, for they say ἤτρωα for ἔτρωγον, I ate, and the ἤλεα for ἔλεγον, I said, ἐώ for ἐγώ, and endless other instances.

Before the word υἱός, a son, they place a hard gamma, which I have not only heard, but seen written in marriage settlements. A mother calls her son Γυιέ μου. Then this gamma is inserted after the diphthong εὐ: for example, they say πιστεύγομεν and δουλεύγομεν, instead of πιστεύομεν and δουλεύομεν. This gamma, I understand likewise, is found in Cypriote dialect, though not in quite so pronounced a degree; wherever it occurs this intrusive gamma is always hard and perfectly distinct from the modern use of the gamma, and reminding

---

[51] The OED gives no derivation for 'canoodle'.

The extensive, ancient site of Vrykoúnda, on the northern tip of Kárpathos, near Trístomo Bay.

one of the change which has made the Latin *vastare*, become *guastara* in Italian, and *gâter* in French.

Excavations on Kárpathos[52]

On this island there are traces still existing of many towns; the first we examined is identified by inscriptions as Poseidonia; old inhabitants still call it by the contraction of this name Posin, but some years ago a name signifying 'drink' appeared objectionable to the sober-minded inhabitants, and they re-christened it, Pegadia or 'wells.' Here there are evidences of pre-historic inhabitants, the graves of whom I was unfortunately unable to open owing to the presence of the Turkish authorities, but I was able to obtain a large stone figure of a female idol, similar to the smaller ones I found at Antiparos, and which were engraved in Vol. V. of this Journal, p. 50.[53] Arkassa on the west of the island is likewise identified by inscriptions, as is also Brykountios, or as it is now called Bourgounta, on the north, but a forth town mentioned by Strabo as Nisyros cannot be found; its site, of course, must have

---

[52] From 'The Islands of Telos and Karpathos', *Journal of Hellenic Studies*, 6, 1885, pp. 233-242.
[53] For the 'female idol', now in the British Museum, see page 152. Theodore's work on Andíparos in February 1883 were his first semi-professional excavations and a major contribution to the early understanding of what was to develop into studies on a distinct Cycladic culture. It can be fairly claimed that his work at the remote sites on Andíparos launched his career as an 'archaeologist'. He published his findings in the *Journal of Hellenic Studies*, Vol. 5 (1884), pp. 42-59.

been one of the three other spots on Karpathos where ruins exist, but where inscriptions have not as yet come to light.

Most of these towns have been roughly dealt with during the Byzantine period, when extensive towns and large churches were built out of the material at hand. Brykountios was apparently the most considerable town during both the earlier and later occupations, and as it was situated at the extreme north of Karpathos, about two hours distant from the Elympos, and several days' journey from the Konak, we were able to pitch our tent there and excavate unmolested.[54]

The town stood on a high tongue of land jutting into the sea; it had a good harbour before the ancient mole, traces of which are easily seen still, was destroyed; the temple and houses have been so mutilated to build the Byzantine town, that it is next to impossible to form any conception of their extent. This town is close to the excellent harbour of Tristoma, and in ancient days must have been a great commercial centre.

The rocks and cliffs around Brykountios are perfectly honey-combed with chiselled tombs of greatly diversified character; on first seeing them I judged of course that they had all been rifled long since by Byzantines and Romans, but on closer examination we found many of them undisturbed, and as to some of them which overhung the sea and were difficult of approach we were the first to roll away the stone from the mouth of the sepulchre. Our finds in these tombs were perhaps not equivalent to our first expectations, the pottery for the most part was but roughly adorned, proving that Karpathos was in its best days, as now, an out of the way spot which had made but little advance in the arts, and the chief interest connected with pottery I brought back is, that it is the first to come from Karpathos and from these rock-cut tombs. But the tombs themselves were extremely interesting, and the great variety of periods of pottery found in close juxtaposition would suggest that the graves had been used again and again, just as the graves of the Karpathiotes now who only allow their relatives to remain a year in the tomb, after which they exhume the bones, tie them up in an embroidered pillow, and throw them into the charnel house.

On approaching the promontory there stands an isolated round rock about thirty feet in height; this is entered by a chiselled passage with tombs on either side, and tombs above these on another level all of which are now empty, and would appear originally to have been closed by an iron or thin marble slab, for round each of the holes is a groove into which a slab has been introduced; close around this rock are numerous shallow tombs cut in the rock, some of which we found unopened, but they contained nothing but one or two coins which crumbled in our hands when we touched them, doubtless the obolos for Charon.[55]

Proceeding along the cliffs we found tombs of every possible description, single chambers, double chambers, tombs one over the other, tombs with steps above them cut in

---

[54] Theodore's clandestine and unauthorized excavations were to eventually lead to him being effectively outlawed from Turkish dominions and he headed for Africa, Arabia, and early demise. The Bents are now at Vrykoúnda, on the northern tip of the island.

[55] Bent's techniques have been widely criticized but A.E. Tozer's contemporary overview of his early endeavours still holds: '[Bent's] inaccuracy in proper names is extraordinary, and this applies to mediaeval and modern as well as ancient ones; and when he ventures on etymologies, they are usually bad... But this does not much detract from the usefulness of the book as a unique description of the life and ideas of a people, which renders it a very storehouse of facts for the student of customs and myths. And in this respect its value will be permanent. Other travellers may follow in Mr. Bent's footsteps, and fill up what is wanting in his archaeological information; but in a few years' time, if any traveller be found so enduring as to attempt once more the task which he has so well performed, it is highly probable that a great part of these interesting customs and ideas will have disappeared.' (Review of *The Cyclades; or, Life among the Insular Greeks*. By J. Theodore Bent', by Henry Fanshawe Tozer, in *Academy* 27 (1885: Jan/June)).

Red-figure oinochoe removed by the Bents from Vrykoúnda, Kárpathos.

the rock, as if for ornamentation, but the most frequent and those which we found the least disturbed were those constructed like this plan:

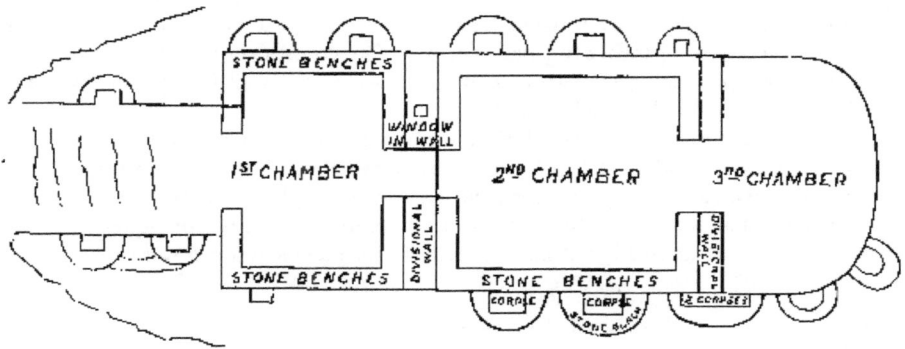

You enter by a sloping *dromos* with walls on either side chiselled in the rocks, in which were generally two or three tombs much ruder than those inside, and invariably containing ware of a much more recent period, Cyrenic was similar to what we have from Cyprus, and objects of pottery of rough material.

After clearing the circular entrance to the tomb from rubbish you enter a good sized chamber. About ten feet square and six in height with stone benches round, all formed by chiselling the rock; the graves are to the right and left and are after a uniform pattern consisting of a chamber cut deep into the rock with a terrace or bench left all round, and the corpse and pottery deposited into a sort of well which was sunk slightly below the level of the floor. These tombs were closed with very large stones and covered with a thick cement, in many cases the outer chamber had likewise been entirely covered with cement, and sometimes we saw traces of patterns and writing of a late date in Byzantine characters. Only one very faint inscription appeared to be of a good period, and curiously enough it was to the memory of a man whose name occurs in the inscription built into one of the later churches, the name was *Aidoios* which I cannot find in any glossary of ancient Greek names. In another grave we found a marble memorial tablet in letters of a good period to the memory of one Menekrates, and in this grave we found a larger collection of pottery than elsewhere, no less than twenty plates, ten lamps, several lamp feeders, and endless specimens of smaller articles. In one grave we found a *pithos* full of calcined bones, and in the middle of the bones a prettily executed *mastos* of black pottery.[56]

To return to the plan, the second chamber is entered by a low door, and in the divisional wall three feet thick are two windows, one over and the other beside the door. There has been a door between the two chambers, the hinge holes of which are still visible. This second chamber is considerably larger than the first, but is constructed on the same plan. The third chamber, which does not seem to have had a door or windows, contained tombs of a later date and was finished off in a much ruder fashion being very much lower, and as will be seen from the plan the tombs around it were never completed; there was a curious long tomb between the second and third chambers with two corpses in it, so that when emptied we could crawl through from one chamber to the other. This idea of connecting two tombs seems to have been of later date, for most of those outside were thus connected.

On the spot on which our tent was pitched there was a quadrangle for tombs, two sides of which had been beautifully chiselled out of the rock and furnished with two rows of tombs, all of which, however, had been opened; it was curious on a vacant space to see the chiselled plan of a tomb which had been designed but never executed.

Another class of tomb we accidentally hit upon consisted of natural holes in the cliff in almost inaccessibly places overhanging the sea; the entrances had been closed with cement and stones, and some of them contained as many as four corpses; the pottery in these tombs was of the best period, big *pithoi* with the maker's mark on, and well glazed things, which as a rule had been rare in the chiselled tombs.

On the small island of Saria, which is separated from the north of Karpathos by a narrow strait, we found similar rock-cut tombs, none of which, however, had more than one chamber with a tomb on either side, and a narrow trench between. All these tombs had been rifled, but amongst the *débris* in them we saw more beautiful bits of pottery than any we had found in the unrifled tombs. On Saria there exists an old watch-tower with a curious

---

[56] The Bents' finds from Kárpathos are kept at the British Museum. Some were purchased directly in 1886. Shortly before she died Mabel, or her relatives, presented a wide range of artefacts to the institution in 1926, cf. http://www.britishmuseum.org/research/collection_online/search.aspx?place=34240&plaA=34240-3-1.

Rock-cut tomb at Vrykoúnda, Kárpathos.

water conduit chiselled in the rock leading to it; this tower was apparently built to protect the only fertile portion of the island. It was Ross's idea that the Nisyro of Strabo was on Saria, but beyond the slight similarity of name there do not seem to be any other grounds for this conjecture.

The Rock Tombs of Kárpathos[57]

During a sojourn of some length in the remote island of Carpathos I was fortunate enough to come across some unopened rock-cut tombs, curious specimens of sepulchral art, which have hitherto been supposed to have been entirely ransacked in former ages. Carpathos,

---

[57] This shorter essay was published as 'Rock-Cut Tombs of Carpathos' in *Athenæum* (Issue 3002 (1885: May), p.606). *Athenæum* was a long-running (1828 to 1921), scholarly news-journal on the arts and sciences. Theodore sketched the article from Sýros on or around 24 April 1885, just a few days after having left Kárpathos and with his thoughts and impressions of the island fresh in his mind. The couple were staying in the Hôtel d'Angleterre in Platía Miaoúli for 10 days before leaving for London: the building still stands (see page 173).

from its peculiar position, has remained out of the beat of exploration; it is a long, narrow, mountainous island, with dangerous seas on either side, which divide it from Rhodes and Crete. In ancient times it had four cities, three of which are to be traced by inscriptions, namely Poseidonia, Arkassa, and Bronkounti; the site of the fourth, Nysyros, is still a matter of speculation between two or three places where ruins, but no guiding inscriptions, exist. Of these Bronkounti was the most considerable, possessing a good harbour, a breakwater, and buildings which offer traces of considerable architectural merit. The rocky ground about these ruins is perfectly honeycombed with tombs of greatly diversified characters. On approaching from the modern village, about two hours distant, you pass an isolated rock, about twenty feet high, which is entered by a chiselled passage, with tombs on either side, but all empty. Near this rock we found poorer shallow tombs cut in the rock, only about a foot and a half deep, which contained nothing but bones. Proceeding along the cliff-side, we came across tombs of every possible description.

Most frequently they had a first chamber chiselled in the rock about ten feet square and six feet high, with the rock left as a stone bench all round, and the graves were constructed in chambers to the right and left. The most common system seems to have been to lay the bones in a chiselled space in the centre, leaving what our workmen well termed a 'terrace' round it. In this space, together with the bones, all the household treasures were deposited. In one grave we found as many as twenty plates, besides jugs and household crockery of every description. The hole was closed up with a big stone, and the whole of the outer chamber was covered with a strong cement of pumice, and on this are still to be seen traces of patterns in red and yellow, circular, toothed, and diaper patterns. In the outer chamber of two graves I found traces of writing, and over one grave was a name which was interesting as identifying it as the grave of the wife of a man whose name occurs in a *psephisma*[58] in the ruins above. I another tomb I found a marble *stele* inscribed with letters of the best period, stating that the tomb was in honour of one Menekrateus, which name occurs several times in inscriptions amongst the ruins.[59] Some graves had much more elaborate designs outside than others; over one was a head made in the hard cement. One grave had three of these chiselled chambers, one entering from the other, with windows on either side of the door. Many of the graves are made to communicate with one another on the inside by narrow chiselled passages.

For some time I despaired of discovering any of these unopened; but, on closely observing the cliff, I noticed that some of these chiselled rocks were nearly hidden by soil, and offered the appearance of tombs approached by a passage likewise chiselled in the cliff. Here we began to dig and soon found chambers in the rocks which were crowded with specimens of ancient Carpathian art.

Furthermore, there is another class of tomb, just one single chamber cut in the rock, with chiselled steps above; but we found none of these unopened. The spot where our tent was pitched was curious. It was a level quadrangle, round two sides of which the rock had been carefully chiselled for tombs; there were only four finished, but there were lines on the rock which showed where other tombs were intended to be made. Tombs of another class at Bronkounti which we accidentally hit upon were made in natural holes in the cliff in almost inaccessible spots overhanging the sea. One of these contained four tombs, and some beautiful specimens of

---

[58] See note 21, page 23.
[59] The British Museum has a marble monumental inscription from the site (1864,1007.54), an honorary decree granting a golden crown to Menokritos for his services as a physician during more than twenty years, and who at 'an earlier period, before he received a salary...gave his services for free while residing in Karpathos, and cured many people of dangerous illnesses'.

ceramic art of a far more finished and elaborate character than any we had found in the chiselled tombs. These holes had been closed up with loose stones and the same kind of cement.

Bronkounti has suffered much from the destruction of ages. There was a Byzantine town built on the ruins, by which most of the ancient landmarks were obliterated. Then, again, I saw the drums of lovely pillars with figures on, after the style of, though much smaller then, those of the temple of Diana at Ephesus, being broken into fragments for the purpose of making square blocks of marble; but there is enough left to testify to the former glory of the place.

'On Insular Greek Customs'[60]

We will begin with the customs concerning the first event in a man's career, namely his birth. In the island of Karpathos, a remote and rarely visited island lying between Crete and Rhodes, last winter, I watched closely all the customs attending birth and childhood, and amongst many strange innovations I found several which have a distinct pedigree from classical times.

A peasant woman when she has a child calls upon St. Eleutherios to assist her in her troubles. He is the modern representative of the goddess Eileithyia, for gender has not troubled the learned men of the Greek Church, who have distributed the old pagan gods amongst Christian saints; thus the attributes of Demeter have been transferred to St. Demetrios, and those of Artemis to St. Artemidos, regardless of sex.

After the infant's birth it is considered desirable that the handsomest man should be the first to embrace it, so as to impart his beauty, and that the strongest and wisest woman should be the first to suckle the child for the like reason. This idea of imparting beauty and strength is an ancient one, for Herodotus tells us a story of how an ugly girl became the most beautiful in Sparta because her nurse took her to the temple of the heroine Helen, whom they met on the doorstep. And the plot of the Æthiopians of Heliodorus turns on the belief that the Queen of the Æthiopians became the mother of a white child because she had an image of Hesione before her when the child was born. We are told by Apollodorus that seven days after the birth of Meleager the Fates told the horologue of the child, and the fire was lighted on the hearth.

There is a ceremony in Karpathos on this seventh day, called in consequence εφτά, which bears a striking analogy to this, when the Fates are supposed to interfere to choose the child's patron saint. The family on this day are assembled, and in the middle of the room they put a large shallow round bowl; if the child is male they put some of the father's clothes on the bowl; if a girl, some of the mother's, and on the top of them they place the child. For this occasion they have previously made a large wax candle, with seven coats of wax; this they chop into seven equal pieces and put the pieces into candlesticks, which are placed round the bowl, and each candle is called by the name of some saint. The family sit around in silence and prayer until one of the candles is extinguished, and this candle determines the patron saint of the child.

In the evening the bowl is filled with food, boiled barley and water, which is stirred till it becomes the consistency of dough, and into the middle of this they pour honey, and

---

[60] Mabel had an opportunity to present a select range of Greek fabrics and costumes before the Royal Anthropological Institute in 1886 (see page 184). Theodore gave a brief presentation at the event and this was published in the Institute's journal (Vol. XV. 4. 1886, pp. 391-403). Extracts from this appear here.

then they sit round to eat. When all this is consumed the doors are closed, more food is put into the bowl, and an old crone is deputed to go round the room to sprinkle it with holy oil, muttering as she does so, 'Come, Father of Fates. Come here Great Destiny, to settle the fortune of this child, that he may have ships, and diamonds, and cattle, and that he may become a prince.' At this moment the Fates are supposed to enter the room, eat of the food, and to give good fortune, or καλομοιράζειν, to the child.

The Fates of to-day are supposed, as formerly, to be three in number, old women who inhabit inaccessible mountains, and none but people versed in magic know where they dwell. 'I shall go to the mountains to call on my Fate' is a common expression of dissatisfaction with destiny. These Fates are always spoken of as spinning, and they preside over the three events of life – birth, marriage, and death. A discontented modern Greek who considers it a misfortune to have been born, a still greater one to be married, and the greatest of all to die, calls them 'the three woes of destiny.'

After the ceremony of the fate-telling is over the guests take their departure, and as they do so wish the mother a good forty days, that is to say, the forty days before she can go to church after the birth...

Such are some of the customs respecting birth and childhood which appear to have survived antiquity; let us now take the closing scene of human life, and in the extant customs attending death and burial we shall find many of a like nature...As an example, I will give you a literal translation of a death-wail I heard last winter in Karpathos: – 'Charon wished to plant a garden; the aged he planted, and they came up as twisted lemon trees, the young as erect as cypresses, and the little children he put as flowers in his vases.'...

In one village of Karpathos[61] they bury their dead in tombs attached to the churches belonging to various families. In these the body of a defunct member is deposited without any earth, and then allowed to decay, so that a noisome odour is generally the result in hot weather; into the cement at the top of this tomb they insert plates. I asked the reason for this, and none whatsoever could be given; it is evidently a survival of the old feast for the dead, which was laid out in the tombs. It was a curious coincidence that in some ancient tombs which I opened not far from this very village[62] I found the plates thus set out with bones of fishes and traces of other food on them which had been there for over two thousand years....

In agricultural and pastoral life we have abundant relics of a bygone age. In Karpathos, for example, before the sowing of the grain they do this:- The farmer takes a portion of the grain that is to be sown and a rose to church. These are blessed during the liturgy. The rose is broken up and scattered about in the first field which is sown that year as a sure emblem of abundance and success. Thus did the ancients at the festival of προηρόσιαι before the seed was sown in the ground...

In Karpathos and Keos[63] they have a curious way of preserving grain; holes are dug in the earth near the threshing-floor, and when the grain is ready they put it in, having first been careful to cover the inside with straw; after the grain has been piled up, so as to form a sort of cone-shaped mound, they cover the whole with straw, and place on the top of this some of the stiff native brushwood, and then they cover their mound with earth. Rain never penetrates these granaries, which are now known as λακκοι, the classical term for them, σιροί, having been changed, while the custom itself has been preserved. [...] In

---

[61] Ólymbos.
[62] Vrikoúnda.
[63] Kéa in the Cyclades. The Bents were there in March 1884.

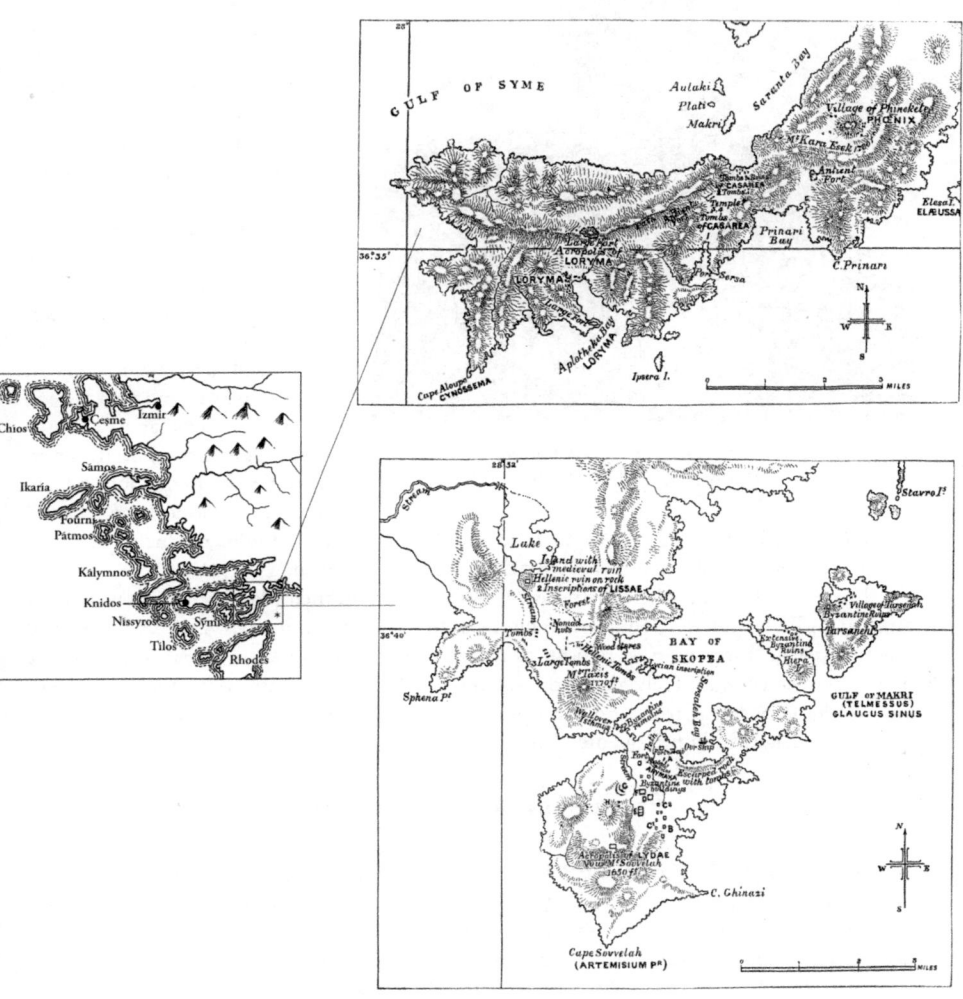

'Loryma', 'Lissæ', and Lydæ' on the Turkish coast. Theodore Bent's own details from a contemporary Admiralty Chart. Originally published in E.L. Hicks, 'Inscriptions found by Mr. Bent at Casarea, Lydæ, Patara, Myra'. Journal of Hellenic Studies, Vol. 10 (1889), pp. 46-85.

The polymath and overseer of Turkish antiquities, Osman Hamdi Bey (1842-1910).

a shepherd's village on Karpathos, where we spent some time, we found many exceedingly interesting words in existence which occur nowhere else in Greece; their mules they term κϊηματα, or possessions, and do not understand you when you use the usual modern Greek word for mules; their goats they call χίλια, or thousands, a truly patriarchal word, pointing to flocks which cannot be counted for number; they have peculiar words for distinguishing the several kinds of goats and sheep which you find in the pages of Liddell and Scott, but in no glossary of modern Greek words. If a woman wishes to carry a light from one house to the other she puts it into a read, which here alone have I heard termed ναρθηκα or ναρθηξ, the same word and the same use for the reed which teaches us Prometheus employed when he brought down fire from heaven.

In their daily life, in their methods of catching fish, in their planting of crops, in their medical and religious lore, endless parallels can be found to antiquity, which prove beyond a doubt that in these islands, remote from the civilisation and alien governments, a race of people live of pure Hellenic blood, unadulterated by admixture with other races; they are not numerous, it is true, and for a pure Greek, as for a pure Celt, you must search in mountain villages and unfrequented bye-paths.

From Sými to Kastellórizo[64]

A short time ago, Mr. and Mrs. F.S.A.,[65] of England, carried on excavations on Egyptian soil, with the full permission of the H.H. the Khedive not only to dig, but to appropriate their finds... Being unable to obtain leave from the aforesaid Turk for anything like a favourable continuation of their work, Mr. and Mrs. F.S.A. determined to become pirates, and unfettered by conventionalities of any kind to wander in a hired Greek boat along the south coast of Asia Minor, in quest of those ancient sites and objects which are so dear to them...[66]

---

[64] An article entitled 'A Piratical F.S.A.' published in the *Cornhill Magazine* (Vol. 58 (11), December 1888, pp. 620-635). These are memories of a cruise through the islands the Bents made in March/April 1888.
[65] Bent was elected a Fellow of the Society of Antiquaries on 1 July 1886, if not a very active one (for them). He made one communication to the Society, concerning his work in Mashonaland (Zimbabwe) in 1891 (Volume 14 of the Society's *Proceedings*).
[66] The tone of this piece is cavalier and one wonders how it would have been received by his peers. Theodore's

Many busy days were spent in the little Greek port of Syra in preparing for the piratical cruise. The F.S.A.'s inspected many craft, and at last entered into a 'symphony'[67] with the skipper of a two-masted Geek schooner, possessing a capacious hold for their workmen and the trophies to be found, a forecastle cabin into which in some mysterious manner four sailors packed themselves, namely, Captain Nicholas, burly and stout; Andres, first mate, bulky; Gregory, second mate, of ordinary dimensions; and Stavros, or Cross, a loutish boy, the slave of everybody, very little higher in the social scale than the ship's dog, Yuruk...

Needless to say, the sails were rapidly unfurled, and the 'Blue Ship' triumphantly put forth to sea, in quest of another hunting-ground. No plan of action having suggested itself during the day, when the anchor was cast at night in a little bay, Captain Nicholas gave it as his advice that the ship should put into a certain harbour on the island of Syme, where there is a monastery, well known to sailors, and that her future course should be decided by the counsel that the Superior would willingly give. Never did monastery appear more lovely and peaceful by the edge of its deep land-locked bay than did that of the Archangel Michael to the wanderers in the 'Blue Ship.' It was built for seafarers such as they, by pious hands, just after the fall of Constantinople,[68] and is celebrated amongst the mariners of the Levant. Around the 'Blue Ship,' as she heaved to, swarmed countless geese – holy geese they are, the private property of the Archangel, and they gain their livelihood by picking up offal cast from the boats which shelter here. None durst do them harm, for does not the legend relate how the first goose came here from Cyprus with an important letter under its wing for the Superior, and also how once a wicked sailor killed and ate one of these holy geese, and the angry Archangel refused to let his boat depart; though the wind was favourable, his boat would not move until he had confessed his crime and paid a heavy fine. No one, so alleges the popular belief, who has stolen anything here he can get away. 'So pirates,' said Captain Nicholas gaily to his men as they got into the ship's boat, 'beware!'

The monastic bell, a very large one, the gift of a sailor saved from shipwreck, rang out a welcome to the strangers as their boat neared the shore; the Superior received them warmly and promised every assistance in his power, and that evening they and all the 'boys,' except two naughty ones who ran off to the town of Syme without leave, attended service in the monastic church, and listened to the monks chanting amid sacred frescoes of the blessed and the damned, fine old pictures, wood-carving, and inlaid work. It was a peculiarly solemn function that day, being the eve of the dead,[69] and many were the baskets of boiled wheat offered, after the custom of the Eastern Church, at this festival, before the Archangel's shrine;

---

flippant reference is to his soured relationship with the Turkish authorities and in particular the distinguished head of antiquities in Istanbul, Hamdi Bey. The Bents uncovered a fine statue on Thásos in March 1887 and had hoped to bring it home to London. Hamdi Bey intercepted it and it is now in the Istanbul Archaeological Museum (see *Chronicles*, Vol. I, p. 201ff. for the details). By 14 February 1887, however, Theodore had admitted defeat as regards returning to Thásos. He writes as much to Cecil Smith at the British Museum: 'Our negotiations with Hamdi have entirely broken down; he is quite inexorable about the knotty point of allowing anything of value to go out of the kingdom... Consequently we have with much regret abandoned Thasos for this year. We stay here until the 23rd and after that go to Syra with the intention of "going on a cruise" for a couple of months... Seriously though I am thinking of Capo Krio and the Doric Chersonese, and if you could manage to get me an admiralty chart of that district and send it to me c/o W. Binney Esq., H.B.M. Consul, Syra, Greece I should be greatly obliged...'

[67] Agreement or contract.
[68] The Bents are at Panormítis on the north coast. The origins are earlier and the present 18th-century foundation and site are built over a sanctuary to Poseidon and a later sequence of Christian shrines. See, e.g. William Travis's *Bus Stop Symi* (1970, 83-91).
[69] The (Orthodox) Lent period includes several 'all souls' events – mostly falling on Saturdays.

and in the gloaming, at the convent door, the pirates ate with the assembled worshippers this holy food, and drank glasses of mastic to the success of their venture.

Very early next morning, stout Andreas came down into the F.S.A.'s cabin to fetch the sacred pictures, for the 'Blue Ship' and all therein were to be blessed by priests from the monastery. A clean towel was spread on the companion, and on it were placed a bowl of water, the sacred pictures, and a lantern; then, punctually at 7 A.M., two priests arrived in a boat, with their red bundle containing stoles, books, and a large silver diptych representing the Holy Virgin and the Lord Michael the Archangel, and various relics of many saints, who were prayed to grant their blessings to the 'Blue Ship,' that storms might not injure her, that the souls and bodies of all on board might be blessed, and that harmony might reign throughout the voyage. Captain Nicholas first received the blessing, accompanied by a whisk of holy water with the sprig of basil and a wave from the censer; then the sailors and the 'boys,' and lastly Mr. and Mrs. F.S.A., who, being heterodox, had modestly retired to a distant corner. Holy water was sprinkled over the deck and down into the cabins with the aforesaid sprig, the pictures were kissed by the orthodox, and then this lovely and impressive service, as the brilliant light of the morning sun glimmered on the waves, was brought to a conclusion by Captain Nicholas, who divided what was left of the holy water between the two water casks, and then brought up a large black bottle of rum with which to regale the holy men.

During the morning, the pirates wandered amid the precincts of the convent, and visited the numerous cells, which are only filled when pilgrims visit the shrine on the Archangel's Day;[70] and this is the reason why there is so large a dining-room, with wooden tables and benches to seat five hundred, a raised dais for the rich, and huge cauldrons in which to cook the food. 'Enough for the meal of forty dragons,' as a fable-loving 'boy' put it.

The Superior, Makarios, who was busily engaged all the morning in attending to the simmering of a savoury pot, insisted on the F.S.A.'s dining with him. And what a meal it was! A huge bowl of rice soup was followed by an exquisitely cooked lamb, stuffed with rice and herbs, which Makarios pulled to pieces with his fingers and distributed to the assembled guests; and into Mr. F.S.A.'s luckless mouth he would occasionally insert with finger and thumb such bits as he considered particularly tit.[71] Scarcely had this course disappeared, than up came a roast leg of lamb, which received similar treatment; then curds, then honey, then cream; and, like Captain Dalgetty,[72] the guests ate gluttonously, not knowing when they might come across so good a meal. Makarios, on parting, gave them his blessing, his best map, and his man John to act as a guide; and when the two truant boys had returned and been well scolded, towards evening the 'Blue Ship' again set sail, and great contentment reigned on board – the joint product of the blessing and the meal. Yet how transient are the effects of even an Archangel's blessing was proved by the fact that the first of a series of brawls took place that very evening between Mr. F.S.A. and Captain Nicholas on the subject of ship-lights, which, for economical reasons, Greek sailors object to carry...

Great preparations were made for the arrival of the 'Blue Ship' at the first civilized port she had visited since leaving Syra. One of the 'boys,' it appeared, understood hair-cutting, and borrowed Mrs. F.S.A.'s scissors for that purpose; beard were shaved, and shaggy locks

---

[70] The great festivals fall on 8 November and Pentecost.

[71] I.e. 'tasty', as in 'tit-bit'.

[72] '[When] a cavalier finds that provant is good and abundant, he will, in my estimation, do wisely to victual himself for at least three days, as there is no knowing when he may come by another meal.' (Captain Dugald Dalgetty, *Legend of Montrose*, Sir Walter Scott, Chapter 5)

reduced with wonderful rapidity, and Hades[73] was strewn with hair. Castellorizo was the port, and it is a unique specimen of modern Greek enterprise, being a flourishing maritime town, built on a barren islet off the south coast of Asia Minor, far from any other Greek centre – a sort of halfway halting place in the waves for vessels which trade between Alexandria and the Levantine ports; it has a splendid harbour, and is a town of sailors and sponge divers.

Captain Nicholas knew everybody. 'Where are you come from, my little captain?' asked they. 'From the sea,' he replied mysteriously, with a sly wink at Mr. and Mrs. F.S.A., to show that he did not intend to divulge their piratical secrets. He, his mates, and the twelve 'boys' went on shore for a day's jollification into the depths of which the F.S.A.'s thought they had better not plunge, so having the red castle of Italian date,[74] and having admired the athletic men and pretty women of the island town, they returned to the 'Blue Ship' for a quiet afternoon....

Every one of the twelve 'boys' and the crew came on board that night with obvious proofs of their merry-making; some even had to be dragged up the side of the 'Blue Ship' and placed on their beds by their more sober fellows; all wrangled and quarrelled for a season, and that night no stories were told, but a chorus of heavy snoring told a tale of its own.

The wild winds at length bore [the F.S.A.'s] to a desert island in the Ægean, called in modern times St. John's Island,[75] from a tiny church thereon dedicated to that Saint; it is almost the most remote spot in all these seas – a lone, treeless, soilless islet, with stupendous rocks overhanging the sea, but interesting to the F.S.A.'s as bearing traces of the stone age, and hence, presumably, one of the stepping-stones by which the earlier mariners made their way to Europe.[76] It is now leased to a farmer for 56*l*. a year, and contains nine souls – an old man and his wife and their descendants, who live in a state of wonderful simplicity in a small cabin of rough stone. The old granny was alone when they visited her, her husband being absent on his dairy on the hills, so they made a pilgrimage to visit him, and found a charming specimen of a bygone age busy making cheese. Of course, he groaned over his excessive rent – what farmer does not in all corners of the globe? And he groaned, moreover, about a recent visit some thieves had paid him, making off with his cauldrons, his milk-troughs, and the fattest of his lambs. Occasionally a priest comes to perform a service at the little church; now and again boats call for cheese and dairy produce – these are their only point of union with the outer world. Mr. F.S.A. admired with a view to purchase some nice-looking loaves of bread, but the honest old fellow told him how a boat from Rhodes had brought some flour to exchange for cheese, with which he had made the loaves in question, only to find them uneatable, for the flour had been kept in petroleum casks! It is to be feared that these good folk often get taken in, and that Matthew's[77] injunction to the 'boys' to pay honestly for the cheese they bought would not be closely attended to.

Next morning, just as the 'Blue Ship' was preparing to depart, the twelve 'boys' came on board with magnificent bunches of yellow marigold, for that night Hades had been visited by an invasion of fleas, caught doubtless in the old woman's hovel, and constant

---

[73] The Bents' term for their ship's hold.

[74] The 14th-century so-called 'red' castle, and giving the island one of its names, was built by the Knights of St John.

[75] The now uninhabited, and nominated bird sanctuary, islet of Sýrna, south-east of Astypálea. The Bents spent a few hours there on 9 April 1888 (see page 172).

[76] Now a widely-held perspective; see, e.g. Cyprian Broodbank's *An Island Archaeology of the Early Cyclades* (Cambridge 2000).

[77] A further reference to the Bents' assistant Manthaios Símos.

were the muttered oaths which told that the 'boys' were suffering keenly from the onslaught of the unwelcome visitors. The bunches of marigold were to remedy this, and a practical illustration of the effects of 'fleabane' was brought before the notice of the F.S.A.'s.

Tossed about again by the winds for two more days, on the third the 'Blue Ship' was obliged to take refuge from a fearful gale in the island of Patmos, a spot which aroused all the legendary lore of the simple-minded shipboy Cross,[78] and, delighted at having such willing listeners as the F.S.A.'s he poured into their ears quaint stories concerning the author of the Revelation: how a rock in the harbour represented the petrified body of an adversary of the exiled divine; and how the shellfish which are caught thereon have a disgusting smell and are unfit for food. Cross, too, in a subdued and awe-struck voice, gave them his opinion concerning those mysterious mast-head lights, the fires of St. Elmo, which appear in storms. He had seen them off Andros, he said, and 'they are,' he added, 'a sort of soft bird with a light on their heads, which sit and eat the inside of the masts, so that they become hollow, and break with the next gust of wind; they are wild things which God sends to punish men.' The boy Cross was quite Homeric in his yarns, and in consequence gave keen delight to the F.S.A.'s...

On the fiftieth day after her departure, the 'Blue Ship' deposited the wonderers once more amongst the busy haunts of men,[79] and the F.S.A.'s one regret in leaving was having to bid adieu to the affectionate ship's dog, which had fifty feast days in his life off their remains, and would probably have no more.

Sýrna[80]

The small island rock, anciently known as Sirina, now as Hagios Joannis, occupies a somewhat important position in the Aegean Sea, as one of the stepping-stones by which the earlier inhabitants of Karia must have travelled westwards; it has two good harbours, one to the north, and one to the south, and is placed midway in a long stretch of sea between Karpathos and Astypalaea, in both of which islands traces of prehistoric race have been found. Having carefully examined Anaphi, an island lying to the west of this line of route, and having found there no traces whatsoever of this early population, and knowing that Astypalaea, Amorgos, Naxos and Paros are full of their tombs, I was considerably interested in discovering in the ruins of a square fortress on Sirina quantities of obsidian knives,[81] which at once identified this rock with the race in question, and proved to us that they made use of it as a halting-place on their way to and from the marble quarries of Paros; in fact Parian marble, objects of which are so frequently found in their tombs, would seem to have been their chief quest in these westward migrations.

---

[78] I.e. the name 'Stávros'.
[79] They Bents have returned to Sýros in the Cyclades.
[80] Theodore wrote these few lines for *The Classical Review* ('Sirina', Vol II, No. 10, 1888, p. 329).
[81] Theodore removed a number of obsidian blades from early graves on Andíparos in February 1884; some are on display in the British Museum, but these 'knives' from Sýrna have not been traced.

'Donkey Island'. Traditional inter-Dodecanesian transport.

Agathoníssi[82]

Whilst wandering for several winters amongst the peasants who sparsely inhabit the islands of the Ægean Sea, I have been enabled to collect much from their daily life and agricultural pursuits which bears the impress of having been directly inherited from antiquity. Religious observances have preserved, perhaps, more that is old, but this has been the case everywhere and in every age. I now propose to treat more especially the daily routine of the Greek peasant's life. This primitive pastoral life may be studied in the Archipelago in either of two ways, by visiting the tiny islets inhabited only by one or two families of shepherds, whose intercourse with the outer world for generations has been exceedingly limited, or by penetrating into the mountain villages of some of the larger islands.

In my wanderings I have visited several of these tiny islets, but of all these none to my mind offered such a complete picture of patriarchal life as did a low, bleak islet some twenty

---

[82] This is the islet of Agathoníssi, east of Pátmos and close to the Turkish coast. The Bents sailed there from Sámos, remaining two nights (3-4 March 1886). The extract is from a longer article in the *Fortnightly Review* (1886, 40:236 (1886: Aug.) pp. 214-224), called 'Greek Peasant Life'.

miles off the coast of Asia Minor, rejoicing in the name of Donkey's Island (Gatharonisi). It is inhabited only by one family, at the head of which is a very aged patriarch indeed, called George, who rules over twenty-two subjects, that is to say, his wife, six sons, seven daughters, and the families of three married sons and one married daughter. Only one daughter is married, it must be noticed, the other six by a custom existing in these remote corners of the world are doomed to single blessedness, for here the matriarchal system is still in existence – the eldest daughter inherits all, whilst the sons and younger daughters have to look after themselves. Consequently, a husband was easily found for old George's eldest daughter from the neighbouring island of Patmos, who was content to leave his home with a view to succeeding his father-in-law in Donkey's Island. The family here have everything in common; on feast-days they all eat together. Day after day the women sit together at their work, sorting grain on low tables, or plying their distaffs; whilst the men tend the five hundred goats which form old George's flock, or till the soil which produces just enough grain and just enough of everything for the wants of the islanders. They possess one caique, in which they visit from time to time the villages of the neighbouring islands, to sell their cheeses and salted dairy produce. This is their only communication with the outer world, and on their return journey they bring back various European productions, with which to delight their womankind, and barrels of water, for Donkey's Island has no wells, and water for drinking purposes has to be fetched from without. Once a year the Turkish tax-collector pays them a visit, and extorts from them so much money that they can barely live. Old George is the very picture of a patriarch, with his brown homespun clothes, untanned pigskin shoes,[83] and long grey beard, as he sits basking in the sun before his cottage. His word is law on Donkey's Island, and his sons dare not so much as smoke in his presence. The various families live in a cluster of wretched hovels, adjoining which is the dairy and enclosure for the goats. After the morning milking they put the milk into large cauldrons, underneath which they light a brushwood fire; as it thickens they take out the curd with a reed basket, shaped like a jelly bag, and then press it into the *tyrobolion*, or wicker basket, exactly like the *tyrobolia* or cheese baskets described by Homer in the *Odyssey*.[84] From this basket the cheese gets a pretty pattern outside; it is then salted, and is ready for sale. Into the boiling whey, when the cheese is all made, they cast a little more milk, and the curd of this makes what they call *myzethra*, delicious when eaten fresh with a little honey to sweeten it, as we had it in Donkey's Island – 'food for the gods,' as they often call it. All their implements are primitive; large gourds are used for milking, the seething cauldron is stirred whilst the milk is thickening with a large vine branch (ταραχτῆς), with the tendrils knotted together at one end. The spoon for stirring and skimming the *myzethra* is made of a vine tendril, twisted round and plaited with esparto grass.[85] They are very pious, too, and never begin to extract the curd without making a sign of the cross three times over the cauldron with this spoon.

There is one little church in a remote corner of the island and once a year a priest is brought from Samos to 'make a liturgy' therein, and to do anything in the way of baptisms or exorcisms that may be required of him. He usually remains several days on the island, and his duties are many, for the performance of which he receives a handsome sum, equivalent

---

[83] The Pitt Rivers Museum in Oxford has a pair of such shoes donated by Theodore, apparently in November 1888 (2006.62.1). The old record card gives Sámos as the place of origin: 'Plain pieces of skin with hair outside, drawn up at the edges with hide thong, which sticks up at the toes. Heels open. Very rough.'
[84] *Odyssey* IX, 248.
[85] The Bents presented such an implement to the Pitt Rivers Museum, Oxford. It bears still an old label: 'Specimen Strainer for Mysethra, very rough. Handle of a small branch the end bent round to form a hoop to wh. is added a number of grass stalks bound tother [sic] at on end...' The inventory number is 2005.68.1. The museum also had from the Bents from 'Gaidaro Nisi Id, S. of Samos' a leather bag or *bouria* (2006.82.1).

to four pounds. Probably in England he would be ducked in a horse-pond as a sorcerer, but in remote corners of Greece the priests are poor and the people credulous, so they are glad to earn an honest penny by incantations. The priest who visits Donkey's Island assists the islanders in their endeavours to keep the eagles from their flocks, by binding to a tree various silken knots, and muttering strange incantations as he does so, which generally depict Christ and the Saints at supper. During the meal Christ notices that St. Mammas, the modern Pan, the protector of flocks, is weeping and refusing food; and on being asked why, he replies, 'because the eagles have carried off a kid.' Then Christ tells him to bind silk to a tree 'that the bird's beak and talons may be bound.' Binding is the spirit of the modern Greek charm. They bind diseases to trees; they bind fleas, bugs, and lice outside their houses, or rather they make ineffectual attempts to do so; and the shepherds of Donkey's Island are careful to bind beneath the knee of a ram or he-goat the bone of a fish or hare, which they believe is effectual in preventing the offspring from being carried off by robbers. The priest before his departure is called upon to bless the flocks and the crops, to exorcise rats, mice, and other vermin from the barn; in fact, his £4 is well earned.

Old Eirinio, the aged wife of the patriarch, is the recognised physician of the community; and during our stay on Donkey's Island we heard from her lips many wonderful charms. She reminded us forcibly of the sorceress Simætha, as described by Theocritus,[86] who could reveal the future from the flutterings of birds, and weave spells to bring back a faithless lover. She has her own peculiar cures for all diseases, for the spleen, for the chest, for fevers, and if she does not understand the nature of the ailment she says it comes from the evil eye, and in this case, says she, 'you must take a basin and fill it with sea or salt water, go down to the shore, and pour it into the sea; then fill it again forty times, and as you go away walk backwards, sprinkling handfuls of the water around you as you do so, and the evil will be cured.' One day she told us, in solemn tones, how once their flocks had been bewitched by those uncanny night birds which they call σκατοπούλα, and which are supposed to have been hatched by a witch, by keeping the eggs in her bosom for forty days. They fly only at night, and I strongly suspect they are bats, but when they settle on a house the milk leaves the udders of the flocks of the owners, and is transported to those that the witch wishes to fill. When this calamity befell the Donkey Islanders they straightway sent to Samos for a priest, regardless of expense.

Pátmos[87]

During a somewhat prolonged stay on the isle which is called Patmos, when my wife and I were the guests of the hospitable monks of the Monastery of St. John, I did not, as most who visit Patmos do, devote my attention solely to the reminiscences of the saint who has gained for the island its celebrity. The monastic life, the life if the people who live around the monastery, the island itself, with its legends and its hermitages, afforded us amusement, which we found it hard to exhaust; and the good monks were greatly puzzled at visitors who did not spend all their time plodding over the manuscripts in their celebrated library, or praying in the Cave of the Apocalypse, but who wandered from house to house, took photographs, and studied the customs of the natives.

---

[86] *Idylls* II. Theodore is taking the classical scholarship of his readers for granted.
[87] The Bents recorded two visits to Pátmos, 5-10 March 1886 and 9-15 April 1888. This first article is from 'Revelations from Patmos' (*Blackwood's Magazine*, Vol. 141, March 1887, 368-379). Like many of Theodore's articles of the time, it was syndicated in the American popular journal *Littell's Living Age* (April 23, 1887, Vol. 173, No. 2235), 243ff.).

Patmos is as barren and drear a spot as can well be imagined – mountainous, treeless, and productive of little else but aromatic herbs. Its coast-line is marvellously indented, and at the central harbour the island is divided into two almost equal parts, joined together by a narrow tongue of land. On this isthmus rises a hill, crowned by the ruins of an old Greco-Roman town, hidden by the grain which is grown thereon. This spot must of necessity be more genuinely associated with St. John than any other, seeing that it was the only town in the island at the time that he was brought here as a prisoner; but legendary history was preferred to ignore this fact, and the worship of St. John, as it exists now on Patmos, is purely legendary.

The monastery itself is a vast mediæval fortress, crowing a height on the southern portion of the island some thousand feet above the sea, around which the white houses of the inhabitants cluster like limpets on a rock. Patmos at various eras has been colonized by Greeks; but when in the eleventh century a saintly anchorite, Christodoulos by name, founded the monastery, the island had for centuries been uninhabited, and from this fact arose his desire to secure it from the emperor as a fitting spot for the pursuit of an undisturbed religious life. He brought with him fifty workmen and their families, and by so doing formed the nucleus of a new colonization. The families were obliged to live on the northern portion of the island, and no women or children were allowed across the narrow tongue of land. However, in succeeding ages this village suffered so much from marauders, that, by special indulgence from the patriarch of Constantinople, they were allowed to build houses under the wing of the monastery. After the fall of Constantinople, a large number of refugees sought an asylum at Patmos; and again, after the capture of Crete by the Turks, large numbers of Cretans came here, so that Patmos, under the favouring wing of religion, was repeopled and grew prosperous. Furthermore, a religious atmosphere is always the most favourable for the conservation of ancient habits; consequently, in their isolation from the world, the Patmiotes live as their ancestors lived, in the possession of charming customs, which even this nineteenth century has not been wholly able to obliterate.

No steamer touches at Patmos, so he who makes a pilgrimage thither must do so in a sailing-boat. Ours was a capital Samiote *caïque*, which landed us at a flourishing village which has grown up round the harbour in these days of greater security. We determined to set off at once on foot to the monastery, after entrusting our letters of introduction to a funny little deacon, who appropriated us on landing. We were rather ashamed, too, of our luggage, for in the Greek islands it is necessary to travel with food; consequently a frying-pan full of fish, a raw leg of lamb, and a bottle of honey were treasures with which we dared not part, more especially as the Lenten fast was imminent. These articles were confided to the care of an agile boy, whilst a donkey carried our weightier goods; and thus we commenced to toil up the road which leads to the monastery.

Somewhat breathless with our climb, and having been conducted through endless passages and up innumerable steps, we became aware that we had reached the superior's door, and that our procession had arrived in the reverse order to what we had intended, for we found his worship in a towering rage with the agile boy for bringing into the monastery and depositing at his door such things as we had entrusted to his charge. Consequently our reception was an exceedingly cold one, and not until half an hour later, when the deacon arrived with our letters of introduction, did the great man relax his severity. Then, indeed, he grew very benign; his servant was sent for coffee, jam, and *rakki*; the treasurer, the librarian, the ex-superior, and other leading monks were summoned to greet us; and their eyes wandered eagerly from us to our luggage, to our frying-pan, and our lamb.

'It is a wet, cold night; you cannot go outside again,' replied the superior in answer to our inquiries if apartments could be found for us in the village. Then followed a private colloquy amongst the monks, during which they continually looked at my wife, and made frequent allusions to that forbidden thing to monks – woman. What would St. Christodoulos, who made such stringent rules for his monastery have said, if he could have known that a man and wife were to be housed for days within its actual precincts? It was enough to revivify his embalmed body, which now reposes in the monastic church. We were given a cell belonging to an old monk, Gerasimos by name, who was absent just now doing penance in a hermitage. A cell indeed it was only in name; in point of size and convenience it closely resembled a flat. There was a large sitting-room with five windows, furnished with a divan, and quaint old pictures on the walls; through this opened a good-sized bedroom. We had a kitchen, a room for our servant,[88] a door, and a latch-key. Our flat was situated on the highest floor of the monastery, so that we could wander at will, when the wind was not too boisterous, over the terraced roofs, and enjoy delicious views over the land and sea. We could see the mountains of Asia Minor, and most of the islands of the Archipelago; we could converse with the monks as they paced to and fro, idling away their time with their beads, and basking in the sunshine. The utter waste of a life spent in a monastery was vividly brought before our notice, for there is absolutely nothing for them to do except to pray and fast; and I question if they adhere as strictly to the former occupation as they ought, otherwise I am at a loss to account for the existence of those fine bow-windows which many of them have thrown out.

The librarian is the busiest of them all, which is evidenced by the fact that he has only got one eye, having, as he said, worn the other out with study. He was one of our earliest visitors, and took it for granted that the object of our visit to Patmos was to live in his library and copy manuscripts. We did visit it, indeed, and were shown the few valuable books which have escaped the many depredations of bibliophiles. Amongst the oldest of the manuscripts we found a St. Mark's Gospel, written in 953 A.D., before the Alexandrian Codex. The initials to the names of God and Christ are in gold, and all the letters are in silver, on rose-coloured parchment. It finishes at the twenty-second verse of the fifteenth chapter, as the one in the library at Vienna. The history of Job is a manuscript of the ninth century, and is imperfect, some of the earlier pages being lost. The painted illustrations are most beautifully done, and the representations of Job's flocks, and his daughters, still preserve their original richness of colour. Some of the later volumes in the library are very interesting from the richness of their Byzantine bindings, notably a Gospel written in 1335, and full of lovely pictures. Unfortunately, many of them have suffered much from damp and want of care; but of late years, owing to the realization of their value, the librarian is much more careful of his treasures, and handles them with infinite pride. But instead of going into ecstatic raptures over the lovely Job and the ancient St. Mark, we, I fear, rather insulted the librarian by becoming deeply interested in two manuscripts describing the wanderings of St. John, and purporting to have been written by two disciples of his, Prochoros and Nicitas. These books form the foundation for all the legends which the Patmiotes still firmly believe – the basis, in fact, of their religion. These works are obviously spurious, full of anachronisms and contradictions, and have been too clearly written to assist in the production of sacred spots, which is a favourite system in the Eastern Church. A priest will say he has found a picture of the Madonna in a tree; a man will dream a dream that a sacred picture is at the bottom of a well; he will proceed to draw it up, and then the churches will be built in honour of the Madonna of the tree, or of the well, miracles will be wrought, and a centre for pilgrimages

---

[88] I.e. Manthaîos Símos.

established. An apt illustration of this idea came to our notice when at Patmos. Our servant, an intelligent and generally well-informed Greek, but not much of a theologian, was exercised in his mind respecting the history of Patmos, as connected with St. John; so one day he asked me, 'Did St. John find the Gospels in the Cave of the Apocalypse?' There is a very close analogy between this system of finding sacred objects and that which taught that images 'fell down from Jupiter,' and that the sacred books of the Sibyls were found.

The most amusing story which Prochoros professes to tell in his account of St. John is the contest which the saint is supposed to have had with a magician called Kynops, who was deputed by the priests of the temple of Apollo at Patmos to do what damage he could to the Roman prisoner, whose teaching interfered so much with their trade. Kynops lived in a cave to the south-west of the island, where he kept an army of demons. The Patmiotes of to-day show you the cave of Kynops, in a wild dreary spot overhanging the sea; and even in these latter days none dare enter it for fear of the demons, which are still supposed to haunt it.

On the day appointed for the contest, St. John, Kynops, and a large crowd of lookers-on repaired to the shore, where Kynops wrought many miracles, diving into the sea and bringing up the dead, whilst St. John merely looked on in dignified silence, and permitted his adversary to gain a complete triumph. The people thereupon fell to worshipping Kynops, and stoned St. John, whom they left for dead on the shore. Prochoros then relates how, whilst he was standing by the supposed corpse and weeping, St. John suddenly arose, walked up to the town without aid, and challenged the magician to a renewal of the contest.

Next day Kynops and his friends came down in the full confidence of another triumph. The magician again dived into the sea, as he had previously done, whilst St. John was engaged in fervent prayer, the result being that the magician never came up again, though the people remained staring for three days and nights at the waves which covered him.

The credulous Patmiotes of to-day will show you the spot on which St. John triumphed, and will point out a submerged rock in the harbour, which they say is the body of Kynops converted into stone by the vigour of the saintly prayers. All the spots connected with this legendary account of St. John are localized by tiny churches; and when I asked how it happened that St. Christodoulos was able to identify the places on an island which had been uninhabited for centuries, I was promptly suppressed by the reply, 'Through prayer and fasting.' There are many other legends connected with St. John and his miracles on Patmos. Before leaving the island, they say the saint went on a baptizing tour through all the villages, in one of which he healed the son of a priest of Jupiter. In another he had to contend with the wiles of and enchantments of a certain Notianus; and on the inhabitants asking to be baptized, he conducted them to a stream – but lo! Notianus by his art, turned the stream into blood. Whereupon St. John prayed fervently, and the blood turned into water again. Notianus was struck with blindness, and did not recover his sight until he humbled himself before St. John and received baptism.

That an outer world existed on Patmos outside the monastery was brought vividly before our notice on the day of our arrival by the town-crier, who makes use of the parapets of the monastery for delivering his messages. All that is necessary for him to do so is to ring his bell, and scream from the four corners of the building, and everyone in Patmos will hear what he has to say. He is a wild, unkempt object to look upon, with long hair, a red fez, brown homespun clothes, and bare feet. He is the mouthpiece of all Patmiote trade, and announces what captains have arrived with cargoes of macaroni, of beans, of figs, and other commodities. The price of each article is given, and the good folks are instructed to repair to such and such a house, where their requirements will be supplied.

Pilgrims to Pátmos.

There is much more left that is old in the town of Patmos than one usually sees in the island towns, presumably because the presence of the monastery has preserved the place from marauding attacks. Pirates in Greek waters are almost universally pious, and they never start on an expedition without the blessing of a priest, who not unfrequently stipulates for a share of their spoil. We visited several very good houses in the town, the best always belong to those who have been sea-captains, and who have brought back objects from beyond seas to decorate their homes. Of old china, indifferent pictures, carved furniture, and *bric-a-brac*, there is an abundance, probably brought to the island in those days when Patmiote merchants traded with Venice and mercantile ports of Italy. Of late years their wealth has greatly collapsed, and curiosity-dealers from Constantinople have found here a rich harvest.

'There has been a great deal of the evil eye about lately,' an old woman told us, whose walls had been stripped of Rhodian plates and other ornaments to pay for present exigencies. The god Fascinus, in short, has survived here in full vigour. The withering of trees, the ruin of decay, the destruction of crops, – every misfortune, in fact – is in Patmos attributed to the pernicious influence of a demon by means of the eye of a medium, those whose eyebrows closely join being usually selected. The Patmiotes take the greatest possible notice of personal appearance as indicating certain tendencies. The popular saying is 'Red hair and blue eyes – the soul of the devil and heart of Satan.' All marks on the body are portentous, according to the Patmiotes. If you have two lumps on your head, you will be married twice; if you have long ears, you will have a long life; if you have good teeth, you will have wealth; and the excitement caused by the birth of a baby with a caul surpasses anything I have heard in our own country on this interesting phenomenon. A caul supposed to indicate a glorious futures; it must be blessed at three different liturgies, and must be hung up on the wall amongst the collection of domestic saints which every householder possesses. 'May God protect us,' say they, 'from a beardless man and a hairy woman!' In most of their legends of gnomes and magicians, it is the man without a beard and the woman with one who invariably play the most conspicuous part.

The great remedy for the evil eye on Patmos is to go and cut off the girdle of the unfortunate possessor of this unenviable characteristic. This must be burnt in an incense-burner, and be waved before the person or the object which has suffered, and then, by throwing three carnation-leaves into the fire, it can be seen whether the charm has been effectual or not. If the leaves crackle, it is a sign of healing, and someone must spit thrice on the person or the thing, saying, as he does so, 'Uncharmed!' But if the leaves refused to crackle, it is best to go to the monastery at once and secure a monk to come and read a prayer to avert the danger.

The inhabitants of Patmos half worship the monks of their monastery, and believe them entirely devoid of the failings which other flesh is heir to. When a monk passes by or enters a house, it is customary for the people to touch the ground with their fingers, and then to kiss the hand which the holy man proffers. A Patmiote mother's highest ambition is to see her son introduced as a 'reader' into the monastic church, with the prospect of being eventually admitted as a monk when the days of his probation are over. All the monks are now of Patmiote origin. This was not the case in former days, when many came from afar. But of late years many things have been altered. The old-fashioned common life has been abandoned, and the handsome common room, with its frescoed walls, is rapidly falling into decay. Visitors have stolen most of the old tiles which once adorned the common table; the superior's throne is now tottering on three legs; and the fine baronial kitchen, which adjoins the common room, is now used only as a depository for the hateful lime with which they love to besmear everything that is architecturally beautiful.

The monks feed now in their own apartments, to each of which a kitchen is attached. They are attended upon by a novice, generally a member of their own family; and then there are two or three working monk, who do the heavy work of the monastery, such as drawing the water from the well, and occasionally sweeping out and whitewashing the cells. Father John, who performed these menial offices for us, was a quaint-looking old fellow, with tattered cassock, weather-beaten tall hat, and bare legs, very picturesque indeed when seen toiling up the steps with our *amphora* of water poised on his shoulders.

A little tailor called Janko was our guide, philosopher, and friend outside the monastic walls; and when Lent had set in, he it was who brought us our food, for the peasants were afraid that, if they were seen brining good things inside during the great feast, they would incur the displeasure of the monks. Some even refused to sell us milk and cheese, affirming that it was a sin; and if it had not been for our tailor, we might have been condemned to an involuntary abstinence. Janko took us one afternoon to visit the nunnery, where the 'good old ladies' of Patmos retire to repent them of their sins. I feel sure that they fast more regularly than the monks, for a more attenuated sickly collection of women I never saw. We asked on entering for the lady superior, and were told that she was ill in bed, and that the others were in church during their 'hours,' and that if we particularly wished to see them, we might go in too. It was a curious sight to witness about forty sisters, in their long black coats and skirts, with black handkerchiefs over their heads, mumbling, chanting, and bowing; and for us the 'hour' passed agreeably enough as we stood in the stalls, and watched the nuns at their *metaniæ* – that is to say, bowing and kissing the ground three times after every fourth Psalm, and four times after every tenth Psalm. The number of *metaniæ* that it is possible to get through in the twenty-four hours, I was told, is three hundred; but they are by no means obligatory. It is really wonderful to see how active even the decrepit old ones are in these devotional gymnastics; and to hear the rapidity with which they can say their Kyrie

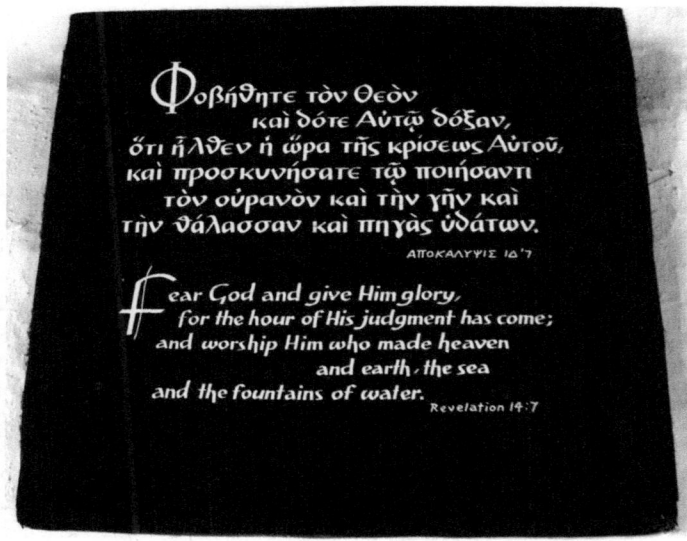

Plaque at the Cave of St John the Divine, Pátmos.

Eleisons almost takes away one's breath. The ladies plod trough the services by themselves, chanting and reading everything. A special priest, however, is kept to perform the incensing and sacred mysteries behind the screen, where it is not lawful for women to enter; but he is carefully locked out of the nunnery at night, and is never supposed to hold converse with any of them.

The lady superior, a wrinkled deaf old woman, received us in bed, where she lay in all her greasy black attire. She was not equal to much conversation; but around us sat other nuns, who made up for the said deficiency. They spoke much at first in hypocritical tones of their 'lovely unworldly life,' and then they proceeded to state their poverty, and finally invited us to their several cells, with the object of inducing us to purchase some of their handiwork. Each nun has her own apartments, most of them clean and tidy, and they support themselves by weaving and working, and by obtaining presents from their friends without and casual visitors like ourselves.

Another day Janko took us down many dark, narrow alleys to visit one of the three old women who still adhere to the picturesque Patmiote costume. Greasy though it was and faded, we could still appreciate its beauty. The petticoat had once been rich red; the jacket was of black velvet, with looped-up sleeves; on her head she wore a tall erection called a *posin*, with a gold-embroidered top; the shoes had once been of white kid, with turned-up toes; but, like the wearer, the clothes were nought but a reflection of past beauty. She lived in a house consisting of one large room with a mud floor, and containing a handsomely carved settee, some fine old chests, and a richly illuminated bed, on which she slept, the sheets of which, though extremely dirty, had valances attached of real Greek lace. The poor old thing was very shy at being thus closely inspected by foreigners, and utterly refused to have her photograph taken, for fear we should work magic with it; and she crossed herself vigorously when we asked her if she herself understood anything about the black art. 'It is a sin,' she murmured; 'the Panagia forbid that I should do such things,' but when we went away, Janko told us that none in Patmos knew more charms or incantations than she did.

Of course the stock sight of Patmos is the cave in which tradition says St. John wrote down his Revelations. There are many caves in the island, and, for my part I feel sceptical as to this one being what it professes; for it must have been exceedingly shallow before the church was built on to it, and, moreover, too much exposed to view for secret meditations, seeing that it is commanded by the site of the old town a little was up the opposite hill on the road to the monastery. At present, however, the cave is sufficiently concealed from view by a pile of buildings fast falling into ruins, where a few years ago existed a school for the education of Greeks; but now that local education is much improved in the Levant, parents do not care to send their sons so far, and the school has been closed.[89]

The care of the churches – one adjoining and one over the cave – is entrusted to a priest, Papa Makarios by name, and his sister Sophia, who occupy rooms in the ramshackle building. On the first occasion on which we visited the cave, we were lucky in finding Sophia alone, for she is deeply imbued with the legends of the place, and the story of Kynops is as much a part of her creed as the existence of St. John is of ours. She is a garrulous, energetic old dame; and, in the absence of her brother, volunteered to show us the cave and the church of St. Anna, which was built up to it by St. Christodoulos. She was almost theatrical in her gestures, as she showed us the points of interest therein. Here was the hole in the rock in which St. John placed his pillow when he slept; by the side of it was the hole, by the aid of which St. John raised himself from the ground when he got up. Over these holes a rude cross was shown us, which, Sophia said, the saint had wrought with his own hands. Then she showed us two holes in the roof, to which St. John was in the habit of tying himself by a cord, so that he might not fall asleep when he said his prayers. But the greatest object of Sophia's veneration, before which she crossed herself and knelt, was a triple rent in the rock, from which she affirmed that the voice of the Holy Trinity had issued with the divine message to the theologian. Every crack and fissure in the cave is associated with something sacred, and, as a remembrance of the place, Sophia presented us with some chips of rock; and it occurred to us that if she did the same to every pilgrim, she must have considerably altered the dimensions of the cave. We bought a pretty little carved bowl, in which the priest kept his incense for burning in the church cave, and then were conducted by Sophia to her appointment, where she regaled us with sweetmeats and rakki, as she related to us wonderful stories concerning the religious ecstasies into which worshippers at the shrine were wont to go. Afterwards she gave us a great description of the festival held here on the day of the theologian – how they hold real vigil in the church during the whole of the night before, and how the monks come down from the monastery with their relics and their banners in grand possession, to worship in the cave.

When we got home, we went to see what Prochoros had to say about the cave, and were surprised to find that he only relates how, before his departure from Patmos, after an exile of ten years, St. John was asked by the inhabitants to write down the events of the history of Christ for their benefit and guidance. To do this, the saint retired to his cave; and after two days' meditation sent Prochoros for ink and parchment, and then dictated the gospel to his disciple without a pause from beginning to end. Prochoros never so much as mentions the Revelations; but Nicitas does, and from his account it is that the *locale* of the cave has been

---

[89] Following the liberation of the island in 1947, this famous school, founded in 1713, was rebuilt a few metres above its previous location.

decided upon. Nicitas, in the MS. which we saw in the library, gives a curious account of the writing of the Revelations, which runs as follows: –

> Having at length reached a grotto which was three miles (?) (σημεία) from the town, with water in it, we tarried there ten days. John remained without food in great quiet, and in prayer; as for me, I went to the town towards evening, and ate with my brethren. On the tenth day, John himself wished to return to the town, and bending on his knees prated; when, all at once, a voice was heard which said, 'John! John!' And he replied, 'What is it, Lord?' And the Lord replied, 'Tarry in the cave yet another ten days, and great and numerous mysteries shall be revealed unto you.' In accordance with this direction he tarried yet another ten days, remaining without food, and became in a great ecstasy, and he perceived great powers, and an angel of the Lord, who related to him what he had seen and heard. And again calling me, he said, 'Go to the town, bring paper and ink, and return here.' This I did. Then he ordered me to write on the paper all the words which came out of his mouth; and we passed thus two more days, he speaking, and I writing. Then we returned again to the town, and we were lodged in the house of Sosipater.

This cave which Nicitas describes, in no way corresponds to the one shown now as the Cave of the Apocalypse. What he means by σημεία, it is of course impossible to say; but the cave where the church is built is not more than three-quarters of a mile from the old town, and has no stream of water in it now.

Very shortly after our arrival on Patmos, Lent began in all its grim earnest, and the first day, which goes by the name of 'clean Monday,' the monks spent most of their time in church. Not so the inhabitants, who make merry on this day; and though they eat no meat, they drink a great deal of wine, and I am uncertain whether the epithet of 'clean' is applied to this Monday because they do not dirty their saucepans, or because they clean themselves out with wine on this occasion. On clean Monday everyone who is equal to the scramble goes down to a spot on the eastern shore, called 'the wood or garden of the saint,' and here makes merry. Tradition says that St. Christodoulos, when he had built his monastery, tried to make a garden here, and his workmen laughed at him for attempting to cultivate so barren a spot. The saint was so hurt at this insult that he prayed fervently, and out from a rock came a spring of water which fertilized the place, and made of it the only productive spot on the island. It undoubtedly now is the only spring of water on Patmos, for the people of the monastery and of the town have only the water which they preserve in cisterns to live on.

On and around this fertile spot, with its carob-trees, olives, and solitary palm, are gathered many little churches, called 'little monasteries,' each belonging to a separate family, and containing the tomb where the departed of each family are allowed to decay, until another member of the same family dies, when they are removed to a charnel-house to make room for the incoming tenant. This system of removing bones in Greece at a given period after burial is truly revolting, and productive of many horrid sights and smells; and if the charnel-house, as happens frequently, is in ruins, the family have an opportunity of viewing their long line of ancestors huddled together in ghastly confusion.

We were told, with much glee, of a great practical joke which had just taken place in one of these charnel-houses. During Carnival time a band of young men, presumably the fast ones of the island, who had visited foreign countries and grown sceptical concerning ghosts and goblins, collected together in a bone-house, and whenever anyone was heard to pass they rattled the bones around them, and sang out in chorus, 'We were all once gay *pallicari*,'[90] the result being that the women of Patmos were nearly all of them terrified out of their lives.

Just below this saintly garden on the seashore all the folks were gathered and enjoying themselves. They sang songs, they danced dances, and time passed so agreeably as we watched them that we had eventually to hurry back to the monastery with all speed, for half an hour after sunset the great iron gate is closed, and ingress and egress is forbidden. Outside this great iron gate is a little church, with a flat space in front of it. Here the monks delight to sit and chat of an evening with the townsfolk as they pass by, and it is quite the fashionable rendezvous of Patmos for the half-hour before the great wooden *semandron* – a quaint species of gong which hangs outside the church, and which is sounded with a wooden hammer – announces the hour for vespers. At this iron gate, in the good old days, the superior used to sit on his throne, and distribute to the poor once a week portions of peas, loaves, and fishes; but this custom has been abandoned of late years, and has been commuted for a distribution of alms at Eastertide.

We had ample time on our hands for examining the interior of the monastery, and for wandering amongst its labyrinthine passages. After a hot climb up the hill, nothing can be more delightful than to sit in the courtyard, which is exceedingly small and vault-like. It is surrounded by an arched arcade, above which rise two stories of cells; in its centre is the monastic well, and never on the hottest day in summer is this courtyard too warm. Along one side of it is the church, rich in every species of Byzantine decoration. Twisted pillars with grotesque capitals support the arches before the vestibule, across which stretches the wooden semandron, which Father John sounds for every-day service. At Easter, and on high festivals only, do they sound the shrill iron one, which hangs inside the vestibule. On the outer wall of the church we see rich old frescoes. The emperor Alexis Comnenus presenting the island to St. Christodoulos, the saint himself and the theologian, and the Creator, are all depicted on this wall in the stiff conventional style of the Eastern Church. Within the church is a labyrinth of colour and richness. The rococo screen which shuts off the most sacred precincts, is covered with lovely *eikons* set in silver; the floor is set with *opus Alexandrinum*; the stalls are richly carved; and the dome is covered with frescoes, but it is dark and small, as are all the gems of Byzantine art.

One day the superior called upon us in our cell. His bow on entering is a perfect study of dignified grace; but his manner is stiff, and we think he can never have quite forgiven the raw leg of lamb and the fishes. We took this occasion of asking for his gracious permission to see the sacred relics of the monastery, which the monks are not fond of showing to the Western heterodox. Our request was granted; and that evening, after vespers, the treasurer came for us with his key, and took us to gratify our curiosity. As the relics are never exposed to view except on festivals, a number of women, who had been attending the evening service, on hearing what was to happen, took occasion to tarry behind, that they might obtain an extraordinary kiss at the treasures.

We were first of all shown St. Thomas's head bound in silver, and deposited in a huge silver cup; then the chains in which St. John was brought from Rome to Patmos were handed to us for inspection; and after these the head of Antipas, 'my witness, my faithful one,'[91] was produced; but I think we were most interested in the embalmed body of St. Christodoulos, about whom we had heard so much since we came to Patmos. Apparently, owing to Saracenic marauders, the saint was obliged to abandon Patmos after building the

---

[90] 'Warriors', 'gallants', even 'pals'.
[91] Revelations 2:13.

monastery, and died in Eubœa,[92] leaving the strictest injunctions to his faithful followers to convey his remains back when a favourable opportunity occurred. This after a few years they succeeded in doing; and the miracles wrought by these embalmed remains have provided material for many volumes, which those who desire may read in the library above. The body is now reposing in a richly embossed silver coffin in a wall-cupboard to the right as you enter the church. Amid much incensing and profound veneration this was unlocked by the treasurer, and a rush was made by the faithful for a kiss and a smell, for, say they, by divine mercy and in recognition of his many virtues, the body of St. Christodoulos has the power to emit a sweet-smelling odour to those who approach it in faith; we, however, perceived nothing of this, for the air was heavy with the fumes of frankincense. Finally we were shown St. Christodoulos's sandals, and his staff with which he wrought in his day so many miracles, and which if placed on a sick-bed, think the Patmiotes, is a more effectual remedy than any medicine their physician may administer; and such is the power of faith amongst them, that I believe there are many genuine recoveries actually on record.

Before leaving Patmos, we felt it our duty to visit father Gerasimos, the owner of our cell, in his distant hermitage, so that we might deliver to him our thanks in person, and satisfy our curiosity concerning his mode of life at the same time. The pious old man inhabits a small stone hut, which he has built for himself on the slopes of Mt. Prophet Elias, the loftiest of the Patmiote mountains. He gave us a hearty welcome, and seemed to revel in his poverty and his tiny church, which adjoins his dwelling. He is getting very blind, he told us; but with the aid of clearers[93] he can still read his prayer-book in church, and the four thumbed and torn works on asceticism which form his library, and which by this time he probably knows by heart; for what else can he have to do without companionship, without employment, except to till a small plot of ground, which produces a sufficiency of herbs for his requirements?

Twice during the day, and twice during the night, he makes the desert around re-echo with his chanting in his church. On great feast-days only does he return to the monastery. He had not been there since Christmas he told us (hence the delightful immunity we had enjoyed from vermin of all kinds), and he should not go again until Easter, during which time he hoped we would continue to occupy his rooms. When we praised them, he told us that he had long since realized that they were too good for erring mortals; and when we asked him if the other monks were not erring mortals too, he replied that he had been so troubled of late years by the frivolity of his brethren, that he had found a religious life amongst them impossible.

We had no means of remunerating our poor old host for the loan of his cell; he wanted nothing, he said, in this world, and we found it out of power to offer him anything towards his requirements in the next. Around Gerasimos's hermitage the configuration of Patmos is extraordinary; massive boulders rise up like genii on the mountain slopes, and in the gloom the spot must be weird in the extreme. No sound is heard here except the cry of the red-legged partridges, with which Patmos abounds, and the tinkling of goat-bells, when on occasion a shepherd may pass by with his flocks. Nature is here seen in her wildest form; and we could not help wondering if St. John ever wandered amongst these rocks, a far more fitting spot for inspiration than the small cave which the Patmiotes of to-day have selected as the scene for the Revelations.

We did not accept Gerasimos's invitation to occupy his cell till Easter, though if time had permitted we would willingly have done so, the further to improve our acquaintance with the Patmiotes and their quaint surroundings. One fine morning, when the breeze was

---

[92] His cave-shrine is still visible near Límni, on the north-west coast of Évia.
[93] Magnifying lenses favoured, *inter alia*, by Lord Palmerston.

Pátmos harbour, looking up to the Monastery.

favourable, we sent for donkeys, and commenced our downward pilgrimage. The superior's farewell was more cordial than his greeting; and Father John, who assisted in loading our donkey was heard to say, 'May the theologian be with you!' An hour or so later we were in a caïque, and rapidly increasing the distance between ourselves and the island so celebrated for its reminiscences of St. John the Divine.

'What St. John saw on Patmos'[94]

During two visits to the island of Patmos,[95] I naturally read my 'Revelation' with a view to local colouring, and having visited at various times most of the islands visible from Patmos, including the volcano of Thera or Santorin, I was able to distinguish them all, and give a name to each as I stood on the roof of the convent dedicated to St. John. One day, as I stood by the sea looking south-west, I distinctly saw Thera, as it was anciently called, rising out of the sea. This island is now also called Thera conjointly with Santorin, or island of St. Irene. Thera, 'the beast' (θήρ, Θήρα), was so called in ancient days because it is naught but

---

[94] From the *Nineteenth Century: a monthly review* (24:142 (1888:Dec.) pp. 813-821).
[95] The Bents made a second landing on Pátmos in April 1888 and were delayed there by bad weather. Long enough, perhaps, to inspire Theodore to write this odd piece.

the cone of a hideous submarine volcano, the slopes of which are arid and composed of black volcanic rocks formed by successive eruptions, awe-inspiring to look upon.[96] Turning to Revelation xiii. 1, I read St. John's narrative: 'And I stood upon the sand of the sea, and saw a beast (θηρίον) rise up out of the sea.' Could 'the beast,' at which I was then looking, be the beast of the Revelation? This question startled me, and in the following pages I propose to put forth much that I have since investigated, confirming me in the theory which then suddenly dawned upon me.

I have read with avidity various commentaries on the mysterious book written by St. John, M. Renan's rationalistic views,[97] theories concerning the reproduction of the plagues of Egypt, a recent notion that the book is a Jewish document of about the Christian era, which an early Christian writer had adopted almost entirely without modifying its Judaism, but interposing from time to time Christian passages. But no theory appears to me so probable as the one, that the book was written under the actual influence of an eruption of 'the beast,' when men's minds were distraught with fear, and the end of all things seemed at hand. By comparing passages in the Revelation with extracts from mediæval and modern accounts given us by eye-witnesses of eruptions of Thera, we shall find, I think, many remarkable parallels, which will go far to prove that St. John made use of phenomena which he saw with his own eyes, to prophetically depict a destruction of another kind.

Others besides myself have imagined that St. John must have been an eye-witness of some volcanic eruption. Sir William Dawson, LL.D., thus writes in *Modern Science in Bible Lands*:[98]

> One would suppose that the prophet had before him an eruption of Vesuvius: the preceding earthquakes, the black pall of ashes darkening the sun, the red glow of volcanic dust tingeing the moon, the showers of hot volcanic stones, the disappearance of the heavenly bodies, the shaking of the mountains and islands out of their place.

And again:

> The phenomena here are those of a new submarine volcano, like that which burst forth in the Mediterranean in 1831, and was known as Graham's Island.[99]

We shall first show that the volcano known as 'the beast' was in active eruption at the time of St. John's captivity on Patmos, and that he must therefore have witnessed it, and then proceed to show how St. John's narrative corresponds with those of later writers, who have witnessed similar disturbances there.

Commentators are at variance with regard to the exact time of St. John's exile in Patmos. An obscure Greek theologian, with the view to arranging certain points of detail in the book of Revelation, stated the theory that St. John was exiled in the reign of Domitian, 96 A.D.; but this, by the consensus of modern opinion, has been held to be impossible, and all the commentators are now agreed that the writer of the Revelation was in exile and compiled his work between 60 and 69 A.D., which is of course more consistent with the probable age of the writer of such a work.

---

[96] The Bents explored Santoríni a little in January 1884.
[97] Joseph Ernest Renan (1823-1892) in his influential *Vie de Jésus* (1863).
[98] Montreal 1888, 58 (both references).
[99] Some 20km off the western coast of Sicily.

The remarkable activity of the volcano of Thera during the first century of the Christian era is related to us by many classical writers. Pliny tells us that an island Thia (θεῖα), or Hiera, was formed by an eruption in 19 A.D., under the consulship of Marcus Junius Silanis and Lucius Balbus. Several authors agree in relating that another eruption tool place in the reign of Claudius, A.D. 46, namely Dion Cassius, Aurelius victor, and Eusebius, when another large island was also formed, and that an eclipse of the moon took place at the moment of the cataclysm. Dekigallas, in his history of the eruptions of Santorin,[100] tells us, on the authority of George of Syngelos, that in an eruption, in 60 A.D., 'Old Burnt Island was increased by a cape on which now stands the Church of St. Nicholas.'

Of the various late eruptions, we have of course much more graphic accounts, all of which appear to have been very similar in their action. The next on record was in 726 A.D., in the reign of Leo the Isaurian; the next in 1457, then in 1573, 1650, 1707, and 1866 respectively. The accounts of these later eruptions are of course more reliable, and will serve our purpose better for comparing with the account in the Revelation. The eruption of 1707 A.D., of which an excellent account was given by M. Delenda,[101] then English consular agent at Santorin, lasted for seven years, with more or less intensity, whilst the late eruption of 1866, which does not appear to have been anything like as severe as some of its predecessors, lasted for four years. Thus we may well surmise, from the evidence given us by the above-mentioned authorities, that Thera was is a state of actual eruption during the greater part of the first century of our era, and consequently would be a conspicuous and awe-inspiring object during the whole period of St. John's exile in Patmos.

Perhaps before entering into details concerning the description in the Revelation, a short account of the island of Thera or Santorin as I saw it will be of use in prosecuting our researches. Taken from a general point of view this volcanic cluster is round; the island of Santorin proper is on the outer circle eighteen miles from point to point, and on the inner circle twelve, and somewhat resembles a horseshoe in form; the remainder of the circle is made up by two islands, Therasia and Aspronisi, and the three channels by which the central basin is entered. All round this basin, which is the crater of the volcano, the island presents a frontage of precipitous volcanic cliffs from 500 to 1,000 feet in height, all in strata of twisted and contorted volcanic lava, red, green, and black, giving the whole place a hideous yet fascinating aspect. In the centre of this large basin lie the active mouths of the volcano, a cluster of three hideous islands, which have been thrown up by the depths of the abyss by various eruptions, and are still steaming with smoke and streaked with sulphur. They are called respectively, Old, Little, and New Burnt Island. The water is too deep for anchorage in this basin, and the ships generally are tied to rocks, and in the vicinity of the volcano the water is bright yellow from oxide of iron which comes out of the cone, which effectually cleans the bottoms of the ships without any aid from the sailors.

The town is on Santorin proper, on the summit of the cliffs round the crater, and from here the land slopes gradually to the outer sea-level and is covered with thin volcanic earth, very excellent for the growth of vines. There is yet another feature: at the south-eastern corner of the island there rises a mountain with two peaks, Mesabounò and St. Elias, about 1,500 feet above the sea. This mountain and its spurs are not volcanic, but consist of a formation common to most of the surrounding islands. It is evident that, before the

---

[100] Joseph Dekigallas, 'Ημερολόγιον περὶ τῆς ἐν ἔτει 1866 κατὰ τὰς νήσους Καμμένας ἡφαιστείου ἐκρήξεως (Sýros 1881).
[101] Apparently in a contemporary Italian MS, according to Theodore elsewhere (1885b, p. 55).

opening of the crater, this mountain was solitary island around which the volcano shed its pumice and gave it a new form.

In the gentle slopes are chasms formed by torrents in the pumice, and most of the villages are in these, the house being cut in the pumice-rock and offering only a frontage of masonry. The ascent of the cliff to the capital is performed by a zigzag path lately cut in the lava, and the town is 950 feet above the sea. On either side of the path stand up huge black boulders, which have been loosened and fallen in time of earthquakes, and frequently cause accidents now. The inhabitants of Thera are perpetually looking out upon the mouths of their volcano in the centre of their harbour. The aspect this bears is infernal beyond description; not a tree grows there, except a few fig-trees, the fruit of which is considered of surpassing excellence. All is black save a few bright-coloured stones and streaks of sulphur; huge blocks of lave and broken volcanic bombs lie about everywhere in weird confusion.

We will now proceed to our comparisons between St. John's narrative and the various reliable accounts we have from eye-witnesses of the eruptions of Thera.

We have nothing to do with the earlier chapters of the book, the messages to the seven churches and the mysterious vision of heavenly things. But with the opening of the sixth seal we are at once introduced to a vivid description of volcanic phenomena, and are given accounts which agree wonderfully with those of later authors, so that we can feel as we read that St. John must have been a terrified eye-witness of the scene, and heard marvellous stories of what was occurring from refugees who would naturally seek the safe harbour of Patmos, as they fled from the wrath to come.

The premonitory symptoms of an eruption of Thera were always mighty earthquakes and mysterious underground rumblings, and on the 5th of July, 1707, says M. Delenda, 'were seen to issue from the fissures in the rocks, great quantities of smoke, which increased from hour to hour.' This smoke killed all vegetation, and the noxious gases greatly injured the health of the inhabitants, the fumes, according to the wind, doing infinite damage to the vegetation on islands thirty and forty miles distant. Fouqué tells us of the volcanic bombs he saw shot into the air like fiery meteors in the eruption of 1866, 'varying in size from a nutshell to several cubic metres.'

Each eruption was accompanied by the appearance of rocks and islands in the sea. 'Imagine their surprise,; says the Jesuit Father Richard, in his account of the eruption of 1573, 'when they saw a great chain of black rocks, which came up out of the depths of the sea, in number seventeen.'

Pliny, as we have seen, tells us of the appearance of the island of Hiera in A.D. 19. In the eruption of 1650 the island called Kolombo[102] appeared, and in the eruption of our own day there appeared an island which was called St. George, but which afterwards became united with the 'burnt islands' and lost its identity.

Let us now read Rev. vi. 12–14 and note the parallels:

12. And I beheld when he had opened the sixth seal, and lo, there was a great earthquake, and the sun became black as sackcloth of hair, and the moon became as blood;
13. And the stars of heaven fell upon the earth, even as a fig-tree casteth her untimely figs when she is shaken of a mighty wind.
14. And the heaven departed as a scroll when it is rolled together; and every mountain and island were moved out of their places.

---

[102] One of the small islets off Santoríni.

The inhabitants of Thera would do exactly as St. John describes in the next verse, and as he doubtless heard they did from eye-witnesses of their terror – namely, 'hid themselves in the dens and rocks of the mountains,' that is to say in their own houses, which, as we have seen, are cut out of the pumice-stone rock.

In the eighth chapter of the Revelation we again discover the continued narrative of the eruption.

> 7. The first angel sounded, and there followed hail and fire mingled with blood, and they were cast upon the earth: and the third part of trees was burnt up, and all green grass was burnt up.

In M. Delenda's account of the eruption of 1707 we read of the flames which issued out of the sea, and of the damage done to the vines and trees by the noxious vapours and by the terrible crashing fall of the volcanic bombs.

> 8. And the second angel sounded, and as it were a great mountain burning with fire was cast into the sea: and the third part of the sea became blood.
> 9. And the third part of the creatures which were in the sea and had life died; and the third part of the ships were destroyed.

'Many,' says Dr. Lee in his commentary on the Revelation,[103] 'see here a symbolical representation of the Red Sea;' but we have not so far to go. Father Richard, in 1573, says: 'The sea was all tinted, even as far as twenty miles distant;' and, as I said above, even when the volcano is quiescent, the sea in the immediate vicinity of the cone is of a brilliant orange colour, from the action of the oxide of iron.

In M. Delenda's account we read of the sudden appearance of a rock in the sea, and how the sea, becoming mixed with sulphurous vapours, became white as milk, and all the fish in the harbour died. When the great masses of rocks and bombs of which the islands were formed came up from the bowels of the crater, great damage was done to the shipping, and sailors who were out in boats at the time were asphyxiated by the noxious vapours. In 1866 a boat with three dead men in it were picked up at some little distance from Santorin, they having died of the vapours and thus drifted away. This is exemplified further by the action of the third angel, when the star Wormwood, presumably an unusually large volcanic bomb, fell into the water and (verse 11) 'the third part of the waters became wormwood, and many men died of the waters because they were bitter.'

The fourth angel produced the plague of darkness.

> 12. And the fourth angel sounded, and the third part of the sun was smitten, and the third part of the moon, and the third part of the stars; so as the third part of them was darkened, and the day shone not for a third part of it, and the night likewise.

The chronicler of the eruption in 1650 tells us how, when the submarine volcano burst and the island of Kolombo was formed, clouds of thick vapour darkened the air, and fifty men and a thousand animals were killed by the sulphurous fumes, many became blind, and the noise of the explosion was heard as far as Chios and the Dardanelles, where they thought a

---

[103] William Lee, 'The Revelation of St. John', in *The Holy Bible*, ed. F.C. Cook (1881).

naval engagement was taking place, and for a whole day and night the inhabitants of Thera could not see the sun, moon, or stars.

The fifth angel had the key of the bottomless pit.

> ix. 2. And he opened the bottomless pit; and there arose a smoke out of the pit, as the smoke of a great furnace; and the sun and the air were darkened by reason of the smoke of the pit.

The actual cone itself, in the middle of the harbour, above described, is thought to this day to be the entrance to Hades, and in the smoke which issues from it the inhabitants of Thera think they see demons coming out. This angel of the bottomless pit St. John tells us was called in Hebrew, Abaddon, or 'the abyss,' and in the Greek tongue Apollyon. On Thera in ancient days there was a temple to Apollo Καρνεῖος, and a propitiatory festival was held in honour of Apollo the destroyer.

The visionary account given by St. John of the sixth angel:-

> x. 17. And thus I saw the horses in the vision, and them that sat on them, having breastplates of fire, and of jacinth, and brimstone: and the heads of the horses were as the heads of lions; and out of their mouths issued fire and smoke and brimstone.

is curiously paralleled by accounts given of the superstitions of the inhabitants of Thera during the late eruptions, who saw, in the pillars of smoke issuing from their volcano, giants and horsemen and terrible beasts. The eruption of 1650, when so many were asphyxiated by the fumes, is still spoken of as the 'year of evil,' even though there have been several eruptions since, and it must have closely resembled that in St. John's day when he wrote (verse 18): 'By these there was the third part of men killed, by the fire, by the smoke, and by the brimstone which issued out of their mouths.'

One can easily imagine how, in a time like this, the visionary spirit of St. John would be keenly worked upon; how he would see in the dense mass of smoke 'the beast that ascendeth out of the bottomless pit' (Rev. xi. 7); how he in Patmos would hear perhaps exaggerated accounts of the mortality (Rev. xi. 13): 'There was a great earthquake, and the tenth part of the city fell, and in the earthquake were slain of men 7,000.' On Thera in St. John's time, as Strabo tells us, were two important cities, Œa and Eleusis, one upon the mountain, which is not of volcanic material, and the other by the seashore, as far as possible from the volcano. Of these cities extensive ruins still remain, foundations of temples and large tombs pointing to a higher state of civilisation and refinement than in most of the surrounding islands. Those cities were doubtless laid low by the 'lightnings, and voices, and thunderings, and an earthquake, and great hail' of which St. John speaks in xiii. 19.

With chapter xiii. opens, as it were, a new phase of the vision:-

> 1. And I stood upon the sand of the sea, and I saw a beast rise up out of the sea, having seven heads and ten horns.

A Swedish lady, Frederica Bremer, who wrote an account of Santorin, thus describes it: 'How strange and dismal it seems as you sail into the many-coloured striped crater, in which you feel yourself as little as a fly in the wide-open jaws of a sleeping wild beast.'[104] Ross,

---

[104] Frederika Bremer (1801-1865) the Finnish-born feminist, novelist, and traveller. The work referred to is

the German traveller, in his *Inselreisen*,[105] likens the mysterious harbour of Santorin, with its layers of lava and pinnacled rocks, to a witch's kettle. Everyone is struck by its unearthly aspect, and from the description given by St. John one might almost imagine that he had actually been into this harbour, a not improbable supposition, seeing that it lies on the route of vessels coming in and out of the Ægean Sea in the direction of Smyrna and Ephesus; and it is also possible that the above-mentioned non-volcanic part of Santorin, with its two-peaked mountains, Mount Elias and Mesabounò, between which the old capital of Thera lay, may have suggested to his mind the second beast, 'coming out of the earth, and he had two horns like a lamb.' In ancient days, as now, Thera was celebrated for but one production, namely wine; to-day the slope of the island is like one vast vineyard, and much of the wine of this island finds its way to Russia and France; in fact an enterprising wine merchant has christened his wine 'Bordeaux,' hoping to be able to sell it as such without passing it through the hands of a French middleman, who would reap the profits. Thus in Rev. xiv. 19, St. John writes: 'And the angel thrust in his sickle into the earth, and gathered the vine of the earth, and cast it into the great winepress of the wrath of God.'

In Rev. xv. 2, St. John says: 'And I saw as it were a sea of glass mingled with fire.' Before the island of Kolombo was formed flames were seen to issue out of the sea, and several eye-witnesses of the phenomena describe the smoke and flames which appeared to come out of the waves at the time of the eruptions.

The seven angels were given vials full of the wrath of God to pour out upon mankind, and the temple*[106] was so filled with smoke that no man was able to enter it until the seven plagues were over, a very possible occurrence, for in later accounts we read how people were asphyxiated as they walked along, and remained in their cave-houses for fear of the sulphurous vapours. The first angel poured forth (Rev. xvi. 2) 'a noisome and grievous sore upon the men which had the mark of the beast.' Dr. Dekigallas made a careful study of the effects of the last eruption on the inhabitants, and found that 'eye affections, biliousness, bronchitis and maladies akin to it, were very prevalent at the time,' and in the account of the eruption of 1650 we are told that 'most people suffered sharp pains in the eyes, which watered profusely, became gathered and closed, so that for a day and a half most of the Santoriniotes were entirely blind.'

The second and third angels turn the sea and the waters into blood. We can easily imagine when St. John saw or heard of the terrors of Santoin he would naturally compare them to the plagues of Egypt. We have seen above how the sea was tinted with bright yellow for twenty miles round – how the fishes in the harbour died; and when he wrote his account he did not exaggerate in the least the horrors of the situation.

> Rev. xvi. 3. And the second angel poured out his vial upon the sea; and it became as the blood of a dead man: and every living soul died in the sea.

This was a phenomenon peculiar to the eruption of Thera.

Of the power given to the fourth angel to scorch men with the heat of the sun we have no parallel in later accounts; but it is possible that the plague of darkness inflicted by the

---

Greece and the Greeks (tr. M. Howitt, London 1863).
[105] See page x.
[106] * We read of a temple built by the Rhodians to 'Poseidon the Preserver' on the crater itself. This during the eruption would be naturally unapproachable. [Theodore's note]

The caldera of Santorini (Thíra).

fifth angel may refer to the darkening of the heavenly luminaries by the smoke, or the above-mentioned blindness.

> Rev. xvi. 10. And the fifth angel poured out his vial upon the seat of the beast; and his kingdom was full of darkness; and they gnawed their tongues for pain, and blasphemed the God of heaven because of their pains and their sores.

The allusion to the drying up of the great river Euphrates is, of course, enigmatical to us. But then the account of the seventh angel is very graphic.

> Rev. xvi. 17. And the seventh angel poured out his vial into the air; and there came a great voice out of the temple of heaven from the throne saying, It is done.
> 18. And there were voices and thunders and lightnings; and there was a great earthquake, such as was not since upon the earth, so mighty an earthquake and so great.
> 19. And the great city was divided into three parts, and the cities of the nations fell: and great Babylon came in remembrance before God, to give unto her the cup of wine of the fierceness of his wrath.
> 20. And every island fled away, and the mountains were not found.
> 21. And there fell upon men a great hail out of heaven, every stone about the weight of a talent: and men blasphemed God because of the plague of hail; for the plague thereof was exceeding great.

In these verses we have an undoubted description of a volcanic eruption, and from the allusion to the islands fleeing away, there can be little doubt that the scene of the eruption was Thera, for no other volcano is surrounded by such a number of islands as Thera. And again, he may possibly allude to the disappearance of newly-formed islands, like Kolombo, which, after its formation by volcanic agency, gradually sank in the waves.

The allusion to the shower of volcanic bombs is again undoubted, 'weighing a talent each,' or as M. Fouqué, in his more modern description says, 'varying in size from a nutshell to several cubic metres.'

The local colouring is constant in every verse of the Revelation; islands, mountains, and seas, noxious vapours, the turning of the sea into blood, volcanic bombs, etc., attesting beyond doubt that the eruption of Thera, 'the beast,' was the one present before the eyes of St. John when he wrote his 'Apocalypse;' and that he used, as is universally the case in Holy Writ, similes from nature and natural phenomena to convey to his readers ideas more spiritual and more recondite.

Finally in Rev. xvii. 8, St. John's description is as follows:-

> The beast that thou sawest was, and is not, and shall ascend out of the bottomless pit, and go into perdition; and they that dwell on the earth shall wonder . . . when they behold the beast that was, and is not and yet is.

From this we may gather that during St. John's exile on Patmos the eruption of Thera was over, smouldering, no doubt, to show that, even though active, it 'yet is,' and men marvelled still at the wonderful things they had witnessed. St. John candidly tells us, too, that 'the seven heads' of his beast are 'seven mountains,' further confirming us in our opinion that the pinnacled rocks of Thera were, according to St. John's imagination, the heads and horns of his beast.

The last vision of St. John – of the angel with the key of the bottomless pit coming down to close the crater – is just what one would expect. Into the abyss he cast Satan, 'and bound him for a thousand years.' The eruption was over, and the evil spirit of the fearful time was 'cast into the lake of fire and brimstone, where the beast and the false prophet are, and shall be tormented day and night for ever and ever.'

The inhabitants of Thera to-day think that the rumblings they occasionally hear inside the crater are the groans of the condemned. As a matter of fact, Thera was quiet for 660 years after this eruption; or rather, we have no evidence to prove that there was an eruption between the year 60 and that which took place in 726, in the reign of Leo the Isaurian.

Astypálea[107]

Some years ago a British man-of-war visited Astypalæa;[108] notes were taken respecting its splendid harbour; an engineer considered the facilities of bringing water down from a mountain source; it was in actual contemplation at that time to make the island part of the British Empire by purchase from Turkey. Its position is excellent, being almost exactly in the middle of the Cretan Sea, a considerable distance from everywhere, just one of those convenient halting-places that commercial England loves to possess herself of. As it is, Astypalæa is one of the most quaint old-world spots to be found in Greek or Turkish waters. Quaint costumes and still quainter customs still reign supreme, as they always will, under the banner of the Crescent; it is the Union Jack which scatters these things to the winds: great though our love is for antiquity, we English have dealt more harshly than any other people with the fashions of the old world. If England had bought Astypalæa neither custom or costume would now remain, for the inhabitants still remember how the British sailors gave fabulous prices for their dresses and laughed at their customs.

---

[107] The travellers were on the island from 21-31 March 1886. Theodore's article is from 'Astypalæa' (*The Gentleman's Magazine*, Issue 262:1875 (1887: March) pp. 253-265).
[108] Most likely Captain Thomas Spratt (1811-1888 and celebrated for his study of Crete) on his survey in HMS *Medina* in the 1850s. Examples of his painstaking research may be seen, for example in his hydrographic chart of 'Anaphi, Pasha and Makrea' in the archives of the UK Hydrographic Office, accessioned 4 June 1860 (Ref. D4737).

The church of the Panayía Portaïtissa, within the Kástro of Hóra, Astypálea.

It is necessary to hire a caïque to reach Astypalæa, for it is far out of the path of steamers, and to spend the night on board if the wind is not favourable. Our caïque was a fairly clean specimen of its kind, with two masts and new canvas bulwarks to keep off the wash of the waves; the small hatch in which we slept only smelt of island bread, an odour which reminds one at the same time of a fox and a mouse, and had no vermin to speak of in it, save regiments of earwigs. In the hold were several old women, some of whom always turn up at the last moment with their boxes, and clamour for a passage every time we voyage from one island to another; we have found it impossible to refuse to convey them, though we object strongly to them for two reasons – firstly, if they are well they get frightened and give constant directions to the sailors, and if they are not well they do not know how to suffer quietly. Another passenger, too, turned up, whom we soon learnt to be a little red-haired Jew from a bazaar in Constantinople, who took this opportunity to make a descent on Astypalæa for embroidery and plates; he was our *bête noire* in the island: whenever we tried to effect a bargain he was always to be seen hovering around, ready to offer more if our price was low, and to chuckle if we gave too much.

We reached our destination early one fine spring morning, and landed at a tiny harbour just below the one village of the island; this village is different to any that has ever been my lot to see, being constructed inside a massive fortress on top of a hill; this fortress has only one gateway, and the walls are built out of Hellenic and mediæval remains. On one stone you read an inscription of the time of Pericles, on another you find the name of some Venetian count who occupied this fortress.

We asked where lived Logothetes,[109] to whom we had a letter, and who, we were told, was the chief man of the island. 'Within,' was the reply. 'Within what?' we asked, and after staring at us for a while in mute astonishment at our ignorance, the peasant added, 'Within, not without.' So we proceeded on our way perplexed up the hill, and soon saw what he meant, for a new village has sprung up outside the fortress in these later years, when pirates have been scarcer; but all the grandees of Astypalæa live 'within,' and have a sort of contempt for those who live 'without.'

Logothetes received us very kindly, and gave us the loan of an empty house which he possessed 'without,' close to a long regiment of windmills, and as a keen north wind blew for a week during our stay in this rickety edifice, we lived as in a perpetual earthquake. The great man was dressed in island costume, that is to say, in cotton knickerbockers, loose between the legs for luggage, which when packed flop about like the stomach of a goose. On his head he wore a fez, and his mien was decidedly dignified, as it might well be, for does he not own all the flocks and herds on the island, as well as most of the houses and most of the best land? We had not been acquainted with him for half an hour before he told us that the Turkish *moudir*[110] could do nothing without consulting him, and that he had a thousand pounds deposited for safety in a church, though he asked many questions concerning banks and investments. I don't think he ever thoroughly got to understand the system. He furthermore told us that he had been once to Athens, and contemplated visiting that city again when his grandchildren were old enough for education; so it was clear to us that he at least knew 'civilization,' as the saying is, and yet his sister Lettuce (Maroulia)[111] and her daughter Emerald, in their quaint red costume, who lived next door to us, and who spent many hours with us every day, are little better than uncultured savages.

A most curious feature in Astypalæa, which was immediately brought before our notice by our intercourse with Mrs. Lettuce, is that the women speak quite a different language to the men, or rather their pronunciation is so entirely different that it amounts to a different language. It was some days before we could properly understand our female friends, and question them concerning their curious custom; all we could learn was this, that it was not considered proper for women to speak like men. Their μ's are converted into $\mu\tau$'s, their ς's disappear altogether; 'the sun,' for example, which a Greek man, like his ancestors, will call it ὁ ἥλιος, the females of Astypalæa choose to call ὁ ἥλτσος. It is quite clear that the men do not speak better by reason of better education and more intercourse with the outer world, for the young shepherds on the hills, who have never left their island, and have never had a lesson in their lives, speak Greek like the neighbouring islanders; but a woman, even if she has been years away and can speak Greek properly, would never think of doing so in Astypalæa; it is some quaint relic of the respect in which females once held the lords of creation, which has quite disappeared in other communities.[112] There is also another custom in Astypalæa which might be said to tell in the other direction, for here it is customary for the eldest daughter to inherit her parents' house and lands, to the exclusion of her brothers

---

[109] Logothetis is an old Byzantine title of office, but it seems Theodore is referring to a specific family name. In her *Chronicle* Mabel mentions 'Mr Logothetis'. Currently there is no 'Logothetis' surname in the Astypálea phone directory (pers. comm.).

[110] The regional government representative or official.

[111] Both Theodore (in his less academic writings) and Mabel (in her *Chronicles*) shared the habit of giving literal translations of personal names.

[112] 'Island dialects are alive and well in many a remote area, and some of them are quite incomprehensible to outsiders (which can mean inhabitants of the next island.' (*Rough Guide to The Dodecanese & East Aegean Islands* (London 2005, p. 532).

and younger sisters; this savours strongly of a survival of the matriarchal system, when the woman was considered as the safest medium for the handing down of property and family honours. Logothetes has only one daughter, by name Peace, and she is married to the meekest of men, whom we only heard named as Peace's husband, or Mr. John's son-in-law; his identity had been quite merged in that of his portly wife, and she herself with remarkable candour told us that her husband was 'a soft man, and only entitled to respect as the father of the future owner of one-fourth of Astypalæa.' Of her father, however, she spoke with the greatest devotion and respect, but as we grew better acquainted with the people, we found that all did not love and respect the great man as his daughter did. 'He is a hard man,' said one; 'he would not give a crust to a starving beggar,' said another; we gathered from various sources that he was unjust, and that he used his financial power to grind down his fellow islanders. But no matter, they all feared him, and all claimed relationship with him in some degree or another. Ties of kinship are not of great weight in a small society like this, when all are relations and intermarry; whereas elsewhere in Greece the ties of relationship are observed with the greatest respect, here, where the society is but one large family, the case is altered. There are no actually poor people as far as we could see on the island, and none actually rich except Logothetes, and there are no distinctions of rank whatsoever; it forms, in fact, an interesting example of the family as the basis of society.

Though the Turks have two representatives on the island, namely the governor and the tax-collector, they trouble themselves in no way whatsoever about the government. So long as the taxes are duly paid the inhabitants are permitted to govern themselves. A council of 'old men of the people' (δημογέροντες) is annually elected, and these councillors are elected not by vote but voice, in a general assembly held in the great porch of the fortress. A name is proposed by the town crier, and the question is put, 'Is he good?' And the people shout 'Yes, he is,' 'No, he is not,' according to their wishes. What a glimpse of old-world custom is this in the midst of ballots and scrutinies in which we live! In Astypalæa the church, which is just over the porch, and which is dedicated to the Madonna of the Gate, is the parliament house, and hither the councillors are conducted after their election to swear before the Madonna's picture to be just and true dispensers of the law.

Amongst the women of Astypalæa we soon made for ourselves delightful acquaintances, and thoroughly enjoyed their quaint perpetuation of many a classical custom. In the evening they will wish you 'a good dawn'; in the morning they will wish you 'a good evening.' They are truly Conservative in every branch of life; and as we watched day by day Mrs. Lettuce and her daughter spinning at their cottage door, we felt as though we were living centuries before our time. Rightly to picture these good folks their dress must be described: a long yellow scarf is wound round and round their heads, the ends of which hang down in loops on their back; from beneath this scarf, over the forehead, peeps a red velvet cap, jauntily worn on one side, and covered with beads and spangles. Very large silver earrings adorn or rather distort their ears. Their dress is like a long shirt, with richly embroidered sleeves, which they tuck up carefully whilst at work, and with inferior embroidery at the bottom of the skirt. Over this shirt, so that no embroidery is hidden, they wear a scarlet garment, the skirt of which on week-days is turned inside out for economy, so that on Sundays and feast days do they appear in all their scarlet magnificence. The jacket is of the same red material, square backed to the waist, when it branches out into two points, adorned with three big silver buttons. In front a sort of bib is worn to the waist, embroidered and bespangled, and sometimes covered with gold coins. At the end of this is sewn a bit of white calico, which looks as if it were intended to tuck in, but it never is.

Nowhere in the islands is the old costume so general as it is in Astypalæa, and the time to see the women to advantage is in the evening, as they trudge along the hillside to the wells for water with huge amphoræ on their heads, some green, some yellow, and some plain unglazed pottery; or on Saturday afternoons at the ovens, for Saturday is the only day on which bread is baked at Astypalæa, and the women are to be seen hurrying to and fro with long boards bearing the week's baking on their heads. On either of these occasions the scene is highly picturesque, and preferable to that exhibited on a feast day, for when busy the women are less conscious, and like the rest of their sex all over the world the good ladies of Astypalæa are fully aware what gay figures they present when dressed in all their finery.

We were lucky enough to see a bride during our stay at Astypalæa, and her wedding garments were extravagantly rich. When new, they told us, a bridal dress costs a hundred pounds, but in their present impoverished state the brides have to be content with imitation jewellery and Roman pearls, unless they are lucky enough to have inherited a costume from their ancestors, which has probably done service for generations of brides. Our bride had for her headdress a sort of mitre of gold, covered with an elaborate pattern in seed pearls. Her dress was made like those the women wear every day, only it was of velvet instead of red cloth, and her jacket was fringed with an endless number of silver ornaments, which jangles together when she moved. The Astypalæotes manage their wedding festivities more quietly than they do in other islands. The ceremony of fetching the vine tendrils for the wedding wreaths is a pretty one: the fathers of the young couple, attended by priests and a large retinue of young men playing the lyre and bagpipe, go down to the meadow where the vineyards are. As they are gathered the priests bless the tendrils, and the party return to make merry in the bride's house. When the bridegroom comes to claim his bride before the ceremony in church, he is met by a bridesmaid in the threshold, who gives him honey with which to make a cross on the lintel, and a pomegranate which he breaks and scatters outside, and in the evening the young people indulge in some curious local dances, in which the bride and bridegroom are expected to take an energetic part.

We never tired of paying visits in the fortress, with its labyrinth of narrow streets, some only sixteen inches wide, and its century-old houses packed like sardines in a box. The doctor soon became a great friend. He is a recent importation into Astypalæa. Five years ago no doctor had ever set foot on the island, and the inhabitants lived and died without physic; but for some cause or another fevers became common, and the 'old men of the people,' in council assembled, decided to send for a permanent physician. He is a queer little man, with a bald head, and a large wart on top of it. He wears 'scissor-made' trousers, as they call our European gear, to distinguish them from the baggy inexpressibles of the islanders, which are made out of one large piece of cotton. He is blessed with a stout European-dressed wife, and he never grew tired of relating to me of the difficulties he has had, and has still, in stemming ignorance of the people, who cling to their charms and incantations as far more efficacious than the physician's nostrums. He has a pretty house 'within,' with a superb view over the sea and the rocky island, but his neighbour Georgiades has a prettier one, and a prettier wife to boot, dressed in the old costume.

This house consisted only of one large room, profusely decorated. The wooden ceiling was painted in little squares, with a yellow and red rose in each square. The walls were adorned with carved ledges for the family crockery. One wall was hung entirely with plates in wild confusion, some modern, some old Rhodian, some Italian, which we coveted, but Georgiades was a well-to-do man, and cared not to sell. Around the room were many gaudily-coloured chests for clothes, and a great settee ran along the whole of one side. The bed, however, in an Astypalæote house is the greatest curiosity; it occupies one entire side, and is raised six feet from the ground. To approach it you have to climb a ladder of boxes, and when you are in you feel in a separate apartment altogether. There is a tiny window to light it, and all around are cupboards containing articles of household use. It is necessarily a very large one, for all the family sleep together, and on my remarking that I should prefer an inside place for fear of a fall, they laughed and told stories of a sponge fisherman who dreamt that he was going to take a dive into the sea, and found himself on the floor instead; and of a priest, who rolled out of bed when drunk and broke his neck. Underneath this bed, concealed from view by boards and a valance, is the kitchen in the better-class houses, when they do not cook in the sitting-room; but in inferior establishments the space beneath the bed is used as a storeroom for all imaginable filth.

Georgiades, his house, his wife and his baby all interested immensely, and when we had exhausted the interests of the former possessions, we devoted our inquiries to the latter, a dear little chubby fellow, whose cap and neck were hung with many ornaments, the explanation for which custom is as follows: when a child is born into the world, especially if it be a first-born, after the lapse of a month its mother takes it to visit all its relatives, which means in Astypalæa a visit to nearly every house. Each relative is expected to give it something; a rich one, presumably Logothetes, gives it a gold coin, which is forthwith tied to its cap, that it may be rich; another, presumably a priest, presents it with a tiny cross, that it may be good, which is affixed to the same garment. Poorer relations are only called upon to present it with trifles: glass beads, cotton, that its beard may grow if it is a boy, that it may be industrious at the loom if a girl, and sugar that it may be sweet. Georgiades' baby was a mass of these things – several coins, silver trinkets, glass beads, and charms. Around its tiny arm was tightly bound the red and white string, or 'March charm,' which is always tied on the first of that month, and is not removed till Easter time, when they tie it to the leg of the Easter lamb before it is roasted in the oven. This is considered most efficacious in warding off fevers. A year after birth they tell its future prospects with a florin and an egg. The father holds one in each hand, and whichever baby touches first indicates whether it will be rich or poor.

Whilst we chatted with Georgiades and his wife we learnt a good many curious things concerning babyhood in Astypalæa. Their child, they proudly told us, had been born in 'a good hour,' it will grow up in consequence of this healthy, wealthy, and wise, but a poor woman 'within' had given birth to a child in 'an evil hour,' and her unfortunate infant had a black mark on its forehead. This, we were informed, was a sure proof of a terrible calamity called 'brother bann' (ἀδελφοδιωχτῆς), and indicates evil or death to the children which are yet unborn, unless by charms the bann can be removed. To effect this a priest is summoned, whose first care is to burn out the black mark and then to curse the bann; having done this, they take the child and place it either on an oven or on a dungheap, and whilst it is there a perfect stranger, if such an individual can be found, must go through the formality of purchasing the child from its mother with a small silver coin, and thus the stranger is supposed to change its luck and to avert the future influence of the bann.

As soon as the poor child can speak it is taken to a lighted oven, and the mother threatens to throw it into the flames unless it says which it prefers, 'brother bann' or 'dolls.' If it speaks at all, it of course says 'dolls,' but if by chance it says 'brother bann,' or is so terrified that it does nothing but cry, then it is clear proof that the bann is still existing, and it is necessary to collect small silver coins from forty once married women, out of which a cross is hammered. This cross must be blessed at forty separate liturgies, and must be worn as a phylactery. When a mother loses several children in succession, she knows that it is this fatal and mystic 'brother bann' which is pursuing her.

The reverend priests of Astypalæa are a more than ordinary uncultured set, deeply superstitious, and living by superstition, the avowed and open enemies of anyone who wears 'scissor-made attire.' Their stipends are nothing; their living is made by what they can collect at the liturgies, their food is supplied by the offerings of bread on saints' days, and cakes at funerals, and as the doctor interferes with their sale of charms and incantations they must naturally dislike him as bitterly as our parsons dislike marriage licenses.

A glance at Astypalæa is sufficient to prove how piously inclined its inhabitants are, for never in my life have I seen so many tiny vaulted churches as there are clustered together between the harbour and the town. One cluster of churches alone consists of ten, each dedicated to a different saint, and constructed out of old Hellenic and Byzantine remains. I entered on the arduous task of trying to count all the churches in and around the village, but gave them up in despair, and contented myself with counting the windmills, of which there are fourteen. Anyone who saw only Astypalæa from the harbour would go away with the impression that the island was devoted only to the production of churches and windmills; they told me that there were considerably more churches than houses on the island. This statement I was willing to accept as true without taking the trouble of counting either, but to the question I put why there were so many near the town I got only conflicting answers; one said, 'because our ancestors were so pious'; another said, 'because everyone who has committed a sin has to atone for it by building a church.' I am inclined to accept the latter theory, knowing that the last generation, before steamers had made the trade both dangerous and unprofitable, had lived by marauding.

Concerning the churches, which are scattered over the whole of the island, I got a much more satisfactory explanation; they are built for two purposes, namely to drive away the Nereids and other phantoms which haunt the streams and cliffs, and to afford a refuge for the peasants in case of storm. I have spent nights in these churches myself when on journeys in the island, and consider them admirable institutions. As there is only one village in Astypalæa, and as it is an exceedingly widespread island with tiny oases of fertility here and there, the men who cultivate the soil are naturally much away from home. Each man possesses a goat's skin knapsack (βούρια), horribly life-like looking things when full; to the four legs of the animal are attached leather thongs by which the knapsack is slung to the shoulders; the back is frequently adorned with a fringe and with the bones of a hare's leg and other well-known charms, and with these filled with a sufficiency of bread and olives to last for several days, the labourers will start off on Monday morning and spend the days of work from home; if there is no church near they will sleep on a bed of brushwood in the open, always careful before lying down to say the prayer against scorpions which their mothers have taught them in infancy. It runs as follows: 'The earth sleeps, the earth sleeps, may the creeping things of the earth, the scorpion and the serpent sleep too.' When this has been said and the sign of the cross made three times, no one fears to be bitten in the night.

The priests are all of them labourers. Papa Demetrios has his vineyard and his garden down on the little meadow, where he may be seen most days digging and delving, an extraordinary and unreverend-looking object, with his cassock off, his sleeves tucked up, and his tall hat bobbing up and down. Papa Andreas is a fisherman, a genuine descendant of the apostle whose name he bears; he is the priest of the sailors' church down by the shore, which of course is dedicated to St. Nicholas, the mariner's friend, the modern Poseidon, the saint who is said to have invented the rudder, and whose picture is to be found in every caïque and in every fisherman's house, sometimes painted in the inside of a gilded crab-shell.[113]

---

[113] The Bents were given such a shell on Mýkonos in 1884 (*Chronicles*, Vol. 1, p. 47).

I went down to see Papa Andreas on a Saturday evening in Lent, when he was busy selling to numerous customers octopodia, cuttle fish, and limpets; his cassock was turned up, revealing a dirty pair of drawers beneath. He was too busy to pay any heed to me at the time, so I waited patiently till his sale was over, when as a preface to conversation I in my ignorance asked him if he had caught many fish lately? 'Fish,' he replied with supreme contempt, 'of course not in Lent.' 'Is this not a fish?' asked I wonderingly, as I pointed to a wriggling octopus, which had obviously been caught since the austerities of the Lenten fast began. 'Oh dear no,' he replied with something of a smile, 'it has no blood in it.' So I stood corrected, and gained a clearer understanding concerning the principles of fasting as inculcated by the Eastern Church.

Papa Andreas then took me into his house, where his wife was employing herself in mending the old nets which I was told would not be wanted till after Easter; around the room was the tackle which present necessities required, the tin can with a glass bottom with which the fishermen inspect the bottom of the sea when in search of sponges or shell-fish, the iron rake which they drag along the rocks to loosen the same from their holdings, and the block of wood with bits of looking-glass on one side and a rude representation of a cuttle-fish on the other, which they drag slowly through the water to attract the cuttle-fish from its lair.[114] Papa Andreas was very proud of his church. It is a building of comparatively modern date, and boasts of an elegant three-storeyed bell tower; inside the church is hung with every imaginable form of nautical offering, miniature silver boats and oars, pictures of escape from shipwreck with the Madonna hastening in a cloud to the rescue. Before the high altar were enough sponges to have stocked a barber's shop, presented by grateful sponge fishermen to St. Nicholas. I fancy the temples of ancient days must have offered much the same appearance as this, and I am sure Demetrius the silversmith made many similar silver objects to be hung up in the great temple of Diana at Ephesus.[115]

Having inspected the church of St. Nicholas, Papa Andreas volunteered to conduct me to a breezy height above, where stands a small vaulted church dedicated to the Prophet Elias, whose jurisdiction over storm and rain is held supreme. It was altogether bare of offerings, and contained only three sacred pictures, one of the Virgin and Child, one of Christ, and one of the Prophet, which last, by way of distinction, was decorated with a frame composed of yellow chintz. When drought falls upon Astypalæa the people go in a body to this mountain church to pray for rain. Archaeologists assert that wheresoever in ancient days stood a temple to the god Æolus, now stands one to Prophet Elias; the names are similar, and during the transition from heathendom to Christianity the early divines doubtless availed themselves of this similarity. When we were at Astypalæa the inhabitants were complaining of drought, and said that unless rain came the grain could not grow; consequently a pilgrimage to the mountain church was in contemplation, but rather to our regret the north wind changed, and with a southern breeze came the longed for rain, and the prayers to Prophet Elias were never said. Prophet Elias in Greece is something like our St. Swithin: if it is cloudless on the prophet's day, a mild winter and a fruitful season are foretold – for, as the saying goes, 'Prophet Elias puts the oil into the olive.'[116]

---

[114] The Pitt Rivers Museum in Oxford has a 'cuttlefish bait of wood coated with wax in which pieces of mirror are embedded' donated by the Bents in 1888 (item 1888.37.1). The findspot is given as the 'Furni [Foúrni] Islands'.

[115] An oblique reference to Theodore's contemporary, the antiquarian and engineer John Turtle Wood (1821-1890), the excavator at Ephesus. See his *Discoveries at Ephesus: Including the site and remains of the great temple of Diana* (1877), and Acts 19, 21-41.

[116] In such sayings as 'Το σπερνό του Ἀι Λια / μπαίνει το λάδι στην ελιά / και τ' Ἀι Λια το βράδυ / μπαίνει η ελιά στο λάδι...' and 'Δευτερογούλη τ' Αϊ Λιά μπαίνει το λάδι στην ελιά...'

Distaff acquired by the Bents.

Drought is not the only difficulty with which the Astypalæote farmer has to contend. In spring-time flocks of small birds alight on this island on their northward passage; these they call indiscriminately 'grain-eaters,' and on their arrival the priests are despatched to various points in the island to make a sacred anointing of the crops by sprinkling them with holy oil and water. When this is done they believe the voracity of the 'grain-eaters' is checked. Thus do the priests gain money, but this is nothing to the solemnity connected with the priestly charm which arrests the ghostly wanderings of those who have died in their sins; the remains of such an individual are deemed altogether unhallowed, the spirit cannot rest in the grave, it returns to its whilom[117] home and haunts the abode of friends of former days. These much dreaded ghostly wanderers are called in Astypalæa καταχανάδες, and a priest alone can cause these evil spirits to rest. He sprinkles the grave with holy oil and water. He offers up a long prayer thereon, and if this is not sufficient he will remove the bones away in a sack to some rocky uninhabited islet, for ghosts they say cannot cross water. The superstition under different names is common all over Greece, and the privilege of becoming a καταχανάς belongs solely to those who have received Christian baptism. A Turk if he dies in his sins, is condemned to wander about as a black dog, which howls dismally all night.

Of all our friends at Astypalæa we liked none better than Mrs. Lettuce. She was with us for hours together and always brought her work with her, for she was busy at the time embroidering a new dress for her daughter Emerald to wear at Easter; and I think we liked Mrs. Lettuce all the better because she embroiders still in the good old patterns, and does not affect anything European, which has been the ruin of Eastern embroideries of late years. She would ask us questions innumerable and very puzzling concerning our country; for example, her curiosity was great to know all about 'land-steamers.' She had seen steamers on the sea, but how they could be made to go on land puzzled her exceedingly, and I doubt whether our explanations concerning the working of railroads threw much light on the subject. Having patiently waited until the thirst for knowledge was somewhat satisfied, we felt emboldened in our turn to put many questions to her, and good Mrs. Lettuce took a

---

[117] Former, erstwhile.

delight in telling us everything we asked. 'She knew many charms, indeed she did; she could tell any girl how to win a husband, if she was in love. Get a scrap of his clothes, tie it to your spindle, and whirl it round, saying as you do so, "May the love of my man turn to me."' 'Had Emerald tried this plan?' 'No; Emerald had never been in love,' and so we went on. As this was the first Greek love charm I had heard, which was capable of being repeated, I entered it in my note-book[118] with a degree of pleasure which vastly amused Mrs. Lettuce. Then she told us of a certain plant Βρομος, which she knew well, and which grows up in the mountains; if you put it into the hair of a woman without her knowing it she will see visions of the future. But one of the head-bones of the *scaros* fish is one of Mrs. Lettuce's favourite divining rods; when any friend of hers is going to have a baby, she goes to call upon her and secrets the bone surreptitiously in the patient's hair. Then she waits to hear whether the woman will first mention the name of a man or a woman, and whichever sex is first alluded to will be the sex of the expected infant.

Mrs. Lettuce was kindness itself. She gave me her handsomely carved distaff, to which I had taken a fancy;[119] she brought us salads and trifles to eat, about which we did not always care so very much. One day I was watching her grinding peas with her stone hand-mill just like a quern. 'Do you have peas in England?' she asked. 'Oh, yes!' and I foolishly added, 'we eat a great many of them.' So that evening, when we had despatched a partridge and were about to turn our attention to some curds and honey, in walked Mrs. Lettuce with a dish of boiled peas swimming in oil and flavoured with the coarsest pepper, nor would she take her departure until we had done ample justice to her present.

As for Mrs. Lettuce and her family – husband, two daughters, and three sons – their evening meal always consisted of peas thus cooked, and nothing else. A large bowl full was regularly placed on the mud floor in their midst; the family squatted on the ground, the father and mother each had wooden spoons, but the youngsters went at their meal with their fingers only; these they sucked and dipped in again, this primitive process having one advantage, that previously dirty hands were after dinner always clean. We watched them thus feeding evening and evening by the light of the brushwood fire on which the peas had been boiled, and they reminded us of a Dutch interior in Greek garb.

Mrs. Lettuce we soon found did not like the doctor, and always left us if he came to pay us a visit; she was in fact a leading member of the party of obstruction. 'How Mr. John,' she would say, alluding to her brother the great Logothetes, 'can believe in his physic, I cannot think.' And after a moment's reflection she looked up triumphantly and said: 'But he cannot cure *drymes*, and says that those who suffer from them in Lent should not fast; he is a wicked man, and he will become a καταχανάς.'

Now *drymes* are sores and abscesses which are very commonly seen on the bare feet and legs of the islanders. The doctor says they come from the poverty of blood and poor living; but they say they come from washing on the three first days of August. Linen, if washed on these days, gets holes in it, and legs get *drymes*. This is their theory, and some go so far as to call them 'devil's touches;' but no matter how they come, every old woman knows how to cure them by putting their hands on them and muttering certain words as they do so. Mrs. Lettuce was very shy about telling me these words, for she imagined, and

---

[118] Only a couple of Theodore's personal notebooks remain in the archive of the Hellenic Society, but these do not include his Greek island tours.

[119] This distaff may well be the Bent donation now in the British Museum and suggested as being from Kálymnos. Its accession number is EU1972, Q.2511: 'The centre of the head wrapped with linen to which is attached a tuft of grey and white wool. The linen has remains of a printed pattern or possibly writing. The top of the stem is decorated with an incised geometric pattern.'

with a certain degree of correctness, that I only wanted to laugh at her. Eventually, the day before we quitted Astypalæa, I grew desperate and offered her in exchange for these words a packet of English needles; the needles gained me my point, but I am inclined to think that Mrs. Lettuce got the best of the bargain. As the aged female physician touches her patient's wounds, she crosses herself and says: 'In the name of God, my master Christ, and Holy Panteleomon, first physician of the world; down on the sea-shore St. John is baptising and teaching thousands of heathen. On Friday the Jews crucified Christ;[120] on Sunday He rose whole without spot, and without blood. Thus may the leg of thy servant be healed.' In obstinate cases these words must be written down and tied to the wound with a handkerchief, and then the *dryme* is sure to disappear.[121]

Those who go to Astypalæa must be people of a patient disposition. We packed our things to leave on a Wednesday morning, the caïque was in readiness and so were the old women with their boxes, but the wind was unfavourable, and it was not until that day week could we start. Mrs. Lettuce rejoiced in our delay, she told us, and when we did start I am sure she was genuinely sorry, for we saw two scarlet figures, which we knew to be Mrs. Lettuce and her daughter, standing waving farewells on the hill side long after any demonstration of that kind was necessary.

J. Theodore Bent.

---

[120] Actually in Orthodox belief He was crucified on Thursday and died on Friday.

[121] A similar reference appears in James Rennell Rodd's *The Customs and Lore of Modern Greece* (1892), page 135: 'These sun-rays are sometimes personified under the figure of old women, known by the name of "Drymes," who will make sore places in the skin of those exposed to them, and will most certainly pierce holes in any linen put out to bleach.'

The Travel Chronicles of Mabel Bent

Mabel Bent began her notebooks – she called them her *Chronicles* – for the couple's second visit to Greece, in the winter of 1882/3, to the Cyclades. She was to continue them until the year afer Theodore's death only. They were never intended as intimate records, but rather as *aides-memoires* for Theodore to consult later when preparing his talks, articles and monographs (often taken verbatim), and as travelogues for her sisters, nephews and nieces in Ireland. Included in one of the volumes is a letter from a friend, a Mrs Graham, who writes: 'Why oh why don't you publish it? It simply bristles with epigrams and I am certain would be a great success! You ought to blend the Chronicles into one and I am sure everyone would buy it.'

Mabel starts her 1886 notebook: 'I must begin my Chronicle somewhere if I am to write one at all, and as in this matter I am selfish enough to consider myself of the first consideration, because I write to remind myself in my old age of pleasant things (or the contrary), I will begin now.'[1]

It is to be hoped her written memories did console her lonely later years. She died in in some distress in 1929 and presumably her *Chronicles* were presented subsequently to the Hellenic Society by her nieces.

Three of Mabel's notebooks cover the couple's explorations in the Dodecanese:

1885, Rhodes and nearby islands: Mabel's 1885 *Chronicle*, her second. The *Chronicle* is written in a dark-blue leather notebook (185 x 120mm) with marbled endpapers and edges. There are 170 lined pages and Mabel fills 115 of them.

1886, Pátmos and nearby islands: Mabel refers to this 1886 *Chronicle* as her 'fourth', but it is actually the third of her notebooks. This *Chronicle* is written in a dark-red leather notebook (180 x 115mm) with marbled endpapers and edges. There are 192 lined pages and Mabel uses all but 10 of them.

1888, a cruise south to Kastellórizo: Mabel's notebook for 1888 is *Chronicle* V (the numerical sequence is restored). She writes in a dark-red leather book (180 x 115mm), with gold lines on the spine and covers. The endpapers and edges are marbled. There are 192 lined pages, of which Mabel has used 182.

---

[1] 'Tuesday, February 2nd, Hôtel de Byzance (Room 2), Constantinople'.

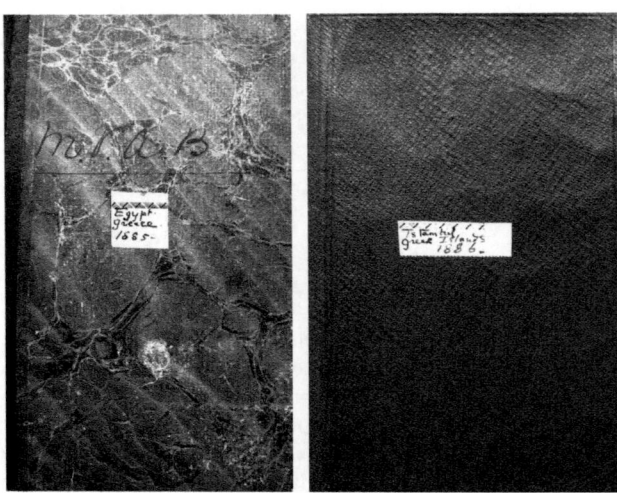

Mabel Bent's Chronicle covers for the years 1885 and 1886.

Mabel V. A. Bent her
Chronicle in the
Sporades, etc.
1885

February 1885 – *en route* for the Dodecanese

Thursday February [5th].[2] I am writing against much rumbling of the screw of the Austrian Lloyd S.S. *Saturn*.[3] We are having as calm a voyage as needs be but not without its hopes and fears.

We left Cairo on Monday evening at 6, seen off by Major Dawson, and 'took up with' a young Mr. Tucker who left the hotel with us. We luckily had dinner enough with us to share with him, washed down with coffee at Damankoor (halfway), and reached Alexandria at [time illegible]. We were greeted with the unpleasant intelligence that the Austrian would not call at Rhodes this week, so we went to bed with the half formed intention of going to Smyrna by a Khedivieh ship and trusting to luck for a passage to Rhodes. However the belated *Saturn* came in early next morning and we left at 4 on Wednesday afternoon. We had a whole day in the very uninteresting Alexandria and took a drive.

Yesterday it looked quite black all round when we embarked and began to rain and the harbour was full of gulls – 17 sitting in a row on the rope mooring a ship near. So we felt very gloomy knowing that if it were too stormy we should not touch at Rhodes but be carried to Smyrna. But the sun came out and all became bright as we steamed off 'adagio adagio'.

---

[2] Mabel's dates can be problematic – with Mabel often 'catching up' at moments of relaxation. Readers should also be aware of the calendar differences in effect then between Europe and the Eastern Mediterranean. Place names present the usual difficulties of phonetic variations. Editorial intrusions within the text itself are limited and placed within square brackets.

[3] More likely the *Saturno*, 1845 tons, built in 1868, in service until 1910.

You would think all our fears were at an end as we have had about 20 hours of excellent weather and hope to be at Rhodes by tomorrow morning, but no! there is 24 hours quarantine. If we could feel sure of remaining on board we should not so much mind, but if the Captain thinks it will be dangerous for the ship to remain in the roadstead he will be off, leaving us in the lazaretto, and if a sudden storm springs up we may not be able to disembark but may have to be left at Leros.[4] There are only 3 Greek 1st Class passengers for Constantinople and the captain, who does not seem to think himself an 'unredeemed Italian' at all, and an ill-tempered German Austrian Doctor. Of course Egyptian affairs have been discussed but in a much more generous spirit than by the French. We hope to meet Manthaios, our servant, at Rhodes.[5]

We had to pay 11/6 duty on some baggage that was not new and never got beyond the customs house. The official, a German, explained that it was a mistake charging more than 1 p.c. and acknowledged that T was owed the rest back, but as so many papers would have to be paid for to reclaim it that only 2/- would remain, and as the formalities would take a whole day, of course it was hopeless to do anything.

Friday [February] 6th. Day seems quite over, it is half past six, and a most anxious day we have passed with the yellow flag waving us. We got to Rhodes about 3 but did not settle till 5 and the health officers did not come till 7. The Captain asked leave to go to a bay to shelter if storm came on, or the open sea, but they said no, if we wanted pratique he must remain there. But the Captain told us that sooner than lose or damage the ship he would go off with us and the two guardians to Smyrna. Great therefore was our horror at 3.30 p.m. to hear all the noises of a start, after having observed that it was getting rougher, but we only went round the corner of the island to shelter on the eastern side and hope to be returned to the capital tomorrow morning. In the mean time no one has been able to communicate in any way with the shore. It has been pouring most of the day. One of the Greeks recognises us, having seen us on Scio 2 years ago. They are most friendly and drink brandy before each meal and T to his disgust has had to accept twice as they always offer it to us.

Thursday Feb. 12th. Here we have been 5 days in Rhodes, having very bad weather in this favoured isle, 'where there is rarely a day without sunshine'. We are right glad and thankful to be here for it is not granted to everyone who arrives here to get ashore. A week or two ago the boat with the doctor in it was upset in returning to shore. The said fat old Turk kept us a whole hour waiting, and it would really have suited us to land a little later, but the Captain constantly feared he could not land us. However after a parade of the passengers we did get to land, though it was very rough. Of course we knew a passport would be demanded and we had lost ours, so when something was said in Turkish which we knew must be this request T solemnly handed them an old letter of credit which he held in readiness. They were quite satisfied and as I was dancing with Kyrios Aristarchis, the Government Dragoman, I explained it all to him and he said 'the trick was so good that it should be duly honoured' and he would receive it as a true passport and now we have it back.

We have actually been to a ball at Mr. Calvert's, our V. Consul's. There were Greeks and Levantines. All the ladies had handsome faces but bad figures. The dresses were very various, some good, some bad, and some in fancy dress because this is the Greek carnival. The prettiest girl in the prettiest dress was a French one dressed like a gypsy. Amongst

---

[4] The Bents seem never to have explored Léros.
[5] From Anáfi in the Cyclades, Manthaios Símos, the Bents' guide and interpreter on and off from their Greek tour of 1883/4 until their final visit to Aden in 1897. The weather delayed him at Makri (the ancient Lycian Telmessus, now the area of Fethiye).

Along the lanes of the Old Town, Rhodes.

others were Kyrios and Kyria Philemon. We had met him in Samos two years ago. He is Greek Consul and they seem to be nice people. When I went to call he sent me a nice little old terracotta jug. Mr. Aristarchis's brother had met us in Chios, so they knew all about us.

We are at a clean little inn in the separate village called Neo Marás, the Christian quarter quite close to the sandy and windmilly point Kum Burnú at the north of the isle. It is quite a little walk to the town where no one but Jew or Turk may remain after sun set. The town is very interesting and full of coats of arms and bits of carving and other traces of the Knights, but see Murray.[6] There is a charming walk along the sea towards Trianda on the west coast. There are big rocks of Puddingstone tumbling about which must once have been shingle and sand and now for a second time are returning to that state. There are quantities of smooth black and white shingles which are extensively used for paving floors and court yards in all sorts of designs. The passage outside our door and the dining room too have very pretty patterns.

All this time we are without M. First he was stormstayed at Anafi and then he arrived here on Sunday evening but could not touch so he is at Makri in Asia Minor and is due to make another attempt tomorrow.

---

[6] Murray's *Guide to Greece* with its reference to Rhodes as an isle 'Where there is rarely a day without sunshine'.

Fancy my feelings on Monday morning when I heard 3 Turks talking in the passage. All I could make out was Theodhoros so I looked expectantly at them and they came in with a telegram addressed in Turkish and began to read 'Mylordos Theodhoros…' I said 'Bent,' and they said yes, 'Bendi,' so I put out my hand, took the document, opened it and found more Turkish so I handed it to them and said in Greek, 'Please tell me what it is, for I can't read it'. Then they handed it to each other – all read it aloud and at last one said he was afraid he could not exactly make it out but any how I made out that it was from poor M telling of his trouble. All the time we are eating we hear Turkish spoken and when any one of the dozen detached words we know turns up we are delighted.

Thursday [February 19th?]. M arrived on Monday morning; he ought to have been here on Friday. With him came the north wind and consequent fine weather. Last Sunday was quite the worst day. Thunder, lightning, hail and rain all day. We spent another evening at the Philemons and took several walks, and also on Tuesday went to Phileremo at the top of a mountain, about 12 miles. Mr. James Aristarchis, the Chios one, who talks English perfectly, came with us. I rode a mule and the others and M walked. I had a European saddle but it had no crupper. So going down hill the saddle turned and I had nearly reached the ground on the near side when Mr. Aristarchis caught me. A fortunate thing as my leg was caught in the pummels. A few steps further he could not have got between me and the precipice. So a rope was tied to the back of the saddle and M held on behind till we reached the plain. The view from the top of the hill is lovely: the coast of Caria and several islands. It was formerly the acropolis of Old Ialysos. There was a ruined church of the Knights and a subterranean Church, Greek, frescoed inside.[7]

On Monday we had been to call on the Pasha, Khamel Bey, with Mr. Calvert and Mr. Biliotti.[8] He was not at home but his plump 18-year-old son Khem Bey was there. I went to see the Harem but was much disappointed. The rooms looked very meagrely furnished. I saw the only wife and other very old and ugly ladies. The Khanoum Pasha only could talk very little Greek so Khem Bey did dragoman in French till the others wanted to come in. They were all 90 at least.

As the Government steamer is going to Karpathos we begged to go in her. But instead of saying straight out that it was impossible, as women are not allowed on these ships, which if such were the rule they must have known, we were kept waiting for an answer till yesterday and further told that a great row was made because some women took refuge on a man-of-war during the earthquake of Chios. Furthermore the Pasha has not returned our visit yet nor sent the promised letter for the Kaïmakam of Karpathos.[9] The real reason for all this is that 2 years ago when we were in Chios we heard in travelling over the island dreadful stories of oppression of the Greeks by the Turks which these wretched creatures begged T to expose in England. When we reached the Chora we were on our way to ask our Consul about it but he was not at home. Mr. James Aristarchis, who speaks English perfectly, came up and asked if he could do anything for us. Theodore told him what we were about and he took us to his father (he was once Prince of Samos) who was the Pasha's secretary, in the *Konak*, or Government house. He of course being a Government official did not like to say too much, but between them all we were told to go to the Pasha. So Mr. Bent asked to see him and in walked to his amazement Mrs. Bent. T said that he had heard such bad things that it was impossible to believe them and as he did not like to go to England with a false

---

[7] Mabel is visiting the acropolis site of ancient Ialysos (Filérimos). The underground and frescoed chapel is that of St George.
[8] The senior wife of the pasha has the title 'Khanoum'.
[9] The Kaïmakam is the main Turkish authority or governor.

impression he should like to hear them contradicted. But the Pasha said all was true and T said he would make things known in England.

We were given unpoisoned coffee and left. After we had gone Hashid Pasha was in a towering rage and said 'Fetch this one! Fetch that one! Fetch the other!', all high officials, and said, 'What do you think has happened? A man has been here asking questions! And a woman! What did that woman want here? They had better learn to govern Ireland properly.' And in half an hour he wished he had asked for the papers which authorised T to ask such questions. He did not get over it for a long time, Mr. Aristarchis says.

When Theodore got home he spoke to Mr. Pandeli Ralli M.P. about this affair, also Lord Edmund Fitzmaurice. Mr. P. Ralli asked a question in Parliament and Lord Granville told Lord Aberdeen to enquire about it. The Pasha was moved to Smyrna and Mr. Anamesaki, our Consul, who rather threw doubt on T, and I believe made himself out to have done most, got the Order of the Saviour, which we have often heard that T should have got instead. Besides this he wrote an article in 'Macmillan' 'Two Turkish Islands Today' i.e. Chios and Samos. This was at once translated into Greek and got about, though the Government tried to suppress it, and in Turkish, which enraged them much.[10]

Khamel Bey was then Pasha of Mytelene and is a very clever literary man and a great poet and gets a pension to keep his pen off dangerous subjects. He was deputed to answer T and telegraphed to Mr. James Aristarchis to come and help him. But Mr. Aristarchis said it was a whole year since the article came out and what paper did he mean to write his answer in? And who would read it? So he gave it up but Hashid Pasha did write something very rabid about T in the Villayet paper.[11]

This is the origin of Khamel Bey's rudeness, and we are assured that we should have spies set on us in Karpathos, and not be allowed to dig, and that as the steamer would get there before us and give warning we have determined to give them the slip and get them off our traces. So we never have said all day that we are giving up Karpathos, which we must get at some day from Crete. Instead of spending more than a night and a day in a *kaïke* we only say we must go by Chalki, an island half way down Rhodes on the west and more than ¼ of the way to Karpathos. We can get there by a Greek steamer, then turn north to Tilos, and together with all the letters for Karpathos we are asking for others in case we may go to the islands, and we have got a new passport for 'Karpathos and other islands'.

It is now past 5 and we do not know when the steamer will come, if we shall sleep on board or what hour we shall start. Knowing how little chance there would be of getting our letters if we wished to, we have said they are not to be forwarded. We feel very mysterious!

Nisiros [Monday] Feb. 23rd. We left Rhodes on the night of the 20th. We went on board the Greek steamer *Roúmeli*[12] at 6 o'clock after waiting in expectation of its arrival all day. The evening before, just as we were going to pay an evening visit to the Philemons', they, thinking we should be busy, came to us instead and Mr. Mitso Aristarchis, who is engineer in chief to the Porte at Mytelene, joined us.

---

[10] Issue: 48 (1883: May/Oct.) pp. 299-309 and reprinted in *Littell's Living Age* (September 15, 1883, Vol. 158, No. 2047, pp. 682-691).

[11] The Bents visited the island in 1882/3 on their first trip to the region; Mabel kept no *Chronicles* on these early visits.

[12] The small steamship *Ρούμελη* (297 tons, 155 feet) linked the smaller islands of the eastern Mediterranean, passing through various owners over long years of service from 1881. Originally named *Operculum*, and Clyde built, she comes into view several times in Mabel's pages. She was ultimately broken up at Savona in 1933, a few years after Mabel's death.

Sými harbor.

Well! The *Roúmeli* is a dirty little ship, and T and I slept in the very smelliest cabin, destined for ladies by the English builders. As it was a passage room for all the passengers a quilt was hung across, but the steward was often within our side. At 11.30, two hours after we left Rhodes, we reached Simi and in the dark and by starlight I could see that we remained in a little land-locked bay for 2 or 3 hours. It looked lovely but no doubt by day it looks bare enough and like Chalki, which we got to about 7, a most hideous island, stony like Syra and not even the picturesque town to redeem it. We did not land there; there is a revolution about the tax on sponges and the Pasha of Rhodes was just going there so we came on to Nisiros, which we reached about 12.30.

We passed Tilos on the way and had to come half round this island to get to the NW side, where this little town of Mandraki lies. The island is only about 8 miles across and quite round. It has been a volcano and there are no springs on it – cisterns are used. In the middle of the island is the sunken crater with a pond of sulphur. One can smell it more than a mile off.

Once more, and for the first time during this journey, we found the very narrow little streets, up and down steps, and sometimes rocks a foot and a half high, and full of pigs, like on the Cyclades. We were taken to the house of the schoolmaster, Logothetis (layer-down of the law) and given coffee, *loukoumi* and almonds, but he was absent as well as Kyrios Apostolides to whom we also had a letter. The Archimandrite of the monastery, situated on a projecting rock among the ruins of a medieval fortress, was soon on the spot and our baggage ordered up the hill. We followed up steep steps and rocks, winding in and out under arches, and with joy found we had a room really to ourselves, large and clean enough, and with lovely views of Kos, Ialé[13] and Kalimnos.

---

[13] Yali, west of Bodrum.

As the only bed was small and dirty I have slept in my hammock very successfully these two nights. The down quilts covered with white to serve as sheets make it look as if it were full of whipped cream. I can now get in without untucking the bedclothes.

The women here wear a very pretty dress, and now we know why 'Turkey red' is called Turkey red, i.e. because all the women in this Turkish island wear an open sleeveless gown of it with a very full skirt a good deal shorter than the thick cotton shirt with handsome silk embroidery round the tail, 1½ yards round. The sleeves are splendidly embroidered. We have bought 5 of these underdresses, 1 pair of sleeves, a pillow cover, and a bed valance for £3.15.0.[14]

Yesterday [Tuesday, February 22nd?] we went to Emborios up in the mountains, about 1½ hours, a place exactly like this. I rode, or I may say I bestrode, a small donkey with a large mule packsaddle. The donkey's and my difficulties were increased by having to squeeze through bushes of prickly dwarf holly up to my knees. My feet and knees often got knocked on stones and rocks, and altogether it was not a very pleasant ride for me. When we started home with the bundle of clothes the muleteer lent his sash and the clothes were slung on to M's back. It was not a very interesting expedition.

We dine in another room very bare, but most thankful are we not to be in a family and obliged to talk when we are tired. The first evening we had to eat soft eggs without spoons as ours were not out, and we had no glass in the windows, but were tolerably comfortable for all that. On the 23rd we paid several visits, engaged a boat and wished to leave as the wind was N., but we were persuaded to put off till next day.

Tilos [Wednesday, February] 25th. We left Nisiros yesterday at 9 a.m. but not for 7½ hours did we step down an oar on to this island.[15] We had calm for most of the 15 miles. We came round the E. so now we have completely circumnavigated Nisiros. We saw a good many people on the shore as we approached, but by the time we landed not one was in sight. The boatman then holloed out 'Come near, fear not! We are from Nisiros, you may come safely!' So out they came and we went to meet them and they said, 'What people are you? From *The Town*?' We said we were not from Constantinople but from England, but this did not enlighten them much. They asked if this were our first time coming to the island and after we had said 'yes', T asked something about the other port and they wanted to know how we knew there was another port. Today T said something to the superior of this monastery[16] of the vineyards near the Limena and he said 'Did you guess of yourself that we had vineyards there or have you been told?' We had passed the Limena on the steamer. There is no post here.

It was 4.30 when we arrived and we at once dispatched M to the town to see after a lodging and take our letters of introduction to the Superior or Egoúmenos of the monastery and Kyrios Kamá, and off he went bearing his coat, half a kid in one hand and a tied up bundle with his favourite scraps for his own eating. He is certainly cheap to feed. He eats all the fishes' heads and yesterday lunched of cold lights.

We left our very voluminous baggage on the beach and went off to look at a young woman we had observed from the sea, stamping like mad upon something black. This was a brown goats' hair coat, which was wet and put on a board, surrounded with stones to keep

---

[14] See page 185.
[15] The couple have arrived on Tílos, at the small northern port of Ay. Andónios, facing north towards Níssyros.
[16] Mabel specifies below that they are staying at the little monastery of Ay. Pandelímona (just before the lane turns up towards Megálo Horió and not to be confused with the remote and fortified large monastery of the same name behind Profítis Ilías). The Bents' temporary lodgings can still be accessed.

The small monastery below Megálo Horió where the Bents roomed on Tílos.

it steady, and the woman had been kneading and grinding it 4 days to get the long hairs off. She said it was cold work and her feet looked quite sodden.

At about 5 all the people began to assemble to go up to the town for no one sleeps by the sea, and they begged us to come too. We said we would wait for M and we could not think why he did not come. The people seemed unwilling to leave us and frightened to stay, so we consented that they should not divide our luggage among them, and they all shouldered the heavy things quite easily. Quite an old woman took a big carpetbag. I took 3 loaves and the honey-bottle, and we were a most queer procession.

It was most fortunate we started. We were not a moment too soon, for it is a mile to the town and we might have at least sprained our ankles, for most of the way is covered with loose stones of various sizes, and then we might have lost our way over rocks and not have hit off the road again. And it was dark by the time we got to the town, besides we had to go so completely round a mountain that we did not see it till the last minute.

When we were ¼ mile off we met M and the schoolmaster Spirídonos clad in black European dress, and we went first down a great many narrow piggy streets and rocky stairs to the café, and we sat for about an hour on a balcony, homeless for one of our friends was absent and the Egoúmenos out. At last the schoolmaster asked us to come and sit in quiet at his house, which consists of one small room, half of it being according to the usual custom at 26 inches higher than the rest. He had been married 40 days he said, and had that morning returned from Kalimnos with his pretty bride, after 8 days of sea-sickness. Twice had they reached Tílos and had to return as far as Kos. So it was hardly a lucky moment to intrude on them, but they were most kind and Mrs. Kaliópe unpacked her box and took out tablecloth and napkins and told us tomorrow she should tidy the house, and seemed rather disappointed that it had not been whitewashed. However when a saucepan of soup, once 'portable', was brought we felt such bores, we declared we would go and dine in the *kafeneion*, but we were told by our host that we should offend them much if we did. So we remained and ate off our own tin plates, etc., and used their pretty painted wooden spoons, which imparted a flavour of varnish to our soup.

After the Egoúmenos came and took us to the Monastery of Holy Pantaleomonos in the valley about ½ a mile from the town. We have a little house to ourselves, one room opening into a sort of court or cloister. One end is 18 inches higher and has a dusty carpet and T sleeps on the floor, his bed full of fleas but he does not mind them. We have 4 windows without glass and the door, so on 3 sides we can have air, which they tell us is charming in summer, but we like it better when we are shut up for the night as well as we may. After being homeless for a few hours very thankfully did I lay myself in my hammock.

Thursday 28th [actually February 26th]. We could not shut our door the first night and about 6 a man came in to find the 'Blessed One'[17] and left the door open. We did not wish to move but when hens came in I had to drive them out, indeed we had to keep constant guard against hens, dogs and cats. We had the room washed after a very slight fashion which did not kill the fleas. We paid visits in the morning with the Egoúmenos and Papa Nikolaos, both very nice men, and in the afternoon stayed in as T had a little fever.

This morning we set forth with 2 men, spades, and high hopes and dug 2 graves close by the sea shore where we landed on the North. A very strong N. wind blowing all the time. We found nothing but bones and 2 little earthen tear-bottles, one broken, and a lamp – all coarse, about 4 feet down. The opening of the tomb was 7 feet down and closed with a stone in the side of the hole that was dug. We came away disgusted. One of the men has brought in a good little black lamp.[18]

The men dress the same as all the other islanders we have seen, but the women look very like Laps. They wear a very rational dress. A shirt which comes a little below the knee, embroidered all round with red and green. Over this a light brown coat is wrapped by a scarlet belt. The shirt has a small square sailor collar of yellow and the open front of the shirt is filled with a piece of coloured embroidery, almost hidden by the great number of necklaces of different colours composed of numerous strings of glass beads, reaching nearly to the waist. On their heads they wear red pointed caps of red cloth with a bit of gold braid straight up the front and down the back. A handkerchief with the point turned up is tied across the front, and the hair, which is plaited rather high in front, is brought low over the ears and behind below the cap. Over all they tie a towel by its 2 front corners and sometimes also by the 2 back ones. Babies are carried in little cradles like the Laps' and hung over their mothers' shoulders.[19]

[Monday] March 2nd. Yesterday we had not a very satisfactory day. T sent and went to the Mudir, Sapré Effendi, and asked permission to dig, but no answer came and he sent 3 *zaptiehs* or policemen after the diggers and we gave up all thoughts of doing anything so sent M to the other village, Mikró Khorió (this being Megálo Khorió, and both the same

---

[17] The resident saint, i.e. Ay. Pandelímona.
[18] The area around the small northern port of Ay. Andónios, facing Níssyros, where the Bents made their landfall.
[19] Mabel acquired a swaddling band from Kárpathos, '150 years old, cotton closely worked with black and red silk on the outer end, and with a small sprigged pattern on the rest'. She displayed it at a meeting of the Anthropological Institute in 1886, and it is now in the Pitt Rivers Museum, Oxford (1888.37.7) with another example they acquired from Évia (1888.37.8). The Bents had no children.

size) to make a symphony[20] about a *kaïke* for Karpathos, and half a dozen women or so for our luggage. They have one donkey but no saddles. I am to have the donkey. We had a visit from the schoolmaster and one from Papa Nikolaos in the evening. The latter told us the real thing was that the Mudir required *bakhsheesh* and if we gave a *medjidie* (4/-) it would be all right and he would go to the *Kanak* and hold out hopes. However last night all the Turks were too tipsy to be spoken to.

This morning it was announced that the Mudir was on his way to visit us so T hastily ordered coffee, and I got out a little plush case with a comb, looking glass, scissors, etc., and when he arrived with 3 *zaptiehs*, T at once plunged into the subject and said he would give him a *bakhsheesh* and handed him 2 *medjidis* and at the same moment I gave my gift, which he joyfully took but told T to lay his money on the table and called a *zaptich* to take it, and this we hear is in order that he may be able to swear he received no money from T.

He then said he was delighted we should dig and he would go to the other village that he might see and hear nothing of it. He asked us if we had an opera glass we could give him, but we told him we had not, and he begged me to go and see his wife and asked T if I could write, for he knew that all the women of the English family knew letters, so this Chronicle was fetched and T said I had written it all and he looked through it and said it was beautiful and everyone wonders I can write so much. A great blow fell upon us when the smoking began and T fetched our old luminous match box with a cracked glass and offered a match and explained its marvels, for Sapré Effendi thanked T heartily and put it in his pocket. We trembled when he took the revolver to examine for fear he might bag that.

We parted excellent friends. Then it poured, which prevented digging today though it did not last long and we had visits from Papa Nikolaos, the Egoúmenos, and the schoolmaster, who lunched with us and he much enjoyed black caviare and lobster. Since luncheon we first went to see the bride who is very discontented, and then wandered about the town paying visits and being consulted about illnesses. There is no doctor here. One woman has erepipelas[21] in the face. Of course there is no use prescribing unobtainable medicines, so we have done what we could and hope it may be successful. M has delightedly gone off to the sick with pills, vaseline, etc. It is so cold we have to shut our windows and only keep the door open.

Tuesday [actually Wednesday] March 4th. On Sunday we walked up to the old fort above the town on a very high mountain overlooking the sea, as well as the plain, and so steep that the town looked as if it were tucked in under our feet, at least it didn't look at all for we could not see it.[22] The Egoúmenos accompanied us and we took paper, etc., to take squeezes of the only 2 inscriptions known to exist but M and T each found another, so we set to work in blazing sun and in a bed of rue, but before we had finished it came on to rain so we had to spread our things to dry in the ruined church which now occupies the site of a temple of which one wall is still in place and T returned in the evening to fetch them. I in the mean time had visits the whole afternoon, wearisome but no doubt good for my Greek. In the night it poured which caused a hasty rush from our very different beds to secure our things from the water dripping through the roof. T's heap of bedding had to be dragged into safety. He has no sheets, but does not seem to mind and has his pillow dressed in a white garment of mine.

---

[20] Agreement, from the Greek verb 'I agree'.
[21] A skin infection.
[22] This is the acropolis above Megálo Horió.

I forgot to say that a very poor old woman wished to know how much she should have to pay for our medicines. We have heard that the patients are doing well. Also I did not mention that women and little girls wear a quantity of silver wire rings in their ears. I counted 14 in one ear, each wire too thick by half for our ears and each ring too large for a bracelet. They sleep in them and, of course, the lobe of the ear is much disfigured. We saw some wedding earrings which not only had lots of beads strung on of glass and filigree, but about half a dozen pairs of good sized cheap earrings of our ordinary kind tied in.

To return to our history, we began to dig with 6 men who, though engaged to begin early, were with difficulty driven to set to work by being told they were not men at all but beasts (ζόα) and taking a leaf out of their own books, we told them it was evening and M said they were now 'half day' men, so they were got to work by 9, or 3 o'clock as they call it in Turkey. These graves were in a very pleasant place, in a field with olive trees and velanidia, a sort of oak with large acorns; the cups 2 or 3 inches across are used in dyeing.

We opened 7 graves. They had to dig 8 or 10 feet and then there was a perpendicular stone mortared on to the mouth of a cave. We found nothing very fine to reward us – some very coarse plates, one containing the bone of a sepia,[23] some little 2-handled cups, a jug very coarse, and 3 immense pithoi, very large jars with pointed bottoms whole, one broken, and the round copper bottom of some vessel.

We were disappointed and decided that this had been a poor place. The big jars, as T said, we should have liked to keep if they had been dug up in the Park,[24] but not only would they have been expensive to bring home, if they had not been captured on the way, but would have caused a great fuss in Karpathos, where we did not mean to speak of excavations for a week. Hardly did the sun set when the owner of the field declared these were fine and excellent things and wished to be paid a great deal for them, so we departed, and theirs and M's screams could be heard several fields off. We had several people to beg us to take these things and pay, but we said we did not care for them and we would only pay for the crops as we agreed. The workmen also have been here for more money but vainly. A penknife has been given to the Egoúmenos this morning and perhaps in consequence all the small things have been brought us. We are in the act of packing for the Mikró Chorió.

[Thursday] March 5th. Now everything is packed for Karpathos, which we hope to reach tomorrow night, sailing this midnight. We had a very funny departure from the Megaló Chorió. Seven women came from the place and carried our luggage. We were reminded of the processions in the Tomb of Ti.[25] I had a very good donkey. Our way led for a good way along the edge of a precipice formed by what seemed to be a subsidence in the middle of the island about ½ or ¼ of a mile wide and sometimes at the bottom of it. This was evidently a volcano as this side of the island is full of pumice.

On reaching this village we were greeted by our host, a Papas who has been to Alexandria and has a bed! and keeps a café. The captain of the *kaïke* we had engaged, Alexis, who at once constituted himself a 2nd servant and shared all M's doings and became a bosom friend of his, and an old Kyrios Katré, a very cunning and talkative old merchant from Simi who, with the nice priest, clung to us continually. We were given the whole of a house about 12 feet by 9 with the bed in it. It was very tidy and clean looking. The floor had been sponged and a white quilt was got out to make a top sheet for T, as Greeks never have but

---

[23] Cuttlefish: *soupiá*.
[24] Presumably London's Hyde Park. The Bents lived within sight of Marble Arch.
[25] The 5th-Dynasty Tomb of Ti at Sakkarah, near Memphis in Egypt.

The ruined village of Mikró Horió, Tílos. In the Bents' time a thriving community.

one. And a great search was made for a basin, but the only one was broken, so a salad bowl was borrowed and in fact they did all they could for us.

After a walk and some visits and our dinner, eaten very publicly, a band came, consisting of a drum, a bagpipe composed of a whole pigskin, and a *lyra*, a sort of mandolin, with a quantity of little bells hung along the bow – a very pretty instrument to see and hear.[26] As there were ten people in the room, we sat as if we were in the train. Yesterday we went down to the sea, ¾ of an hour's walk, very rough, and dug but vainly. One of the workmen was the priest's brother-in-law. What people would say if they knew one of my sisters is a Papadhiá I know not. All the clergy are quite common people. We passed a ragged old man on the way, I don't say *road*, building a wall, and only by his brown goatskin cap, which represents black, could one know he was a clergyman. The superior of the monastery is a shoemaker and Papa Nikólaos ploughs.

This house is haunted by 4 cats which play about all night to my terror and bump against my hammock. We can't keep them out because they have a way in that we can't stop up. We are offered a barn near the sea but it is full of rats, they say, so we shall go on board at once. The ship has a hole or hold, but we shall lie on deck I think. We are taking about 20 bottles of wine with us as it is good. The people of these villages are very jealous of each other and tell lies of each other and do not intermarry.

Before was came here we were told that all the inhabitants were lepers. Then someone else said 'in only two villages'. Each village says they are all in the other but they live among their families so we really do not know. They speak of them as 'broken people'. Before we left Megálo Chorió our erepipelas patient was so well that she tried to send us a *medjidie*, but we of course refused and are very proud of our success. All the women here are terrified at

---

[26] See page 17.

the idea of being photographed and my camera is rather a 'white elephant'. They are also afraid of T's sketching them and all run away.[27] There is one in particular, Kyriakí (Sunday) by name, one of those who carry our baggage, about 50 and very handsome, in the wildest darkest gypsy style, and when T takes his book out she skips away like a goat.

A dreadfully ragged old priest, the owner of *the* donkey and the one who was building a wall, stood for his portrait in our little house among a jammed crowd, all very much delighted when T said 'Here are his eyes, his nose; he has no mouth on account of his beard'. I espied his house key hanging at his girdle, very like the key we bought from the monks of Paleokastrizza in Corfu – their cellar key – so we offered a knife for it, it was joyously accepted, and in order to express that I was to ride his donkey he made his 1st and 2nd fingers of his right hand ride on his left hand.

Then our host, having been given a knife, gave me half an enormous embroidered curtain. I at once took from my pocket a brooch for his wife, whereupon he flew to a trunk and gave me a little bottle with a few treasured drops of lavender water. He is going to Alexandria, so we may again see Papa Andreas Diakónoudemetríou.

Now I will recount our voyage to Karpathos. We got down to the sea about 2 p.m., as that seemed to be about the time that suited everyone, and the women were sent flying up the mountain by T, who popped out round rocks at them with his sketch book. When it became dark we took refuge in a *magazi* or shed containing anchors, planks, ropes, etc., and M cooked our dinner, which we ate off a bench sitting on a pole. The ship's company consisted of Alexis, his wife, and we suppose 2 sailors, and a young man and a little boy, who were taking the opportunity of the passage.

We had to wait for the moon at midnight, and about 7 T and I clambered down the very steep rocks and were laid by Captain Alexis side by side on the ballast with a carpet over it and our heads on the tent sack. He then proceeded to close the hold, about 2 feet deep, completely up, so we begged for mercy and only had a sail spread over us. I found the shingles awfully hard but T, after a fortnight or more on the floor, was able to sleep and it was with the greatest difficulty I shook him up, telling him he must go ashore for the men as the moon had been up an hour, so he went and found M very anxious to get them off but unable.

We were soon on our way. M crawled into the extreme bow of the hold where he got very wet, for the N. wind freshened and the waves were dashing over us from behind. It became so bad that before we got to Saría, an island N. of Karpathos, it was decided to give up trying to get to Pegádhi, our destination, far down on the E. coast, but to go into Tristoma, a bay on the N.W. We landed there after 9 hours and did not very much mind as we thought we could travel through the island a different way. You will hardly believe we started before the next daybreak without seeing one Karpathiote!

Tristoma [Kárpathos] has its name because 2 islands at its entrance give it Three Mouths.[28] It is a most desolate looking place, there is a little half-ruined chapel, almost in the sea, and there we built our beds, and very damp we, and all our goods, became. A boat from Kasso was there and the men said it was 4 or 5 hours to Elymbo and the road, or what answers to one, washed away so we settled at dawn to set off again to Pegádhi. All around were nothing but steep bare rocks so we 2 chose the softest to sleep on in the afternoon and all the Greeks slept in a heap. The day was enormously long and every one unsettled

---

[27] The first reference in the *Chronicles* to Mabel's role as expedition photographer and to Theodore's skills as sketcher and watercolourist.
[28] The party has landed at the remote northern inlet of Trístomo on the island of Kárpathos.

Trístomo Bay, where the Bents first landed on Kárpathos.

and anxious, and we heard from the men of Kasso a terrible tale of a boat kept 15 days in that bay by a W. wind and next day we wished to go W., N., E., and then S., there were many fears. We lay down in our clothes and at dawn my friend T was in a very obstinate state of comfort, warmth, sleepiness, etc., but I respectfully reminded him that I had obtained leave over night to rouse him up, and that all the others were up, no doubt unwilling to wake us, which proved to be the case.

We got out by the N. entrance, having entered by the S., got through the straits very well, and though there was not much wind, were progressing favourably when a whirling gust came down a gully in the mountains and then another and overboard went the foresail, mast and all. All hands dragged the sail in and the sailors began hacking and hewing with axe and saw, while the male passengers flew to the oars, and the sea so calm all the time. How thankful we felt that we had safely got into Tristoma bay only just in time, for only one more gust such as we had that morning might have done for us. The sail would have filled before anyone could do anything, and the big hole in the deck would have let the hold fill.

After this Pegádhi was out of the question in that boat, so we made for Dhiapháne, where we landed and made acquaintance with some of the inhabitants of Elymbo and promised to go there for Easter. This is their landing place. We breakfasted in the open air and then got into a narrow, very deep boat with so much water in it that it had to have a hearty bailing for 5 or 10 minutes occasionally with a big basin. We had 4 men to row each on a different bench, and we 3 sat leaning against each other in the stern.

It took 7½ hours to get to Pegádhi, coasting closely and landing twice for water, once at Kyria Panagía, a very pretty little bay with a little white church of 'Mrs. All-holy' – the Virgin. All the whole time the men never ceased with every stroke to shout all sorts of verses and sayings. In spite of all the noise no one came out at our approach to help our landing, and we had to call for a lantern and got the boat on a rock. However we landed safely and that moment were asked for our *teskerreks* by a *zaptick*, or policeman. We then went into their café and enquired after various people for whom we had letters, Mr. Manolakakis, the Kaïmakam Mr. Koumpis. The Kaïmakam was the only one down at Pegádhi, and the minute the Turks heard we had a letter for him they demanded it imperiously. T said it was in the boat still but they simply clamoured for it, even a boy of 16 came to me when T was gone out and said 'Give me the Kaïmakam letter at once'. When it came it was taken to the Kaïmakam who was in the upper room of this filthy hole of a café with his Turkish secretary, a very smart young man and his Greek Dragoman, Mr. Frangisko Sakolarides.

T was put on a sofa a yard high near the Kaïmakam, and there I found him and we were given coffee and nothing civil was left unsaid. Mr. Sakolarides always translating from the Turkish into Greek, though both Turks can talk Greek. We heard T mentioned as Frank Effendi, and Lord Bent. They said they would give up the room to us and kindly departed. The room was clean looking and to get at it we passed through a small kitchen where M prepared our supper.

The woman of the house made T up a bed on the high seat, and while doing so quite calmly dropped her 6-months'-old babe into my arms. As he was good, pretty and clean I did not mind, and it seemed quite natural that I should keep him next morning, after he had been dressed only in 2 cotton shirts, quite clean, while his little brother was dressed and the room cleaned. When T went to shut the door of the kitchen, where M was to lie on the floor, behold there was no door to shut but as there was no use saying anything, nothing was said, but I with my hammock quietly removed into the most secluded corner.

We were a good long time dressing as we wished to rearrange our luggage a little and leave some things down there, but about 7.30 the family was at the top of the outside stairs waiting admission, and the Turks all patiently on the beach. They all came up the moment we opened the kitchen door and we packed under great difficulties as they played with our things and unpacked some. The air pillows are a joy to all and my bed, sponge bags, etc. They said the Government steamer would be going to Rhodes and would take letters, so we all began to write, we at the table and the Turks sitting cross-legged and with the papers and a pair of scissors by them with which they cut it down after it was written.

They begged us to wait ¼ of an hour to send M and the baggage by land to Apéri, the capital, and send my mule to meet us at Vrondí across the bay, and they would take us in their boat; so we waited an hour and a half but were saved an hour of rocks by it. My mule duly met me at Vrondí, or Brontë, or 'Thunder', and a very steep ascent of about an hour chiefly up the bed of the river Chaos that led up to Apéri. We all went to the café and sat in the balcony and then went to Mr. Frangisko Sakolarides' house where we found M in possession. We had many visitors including the Turks in the evening in long cotton nightgowns and grey plaid flannel dressing-jackets.

We stayed at that house 2 nights and were greatly bothered by starers and were the objects of great wonder and so we sought for a more private lodging as we wished to remain some time. We could get nothing in Apéri but eventually found a house in the village of Volátha, so close that even I could make the journey on foot. A flock of women, including Mrs. Sophrosíne Manolakakis, the daughter of a very nice man, came and shouldered our baggage; and the way leads up a torrent, hopping from stone to stone, sometimes you walk

Forks from Mabel Bent's own travelling canteen, engraved with her initials.

through a little water. The village is very high up and has most extensive views over sea and land. It is a very pretty island and the mountains we see from here are chiefly greenish and the huge arums in big bunches are quite lovely. No one can think why we have bouquets of them in the house.

All the houses are the same here. One large room divided lengthwise, the side nearest the door has a fixed sofa near the door, very high, a panelling behind it, and a cupboard in it with a small carved door. The back half is raised, the larger part about 4 ft, and the smaller, and further from the door, is raised about 6 feet. All the wall of this is panelling and has doors by which they reach the storerooms and cellars situated inside the sleeping part. There is a railing all along and rafters and bars overhead with towels and sheets and quilts hung upon them. All the pillows and mattresses are piled in a heap and chests and trunks all round containing their clothes. Round the whole house run 2 or 3 shelves full of plates, jugs, bottles, bowls, etc. Our house is like this. Our lower floor is earth but we are pretty quiet and the people are nice and kind. We have plenty of room for our things.

The upper parts are called upper and lower 'sopha' (*áno* and *káto*) and no one goes up there with shoes. We have many visitors and women coming to sell embroideries, also for medical advice. Every time we go out we have to go through the river and some causeway might so easily be made. There is at least a ¼ of a mile of it.

Saturday [March 7th]. On Thursday we went to the village of Spiliés (caves) passing through Othíos. I rode one and a half hours. It was very hot. At Spiliés we asked them to bring things to sell and they did bring plenty, but asked such prices that we bought little. Ten pounds here or there seemed nothing to them and as we shall pass that village again we hope they will have come to their senses. We went into many houses and a woman called Chrysánthe (goldflower) took us under her special care. T sketched a horrid old witch called Marigó and everyone recognises it as a good likeness. We crossed this narrow island at its widest part. It is not so pretty there, more bare.

When we returned we found that a dire disaster had befallen me but which delights T. A cat had got in at the unglazed window, eaten about 6/- worth of Brand's Beef tea and then not feeling very well had taken to *my* bed, and the results were such as to cause shouts of woe from me which brought T, M, and the neighbours. Fortunately my down quilts were sewn up in sheets and everyone set to work to wash, except me. I remained in retirement. Now, however, they have been washed and are not even stained, but I have been reduced to the floor these 2 nights.

Yesterday was really a day to be marked with a white stone. We had a delightful picnic to Kyriá Panagía. The company were 3 Turks, one of whom could speak no Greek, 2 English,

4 Greeks, 3 of whom could speak Turkish. There was also an Albanian cook who could speak no language but his own and that no one understood, and 2 soldiers. We arrived first. I riding 2 hours on a bone-shaking road. The latter part was through pine woods smelling sweetly and with big single white peonies and arums.

M at once set to work to cook a chicken, or rather aged cock, and was ready with brandy to offer the Turks on their arrival, and at one o'clock we all were seated round a waterproof rug of ours with 2 glasses, few plates, and a moderate amount of forks and spoons. We talked English together. The Turks talked Turkish together, but of course Greek was the general tongue. We all of course ate too much after the manner of folks at picnics; all sorts of unexpected things turned up: eggs after we had been eating boiled sheep's cream with sugar and then bowls of rice jelly and cinnamon. So happy were we and so much did we seem to enjoy overeating ourselves, that it was then and there determined to send the soldiers off for a lamb to be eaten *à la Palikári* for dinner.[29]

We 2, the 2 Sakolarides and a certain Manolakakis,[30] in whose house the Kaïmakam lodges, went on a long hot rocky walk, and I think I got a little sunstroke, for I had a great pain in the back of my head which is gone today very nearly. We at length found ourselves at the source of a stream springing out of a bed of maidenhair under great big myrtle trees. It was such an enchanting spot. At 4 o'clock we sat cross-legged round a heap of mastic bushes and rosemary, and on this bed was laid the lamb who had been borne on a spit through his head and his hind feet tied to it.

We then tore him limb from limb by hand and all gnawed. I never saw a funnier scene or a merrier meal. After the lamb's bones were cleaned by the 8 sets of teeth, the Kaïmakam examined the shoulder blades and prophesied peace and quietness, then more sheep's cream and then home. We went half way together and the Kaïmakam and Co. went to Apéri, and we and Mr. Frangisko Sakolarides to Volátha. Having been taking lessons from Hassam Tachrí Effendi, the secretary, I was able to say 'Teshekür edérim', 'Thank you', to the Kaïmakam. We were led to the café by Mr. Frangisko Sakolarides and given coffee and were very glad to get home safely with only starlight to help us, and I had to walk some way.

In the little church at Kyria Panagía, which is quite good and not ruined, there were lots of scribbled names and one of the Greeks said, 'Now we will write up your name' and I said 'Oh, not my name please', they said 'Why?' and I said it was not our custom in England to write our name in churches. So he went out and the Kaïmakam, who had put on an awestruck face, said to me very quickly 'Because it is a sin?' So I said 'Yes, for it is the house of God'. And he said, 'Yes' and I really felt glad he should see that some Christians have a little reverence. The very irreverent jokes the Greeks make and their heathenishness mixed up in their religion must give them a bad idea of Christianity.

Today we are very busy preparing for a luncheon party tomorrow of 7, but are rather in a fix as the people of the house wish us to have our feast under a tree, or at Mr. Manolakakis', who is one of the guests, because their brother died 6 months ago and the neighbours will think little of them if they permit a party in the house. M and I are going to cook, but we have great difficulties; to begin at the very foundation, we must borrow a tablecloth, for we dine off oil cloth off the floor, and food is not easy to get in large quantities. The Kaïmakam

---

[29] Traditionally a slow-cooked dish of lamb, oregano, onions, garlic, tomatoes, cheese and potatoes, similar to *kokinistó*.

[30] Emmanuel Manolakákis published *Karpathiaká* (1896), a monograph on the history and culture of the island.

gave T his beads for playing with, string on leather. T bought 14 good Rhodian plates and 4 broken ones from Manolakakis' mother, but we never got them.

Sunday evening [March 8th]. Our party was over very successfully by half past 2, and surely it was the very funniest feast at which I was ever hostess. A 7 o'clock I went in my crimson dressing gown to the neighbouring mud-floored hut where M sleeps, and which is our very smoky little kitchen – to cook a pudding. Mr. Manolakakis was already there, but we are used enough to the ways of the place not to mind that. So I set about my business. After that he stayed about an hour and we got very hungry and discovered that M thought we would not eat till the midday meal. We became very anxious about a kid which did not arrive till 10.

The people of the house then made a great row, wept, and screamed about our 'making a table' but fortunately our friend said he should be there, and if we wished to sing and dance we should come to his house. In vain we assured them we only wished to eat 7 together instead of 2 and Mr. Manolakakis had dined with us 2 nights ago. However they set about to tidy up the house, and to our amusements the sheets T has slept in nearly a week were spread over the 2 sofas. A tablecloth of calico, very small, was borrowed and knives, etc., from Mr. Frangisko Sakolarides. We put a great many Majolica jugs, of which there are 19 in this room, and a lovely nosegay on the table, and that was all we could do. They say Mrs. Virginía has a mania for flowers and that *stock* is the only one they care for.

Before we were quite ready in came a man, who, when he was asked where he came from, said 'from Apéri, you have been in my house'. T asked which house, as we have been in so many. 'The house with the bed', but we do not know his name and only remember that he keeps a shop. We only imagined him to be a casual visitor, but he remained uninvited for luncheon. The Kaïmakam brought the secretary, who can only speak Turkish, and who we also did not expect, so we were tightly crowded round our small table. The Kaïmakam and I sat on the sofa. The flowers were flanked with wine for Christians and brandy for Turks.

M is considered a first rate cook according to Greek notions. First we had a huge quantity of broth with rice. Our unknown Greek guest was fasting, so it was lucky that we next had lobster salad. Then chicken in some sauce and then lamb in another sauce. Then cheese, then each person got a soup plate *brimful* of solid milk with cinnamon strewed over, then my pudding and then the sheep's cream. Four times we all arose and clicked glasses, and as no one drank ever without drinking everyone's health, we were always saying 'Evcharistó', 'Thank you'. Everyone smoked any time he wished during the meal and we were quite as merry and talkative a party as if we had all been English. N.B. Mrs. Virghinía is the exception as far as talking goes. A tin plate with our alphabet round it and 'who killed Cock Robin?' was a delightful topic of conversation, and after coffee some views of London given to the Kaïmakam with a luminous match box, a plan of London shown, my down quilts to pinch, air pillow to blow up, and my bed to be lain in by several, and picked to pieces, were the entertainments we offered to our company.

Last night a lot of old women spent the evening with us and T drew them. One was quite terrified and all were angry at his doing it and tried to tear up his book. A little child of four whose name is Verghinía says she has the same name as the Frank lady, so she begs her mother to plait her quite short hair on the top of her head like mine.

We think of starting for Arkássa tomorrow and are already provided with a host who hopes we will remain a year if we wish. What pans and jars M will borrow to carry off the 'remains', for he could not bear to leave them behind and indeed it would be useless as everyone is fasting. We have constant patients coming to us and I am sure you would all laugh to hear T's medical lectures – we do afterwards, but at the time we are quite too busy trying to understand and advise. A child born with a twisted foot was brought to me yesterday.

I forgot to say that 2 *zaptiehs* fed in the kitchen and the Kaïmakam is anxious we should have one with us but we don't want one. We should have to give him a present besides paying for a mule and feeding him.

Monday was quite too rainy and windy for us to start when we had a good roof over our heads, and we suffered very much from the cold. We shut our shutters to keep out the hurricane and had a brazier of charcoal, but the door had always to be open for light. We ached with cold, so changeable is this climate, and the damp of all our things is wonderful. We cannot imagine why we do not take cold; all our day clothes feel cold and damp in the morning and at night we are very glad of the flannel gowns we had made on purpose, but which decidedly would want airing before we put them on in England.

Tuesday March 17th. After a rainy night we set off at 8 for Arkássa. At the last moment one mule failed us, but it did not matter. Eventually all the baggage we took with us, my bed, a small portmanteau, and a bundle of cloaks, besides food were piled on all over the mule, so high that it was like a camel. I had to climb a chair and then a wall as high again to mount and sit cross-legged on the pile. We passed Othos without stopping and at Spiliés we stopped to lunch at Chrysánthe's house, and there made some bargains over embroideries.

Arkássa is on the sea 2 hours from Spiliés and the road became much easier as we got nearer the sea. I was dreadfully cold, the wind was so high. About ½ an hour before Arkássa we came to Pheníki, a little bay with very few houses. Having a letter for Kyrios Constantinos Malagarda, who keeps a combination of a café and tinker's and jeweller's shop, we turned out of our way to visit him. He gave us coffee and jam and implored us many times to remain the night, but as his bedrooms were very uninviting-looking balconies, approached by ladders, we, with hopes of better things, said Kyrios.

Polychrónia (many years) was awaiting us. We were lucky enough to get possession of a set of silver and gilt ornaments formerly worn by the Karpathiote women – 3 long chains, 2 frontlets and 2 earrings. Before he left he took us into his garden, and such a garden! It was apparently a barley field in the first instance and all through it, like weeds, were various vegetables, each plant separately had to be hunted for. The only flower a bush of stock. He gave us lettuce, cardamoms, celery, tomatoes, and other things were a great joy to M as we had salads for 3 days.

Arkássa is quite a new place, about 10 years old but rapidly increasing as the masons were busy. It is built on both sides of a steep cleft containing a river and on the neck of a promontory. Mr. Manyyears's house was horrid; the floor damp, sticky and very smelly. It was a general shop with wares of the poorest kind. The 'sofa' had no railing. No window and altogether it was a nasty place but a little redeemed by a good fireplace, the first we have seen and we had a really good fire in it.

I was excessively glad of my own bed. T of course had that combination of 'Bed & Board' which is usual. Next morning we walked about and saw the remains of temples, that is a good many pillars which they are hacking up for building, but we did not think it a good place for excavation.

Next morning, [Wednesday] 18th March, we gladly left our cow-house and started for Menités across the mountains on the other side of the island. This part is not so pretty, it is much barer than the E. side. It was 2 hours' 'road' and Menités can be seen from a distance. It is very prettily situated; the church stands on a high and precipitous rock, jutting into the valley or plain, sloping to the sea, and the town runs up the hill behind it. Here a real mud

Plates and saucers acquired by the Bents from the Turkish coast and Rhodes.

floor seemed quite a luxury to us. There was no window and immediately about 30 people were in the room to stare, which they unremittingly did all day long.

How superior is our treatment of the wild beasts in the zoological gardens! Each one has a bedroom that he can go into when he is tired of being stared at. Yesterday morning as I wished to button on my long gaiters, I retired to the end of the room and sat down with my back turned to the multitude, but as there was a little room between me and the wall, that soon became crowded. Once M said, 'What do you want here?' and a woman said 'Only it amuses my baby to see the man write and the woman sew'.

They brought some embroideries but asked enormous prices. Every man, woman and child seems to wear on their persons all the foreign money they can find and think it very old and tell us it had been found in tombs, an English penny for instance, and such an exalted idea have they of inscriptions that they prize a new coin more highly and think it older because it has *grammatá* on it. The English idea of 'second-hand' being cheaper has no equivalent in Greek. The older, raggeder, and dirtier a thing is the dearer. T took some pretty sketches in the afternoon.

Yesterday, Friday [actually Thursday, March] 19th, we returned to our home at Volathá, which seemed really quite comfortable and grand and clean, which last it really is, though very damp. We passed through Othos, where we lunched amid a crowd in the little windowless hut which serves as a café. A 3 hours' journey over the mountain, very windy and very steep

on the W. side, and more sheltered and an easier road on the E., in and out of the folds of the mountains; each spur much greener on the E. side than the W. At Othos we picked up for 1f. a little Rhodian saucer and some embroidery. Mr.
Manolakakis was here from 7 to 9 this morning.

We start next week for Elymbo and there we hope to get diggers to come to the uninhabited island of Saría with us. We shall use the tent but we hope to find a chapel or some ruin perhaps. M is to make the bread. It is better than the plan of making biscuits of 3 weeks' bread and soaking it in water. Our plan is to get our superfluities and purchases down to Pegádhia and leave them there, to send M for them and 'lie' at Diaphane waiting for them and to go in a sailing boat to Syra.

I have been quite interrupted in everything, and T was packing and arranging our goods when in came a crowd and now he is having Greek poetry read loudly to him and I am trying to write letters and have someone sitting tightly beside me, leaning upon and over me to see my writing. When I was at Menités we were anxious to know about a charm for fever and were just asking about it when M suddenly said the Kyria had caught cold and was suffering, so they said they would fetch a woman. Some time after M said 'Won't you have your cloak, Kyria?' Of course I accepted it and rolled myself up and made an invalid of myself. When the old woman came, she demanded my wrist and took a thread which she began to tie round it. She said 'Where do you come from?' Of course I began to say 'from England' but I was directed to say 'From the Holy Mountain (Athos). A black dog has come near me. Leave me that you may bind that'. I had to repeat this answer 3 times and when I had done so she finished tying the knot, saying I should be better in the morning. As we wanted to see another woman do it, I gave my left wrist and had to say I had come from Saloniki, but otherwise one charm was the same as the other.

On the Saturday after our return we 3 walked down to Apéri, meaning to pack the plates we had bought and which the woman very civilly said we might leave in her house till we were ready for them, but when we asked for them she would not let us have them without our paying much more, so we told her she was a liar, which is commonly done, and does not seem to enrage the person thus insulted the least. We hoped after all to have got them but we did not. [A later footnote, October 1885: We have them now, M having been back to Karpathos in the summer.]

We then went and had coffee with the Turks and to see Mr. Koumpis, who walked home with us. On Sunday, as I said before, Mr. Manolakakis stayed from 7 to 10 while we wrote letters, and was seeing us off to walk to Othos where we meant to lunch, but perceiving M come out with a basket and an earthen dish containing some lamb, he suddenly decided to come too, which bored us rather, and of course the luncheon for 3 had to be stretched for 4. We went to see an old man in bed, said to be a prophet. He had to tell our fortunes out of a book and what struck the crowd most was that T was nice out but unpleasant in the house, and I was disagreeable and stingy to my relations, and an old man afterwards, when I said I liked to travel, said 'yes it is better that you travel as you are not liked at home'.

On Monday [March] 23rd we went down to Pigádia, 3½ hours. It rained a great deal but at last we determined to be off and after 2 thirds of the way it was fine. We sewed up a sack of old dresses, etc., packed a box of pottery, and left these with a bag in the customhouse and carried up the tent and T's bed. I rode and the others walked. At 8 next day, 24th, we had many affectionate farewells and set off with 3 mules, one pack mule and 2 with plenty on them besides T and me. M walked all but about 1½ hour when he had the mule. We went through Othos and Spiliés to the W. coast and then after a little visit to Chrysánthe while M replenished our jar with the good wine of Spiliés. We turned north to Méso Chório, which we did not reach till 5.15, all very tired.

Several times we had to get down and walk half a mile or so as the way was too steep or inclined to slip from rain and once we had a great deal of trouble in getting up a rock much higher than ourselves. We had to dismount and partially unload the mules and we kicked a good deal. Much screaming took place. M told the old muleteer that his mule had no legs (ανάποδος), addressed him angrily as brother, asked him what sort of a man he was and answered himself that he was not a man at all but a beast, and at last we all arrived at the top, beasts and people. There a boy and an old man called Giorgios Barbalagónikou. He told us his surname came from his father, being very good at running after hares (*lagós*). He was called consequently Lagóniko, prefixed with Barba, or Uncle, as he evidently was an old man. Besides there was a woman who had the combined object of dragging T's mule and offering at a church here a candle for the recovery of her son a year ago.

Before noon we found ourselves lost high up on the mountainside when we ought to have been near the sea. So we had to scramble down on foot as best we might, down beds of loose sharp stones over rocks and through thorns and suffered somewhat as I had not my gaiters on. We could see the path beneath us on soft ground. It is easy enough to lose the way on stony ground, for the road is only made by the steps of men and mules. If there is earth among the stones one can trace the track by the splashing of mud on the rocks in rainy weather. When the road gets worn away, or washed away, they step aside and make a new road, even through someone's field with the corn springing up, and indeed sometimes they do this without rhyme or reason, for no one minds walking through quite tall corn.

After we had gone over a quantity of tremendous boulders, we turned up the course of a dry river and despairing of finding water we spent a very merry half hour over our luncheon, consisting of oat bread, sardines, caviare and wine out of scooped out lemon, a delicious cup which we have used before. We passed through a great deal of scraggy pine wood, very difficult to stoop and squeeze through. The sun was very burning and I broke my parasol when it was shut, and I felt it dreadfully and got a headache though I had a white thing on my head. I had the anxious charge of the brandy bottle, which M meant to carry in his hand. I had also our larder on my mule, a hare and a half, a very welcome change from boiled lamb and kids.

We went in and out of folds of the mountains, up and down and across a water-course, then up again, and were glad indeed when we sighted Méso Chório (Middle Village) seated on a jutting rock over a plain, looking as healthy as possible but exposed to fevers. We were first taken to a house of the usual shape, but gaily and wildly frescoed within, and there, to our surprise, were greeted by Hassan Effendi, arrived from Apéri half an hour ago, having left at 11 and come a shorter way over Lastos.

After sitting with him for some time we were led to our home, the schoolmasters' house. It is a poor place but has an outer staircase and that makes us feel more private than if we were on the ground. We have 5 windows so that we can close the door, and indeed have to lock it today as there is no other means of keeping it shut and there is a violent S. wind blowing at it. The bedroom, or boarded part, has no rail and is 2 or 3 inches higher than the table, so it is a good climb as there are no steps.

The bed was laid, very clean, at once, and marvellous to say we were left to ourselves so that T was able to nurse me in peace. I took to the floor immediately and could eat no dinner but arrowroot and became so comfortable, for the pillows were not straw but soft, that I would have stayed there but at 11 o'clock, long after we had gone to bed, bugs were discovered so my own bed was built and I retired to it.

There have been violent showers very often and wind all day, so we only took walks and had a long visit from the schoolmaster, a very pleasant man, and from some old women with things to sell who called us 'my boy' and 'my girl', and in the afternoon from Hussan Effendi, who found me putting the rib of my parasol together with a pencil bandaged on with rag. This is the second I have done and T is darning his umbrella. One of the shutters in this room has quite 2 inches of light round it on 2 sides. A large stone on the window ledge in churches and houses is the recognized fastening.

Friday [March 27th]. We had tremendous wind and rain all Wednesday night, which, however, very suddenly ceased and yesterday, though there were a few showers, was fine. We get up about 6 always and from the moment we were ready people came with their old embroideries to sell; some had washed them and brought them wet. We bought some things and after a good deal of exclaiming that it was now 'evening' and 'night', and 'we were losing all the day', we set off for Levkós (white), a plain near the sea 2 hours off. There are traces of an ancient city whose name is unknown and there is a little rocky island very near the land which has remains of a Byzantine fort; it is called Sókastro.

We had seen the plain below us on our way here. Though I call it a plain it is very rocky and all the fields are terraced up. My mule was led by its owner the parson, Papa Manólis. He had blue cotton bags and his long priest's robe was also blue cotton, patched and faded, but he had a very good hat. T sketched him while we ate our luncheon under the shade of a boat by the sea. It was very hot. We went in a boat to the island and had a very steep, hard, stony climb up and were not in any way rewarded by the ruins. It became quite cloudy on our way back and we saw a water-spout sailing along the sea and then run up into the mountains. We saw one in Telos too and had great rain afterwards. In the evening the schoolmaster, our host, and his father-in-law came and sat and talked.

This morning the house is dripping all over and we have spread all our waterproof rugs, etc., out to the best advantage; a rushing torrent is roaring down the street, a spout pouring off each house and T is at the door sketching with a waterproof hat on his head. I am receiving the sellers and every minute a new drip causes me to rise and move something. I have just been saving the boots. It is getting finer so we hope to be able to get to the village of Spoa where we hope to obtain provisions. This is a very poor place. We can get no milk, eggs, or bread and our kid and other things that we brought here are vanishing, also our wine and the wine here is bad.

Well! We have got back to Méso Chório safely, but not without adventure, and had a very pleasant day.

The plan in this island is to *drag* the mule until the muleteer is tired of it and then to tie up the chain which hangs under the mule's chin and drive him. Today, the minute my mule was released he rushed up a wall about a foot and a half into a field and set off at a gallop and I soon began to feel very loose, so seeing a drop of an unknown depth before me I thought it best to let myself go then as I could not stop the mule, so off I fell easily enough as I had no kind of stirrup. I fell on no stones but on a soft wet bed of vetch and was neither hurt nor dirtied. Away went the mule kicking off all our waterproofs and baggage, very properly so called, and away went the Papas, casting his stick and umbrella behind him, and were some time before they reappeared. We gathered our goods and found that the mule had gone off with the bag containing the bottle of wine, but fortunately, after a bit, I stumbled on it among the vetch.

Spoa is on the other side of the backbone of the island, and as the church is the only thing that is whitewashed it does not show at all at a distance. It has only 40 houses all clustered together. As we entered we asked the villagers to bring things to sell and a crier was sent round to summon folks to bring things to the house of Mr. Pachys (fat), for whom we had a letter of introduction. We lunched in his windowless cottage, which was at the same time a shop, and bought quite a large bundle of things.

One was a gown, whole, the embroidery not very deep but the silk ground good. Of course we only bought it because it was whole, but at the last moment the woman came and said she wished to cut off the plain silk. We refused, she screamed, and so did a number of her friends who followed us to the place where the mule was waiting and they tried to snatch the dress while dire insults were bandied. The mule was finally loaded, for we had bought raisins, sugar, a little tiny kid and 20 herrings, which we had joyfully discovered, and as I was caught by the legs just as the saddle was going over backwards, we reached home safely in time to avoid a shower.

We had a great medical consultation at Spoa, and since we came back a man came with weak knees, and then one to have an advertisement in French of Macassar oil explained.

Elymbo. Palm Sunday. March 29. Yesterday at 8.30 we set off to continue our northward journey. Before starting, at the last minute things were brought to sell and some chamomile brought to know if that was what we had recommended for a poultice. Next, one muleteer, to whom we had agreed to pay what he asked, refused to go without more money so we had to get another mule which M drove or led with baggage. The mules were not very cleverly loaded, which caused us some trouble by the way, but the little excitement helped to pass away the 8 long hours. Everyone told us we could never pass these mountains as the roads are so very difficult, but the wind was too high for a boat and, besides, we should have had to get our baggage down to the sea and up again here from Dheaphani.

We went so completely along the backbone of the island that had our eyes only been like those of birds, we could have seen both seas at once; as it is we had to turn our heads. Once, on the very ridge, the sumpter mule took to kicking and dancing and the string of the tent-sack becoming untied, out flew all around various sardine tins, etc. M rushed about trying to catch the mule. My muleteer helping, with his *skouphiá*, or red cap, blown off and his long hair blown over his eyes. T holding my mule which wished to get into shelter and my few clothes spread out like Prophet Elias, after whom, as usual, the highest mountain is named.

Another time at a very narrow place this mule was in front alone, then came I, and T was very angry with my man for not going in front to see if the path was broken away, for there were so many landslips from the rain, but he said 'Oh, the woman understands it all' and it was impossible to pass. But at last the first mule stopped, no one could see why and my mule overlapped him, then the first *tried* to kick but hadn't room, to my alarm, so T commanded my man to go on and he scrambled round and led the first mule over rather a bad place. T walked more than half the way and I had to walk a good deal. Once we had to build a bridge, or rather viaduct, with stones on a gully of sloping crumbly schist.

We lunched in a lovely spot among trees, in an inner angle of the road. We sat on a large flat stone with water all around it and arbutus bushes and maidenhair, and fir trees. T took a sketch. The wind was tremendous and I am sure I should have been blown off once if T had not held me, but we were so high that the sea did not look rough and we could see the rocks at the bottom for about a mile. Oh! It was a long, long way! and as for the road, there was no *trace* of any for a mile or 2 sometimes, and at other places we had to make one for ourselves as the ordinary one was washed away. We were very glad when a little cairn made us truly guess that Elymbo must be in sight from there. Soon after passing this cairn, which

Kárpathos interior.

holds up a board with a cross in it, I had to dismount again and we had to help ourselves along with our hands, so you may fancy what a road it was.

We entered Elymbo, or Olymbo, amid startled exclamations of 'What people are these?' We went first to the house of the man for whom we had a letter. His house was locked and he was out and we have not seen him. We unloaded at his door, and soon his wife and a dirty priest asked us up. The house was so abominably dirty that T asked the way to the *kafeneion* and demanded the schoolmaster. He came forward and asked him if he could find us a comfortable house for a fortnight, as the only one we could get was too much exposed to the wind, so he very kindly placed his own at T's disposal and M was sent for me and the luggage.

I had not been very happy all this time as the people were not pleased at our deserting them. They asked me if there were Christians in my place and I said 'Naí, málista!',[31] we all were, but I do not think they understood where my place was. They hardly said goodbye

---

[31] 'Certainly'.

to me and I was glad to follow the baggage to the new abode. We have a plain room, 14 ft square with a hard sofa and many rush-bottom chairs and a little very low round table, so that we keep our plates on our knees. This room is too new to be dirty, but the boarded floor streams with damp. It has a large window, one on each side of the door with glass *tacked* in.

M has the neighbouring Karpathian house where he cooks. My bed was set in one of the far corners, T's at right angles as a breakwater to keep off the crowd from rubbing on it. It is a pride and pleasure, if a trouble to M to set up these wondrous beds before a gaping multitude. We had several visitors and were glad to get to bed as all were tired, though fortunately the day had been cloudy.

We dressed in the dark, as if we had opened the shutters we should have a crowd; very soon we had a visit from Mr. F. Sakolarides, and a soldier, who is here on government business. It was Palm Sunday. We walked about; all the houses, including ours, are sunk in the rock behind. The church is the nicest we have seen as it is roughly covered with frescoed pictures; inside the walls are smooth. To reach it one goes through a room, which, though it has 4 sides, is nearly triangular in shape. Here in the afternoon we stumbled upon a parliament being presided over by Mr. F. Sakolarides. He was seated in the extreme corner on the only chair placed on a stone-built bench which ran around the room. He made me sit in this chair and more were brought for him and T.

There were about 80 men seated, some on the bench and some cross-legged upon the rough stone floor rearing and bawling, often all at once, about boundaries, taxes, etc., and often they rose up and rushed at each other with threatening gestures. Then the two soldiers stationed one at each end ran into the midst and separated them. Even when they were forced to the ground they sprang to their knees like jack-in-the-boxes to shout.

Everyone smoked and the government and the opposition, at more peaceable moments, frequently stepped across to get a light from each other's cigarettes, countless ends of which strewed the middle of the floor. The schoolmaster had a very empty inkstand on the floor before him and wrote the proceedings, and whenever he said a symphony had been come to, everyone denied it and at last they came to blows and we unobserved escaped, having long been tired of it.

You must excuse these smudges as I am sitting cross-legged on T's bed in our tent and was just interrupted by a man who came for 2 candles T had sent for that he may explore a cave.

We are encamped ([Monday] March 31st) for 4 days at Vourgounda (Βουργούνδα). We came here yesterday with two mules and 2 workmen to make excavations on the site of an ancient city. We only took our medicines, without which we never move, necessaries of clothing, and books for 4 days, food and bedding; but I had so much to sit on that I had to hold with both hands all the way. As I did not fall off I was pronounced an excellent rider by the men.

There is a long rocky point jutting into the sea on the W. of Karpathos, far N., near Tristoma and covered with ruins. Here everyone lunched at 12 and then T set the men to work and I went to the end of the point and had the tent pitched by a high rock which shelters us from S. winds. As Sunday night was the only rainless one we have had this long time, the ground was dry and by great good luck we have a level gravelly floor. Neither M nor the other two men had ever seen a tent before, so beginning with turning right side out I had to, by example and prompt, instruct them in everything; all in Greek too.

Do not think I had only to cause the pegs to be driven into the ground and put the eyes or guys, or whatever you call the ropes, over, no, only one peg is done like that. No 2 ropes are the same, either as to length or the angle from the tent: some are under rocks, some are round rocks, some are over rocks, and one had to be strung through a hole in a rock. One of those, which support the pole, is hitched over a little cairn; it is fastened so low, while its fellow forms a right angle with the pole. They could not understand the wooden runners and wanted to *tie* the ropes in knots and were amazed at the *mechani* when shown. I was tired enough in my tongue and limbs when after hoisting the Union Jack, I sat down to survey the tent and really the ropes all dancing have a very funny effect. The sun was hot outside but it was hotter still setting up the beds inside, 'tromeró zestë'[32] as they said.

After that I went to the workmen; who had discovered the pavement of a Byzantine church. We turn up our noses at anything 'tes Vizantines epoches', so T took them elsewhere.

Soon after our arrival, a messenger came and brought us 2 letters, the first we have had for more than 5 weeks and our first news of poor General Gordon's death. As soon as we had joyfully read them we began to lament the many more that had been lost, but 2 or 3 hours later another man came with 23, and 2 newspapers, February 7 being the latest, and March 9 the latest letter.

When the sun set we scrambled home. Next to our tent is a little hut built against the wall as a kitchen for pilgrims who come to a little chapel in the cave beneath. A very steep path leads to the small round entrance and several flights of steps lead down into a large cave. The holy place is shut in by a low wall and some pillars which do not touch the roof. Holy water drips into 2 little stone troughs and thither we hie with our sponges and towels to wash.[33] The workmen sleep among the rocks; there are plenty of caves about. When it got dark we went to the kitchen to dine. It was T's birthday.

The sacks of my bed and the tent were laid as a tablecloth on the soft wet earthen floor. We sat on 2 stones. T leaning against the middle post supporting a lambskin full of water, and I, as I found afterwards, very few inches from the lamb of the period. M built a table and seats next day. All the rocks and stones around were full of food and pots and a candle stuck by its own wax to one of them shed a dim light, except once when it tumbled down and went out.

We had a soup of lamb's head and a lot of herbs picked by the wayside, onions, and a handful of peas someone had given to T to eat raw. Then the brains and tongue boiled. Then the liver fried; a bowl of sheep's cream and sugar. Some wine from Samos and coffee. We then strolled on the rocks by moonlight and complained to each other that we did not feel at all excited at the idea of our first night in a tent – indeed, I think all we felt was satisfaction at the idea of a clean, dry shelter.

M spread his bed on brushwood in the kitchen. I undressed outside that I might bring in no fleas. As I had spread all our bedding in the sun, for once it was dry and our clothes in the morning were quite dry too. It rained in the night and T had to go out about 2 to loosen the guys and the N. wind came on in the morning, so they had to be tightened again.

It is a cold dark day and the sea wild and black. We breakfasted outside. T has gone to dig graves today and I am remaining at home enjoying great peace, nooked in where no one can stare. I am just going to have another read of the letters. In the afternoon, or rather about 10, I went and with difficulty found the diggers, as they were in catacombs whose openings were quite invisible from above. They had already begun to find things, though many of the graves had evidently been opened in the Byzantine times. Most things were broken but still there were many whole and during the whole time we became possessed of

---

[32] 'Very hot'.
[33] The cave-shrine of John the Baptist at Vrykoúnda, an ancient cult-site. Theodore was born on 29 March, 1852 (Mabel's birthday being 28 January, 1847).

Vrykoúnda, Kárpathos, the subterranean cave-shrine of John the Baptist.

many earthen plates (20 in one grave), the remains of copper mirrors and boxes, some glass things broken, and some broken but very pretty vases, etc. But the best thing is quite perfect, a bowl shaped like a pineapple about 4 or 5 inches across. Besides this, 3 round boxes and 2 lids made of lead, we think, a sort of button with a hanging ring but we know not what metal, and some little twisted bits that seem to be gold. The prettiest lamp, quite perfect, has a word on the bottom and T copied some inscriptions painted on the stucco of the vaults. We are altogether very much pleased with our success, and if we do not find things on Saría may return.

On Thursday morning (March 21st, I mean April 2nd) [March 21st was a Saturday, April 2nd was a Thursday], I did not go at all to the digging. To get there one must climb up, down, or over 17 walls, and as I did this 3 times the day before, besides wandering in search of tombs, I am sure I had a good deal of climbing. I was not much use as the men preferred grouping themselves round me when T's back was turned, talking to me, looking at my eyeglass, scissors, gloves, never before seen in Karpathos I am sure, and asking innumerable questions. In vain I suggest they should work but when the *Aphentikó*, as they address T, comes it is different.

Besides there was much to do in cleaning out the earth from the pots with very little water. I had to mind the camp while M went to seek a meal in the sea. I had a visit from 5 women and girls who without any ceremony called me nothing but Verghinía. This is the first time I have not been called Kyria Verghinía, but I suppose these people really never have seen anyone superior to themselves and their only idea of a 'Kyria' must be the Blessed Virgin. They said 'come with us Verghinía and we'll give you cream', but they terrified me by playing with the pots and I gave them no encouragement to remain and was glad when they left.

I packed our personal possessions and the more delicate 'finds' and after luncheon T went off again and I broke up the camp with M, though T had sent me a man, which I told him was quite unnecessary. The man was busy all the time turning a lamb into food, which I fortunately did not find out till he was dead.

By the bye, M had not slept a 2nd night in the kitchen, which was really as air tight as a nutmeg grater, but taken refuge in a cave about 30 feet above our heads.

We had 3 mules as we had 2 huge baskets of pots and seaweeds. About 4, T and his men came and everything was carried about ¾ of a mile and they and I were loaded on the mules and we reached Elymbo by dark. Sunny day.

Good Friday was a fine sunny day and we unpacked the panniers, for we were quite too tired to look at anything on our arrival. It is very exciting work digging, first finding something, then is it whole? Then have we all the pieces? The men grind the edges trying to fit them and any metal they cut with their knife. Fortunately they never saw the little boxes. T found and pocketed them.

We cleaned as much as our limited means would allow (a milk jug and a Russian wooden bowl such as grocers have with 2 lbs of tea). We packed the pots into 3 boxes, all except a very large earthenware jug, 2 of which were found whole and one of which T gave away. It is to be carried loose all the way home and now we empty our bowl into it. These two days before Easter are employed making bread and cakes with red eggs stuck into them and every oven is smoking. Elymbo (Ολυμβος) is rather a disappointment to us; we think Méso Chório was a quainter place. This Saturday is a rainy day.

Now here I must I think make a few remarks about the Greeks founded upon my 3 journeys amongst them and staying in the houses of high and low and seeing them in town and country.

Though they have a king, surely never were more true republicans than the Greeks. There appears to be perfect equality among them and a complete mingling of classes, neither dirt, poverty not want of education seems to make any difference.

When we were in Chios we went to see Mr. Choremi who has a very nice house in Athens, is very rich and in the best society there. Phaedros, our dragoman, whose wife is quite a common woman, glad of a very old dress of mine, was treated quite as an equal. Mr. Philemon, who is the Greek Consul at Rhodes, and who is quite a gentleman and whose wife is quite a lady and very well dressed, has a most ragged and dirty old father-in-law, Dr. Klados, and no one would take Mrs. Klados for a lady. Mr. Philemon gave us a letter to various people in Rhodes, particularly to Mr. Manolakakis, evidently quite an equal. He lives with a mud floor. His daughter of 17 with bare legs carried our luggage about a mile for 6d on her head and one of his little boys I saw running about with only a tattered frock open all down the front and bare feet. He is quite one of the chief men of Karpathos and Mr. Sakolarides's children also have bare legs. But these people are not like us in keeping up a good establishment in the country, for though they are as smart as possible in Athens, Syra, or Smyrna, once they get to the country they cast off their civilization with their collars and seem content with any kind of an untidy picnic for any length of time. Mr. Manolakakis has a cousin, a bricklayer, and one of our friends here is a bricklayer that T met at Mr. Manolakakis's house. He gave us letters of introduction to all kinds of peasants, some very dirty, but they all seem quite equal and we always noticed in the Cyclades that our muleteers used to sit down in any house and help themselves to tobacco. Certainly whatever their education is, they all seem to have good manners, if not quite according to our notion.

We are expected to know any English engineer on any steamer, etc.; in fact they do not seem to recognize difference of rank at all. As to our being 'a nation of shopkeepers' the Greeks cannot understand our buying anything for ourselves and think every bit of embroidery and everything else is bought for sale, and they often ask us if we have different things with us to sell. The women are quite like animals and are very much looked down on by the men (violent hail). Every man but a priest or two and a few old men leaves the island every summer for 6 months or more, chiefly as bricklayers, and every field labour, wine making, etc., is done by the women. There are no girls' schools and few of my sex can read.

Here the women's dress consists of a pair of full white trousers and a white night gown flowing open to the waist. When cold they wear a blue wadded-cotton coat, rather shorter, and then both men and women have a coat of brown goats' hair with a hood. Sometimes they wear brown leather top boots, sometimes not.

All these Greeks seem to love money dearly and always are wondering what everything is worth. They seem to like to 'go back of their bargain' too. Twice have women come demanding to cut all the plain silk off dresses we had bought. Once having bought a worked sheet because it had good lace on it, after the money was paid the seller asked to cut off the lace and once or twice after we had bought a bundle of bits they tried to remove one or two.

Easter Sunday, April 5th 1885. This morning was sunny after the first two hours so we opened all our windows and the door and tried to dry our things. Though T forgot to put out the brazier for the night and though it was still burning in the morning, some *clean* clothes hung *over* it on 2 chairs in the morning. We hung out the Union Jack in honour of the day. We had a visit from the schoolmaster, who is being doctored by us and is the better for our treatment, and took a walk with him. By the bye, one of T's patients (cold tea for the eyes) brought 2 eggs as a thank offering.

A little while after our return M came to say luncheon was ready if we were, for he thought it must be noon. T looked at his watch and found it to be half past 10; however we agreed our appetites were ready, so to our amusement we found we had everything cleared away by 11.30.

We spoke over the difference we observed between the inhabitants of Karpathos and Tilos and the Cyclades and the other islands we have visited, i.e. Nisiros, Rhodes, Chios, Samos, and Mytelene, in their not offering coffee, etc. to visitors. In the other islands we were always at once brought coffee, or jam and water, or *raki*, or almonds, oranges, or pomegranates, but here the only one who had offered us coffee was the Kaïmakan and the wicked owner of the plates who is a Greek from Syra. I agree with T in thinking it a Turkish fashion, but it is odd they never have offered us any thing till about an hour or two after this conversation when we were asked into a house, which we entered, and very soon a large dish of sheep's cream was placed before us and a *kouloúri*, that is one of the wound-up serpent-like cakes they make in great numbers for Easter, generally with coloured eggs in them. I could hardly get any down so soon and my horror was great when she said, 'now you must eat some lamb!'

Such cooking is going on these 3 days. First bread and *kouloúris*, then yesterday and today lambs, and we see the lambs come out of the oven in every imaginable shape in which they may have been flung in. Well! She fetched the family lamb and tore us off bits. She handed me a whole leg, but I cried for mercy and was let off with a smaller bit. It was very tender and I gnawed away industriously till the kind woman took my bit and rubbed salt into it with her thumbs, having been to fetch a handful of salt. I managed to continue eating inside bits till, when everyone was excited over my gloves, I squeezed up my lamb and bread into a tight ball and pocketed it.

Since this we have been to church. Only men and little boys go into the church, the women remain in the outer room where the parliament was, but as I count as a man, sitting at meals, etc., they invited me in. In I went. All the little boys stood in front, some very small and very pretty – indeed there are lots of pretty children here, though their elders are not handsome.

Everyone but we had a candle, but just before the time for lighting them came a man with two very large ones, hot and newly made so that we were glad to have them in the tray in which they lay, they were so soft. Of course, when they were so kind we lit up like the rest and I consoled myself by remembering that it was in honour of a truly Christian feast in which we could take part, in fact we recognized many parts of our own service.

There were 5 priests with such dirty rough-shock heads of uncombed hair. Their poor robes were made of printed calico. People chatted a good deal and we often heard a loud 'shsh!' It was very odd seeing the priests dressing and undressing inside the *tembelon* (τεμβλον) or screen. They walked about a good deal in a way I could not understand and 2 or 3 young men stepped about with large prayer books and repeated 'Christ is risen from the dead' (Χριστός ανέστε εκ νεκρον) and wherever they went the bystanders looked over and raised their voices.

The gospel was read on this wise: one papas read a verse or two in Greek, then each of the other 4, and then a young man read them in French! We did not discover this till the very last set of verses, as the French was very bad, but the last set but one I began to suspect. M tells us each of the priests ought to have read in a different language if he could, Turkish, Arabic, etc., that all the world might understand. A very good idea I think.

After the service was over all the papas came out and, clearing away the candlesticks, etc. which stood in the way, and holding up a silver-bound gospel, cross, and other things, they stood in a row and the men who wished passed before them kissing each object in hand once, and the papas once on each cheek and on the mouth. We did not perform this ceremony.

'This the men shot at, getting nearer and nearer till he got on fire.' Modern islanders shooting an effigy of Judas Iscariot at Easter. The Bents witnessed a similar traditional event in 1885.

When we got out there was a wonderful sort of a 'guy' set up over the gateway of the church to represent a Jew. His head was an earthen jar and he had a child in his arms. This the men shot at, getting nearer and nearer till he got on fire. I was sitting among the women who constantly begged me not to fear and thought I must be cold as I had on gloves, but I answered, 'Είναι συνήθεια μας', 'It is our custom', which finishes off all discussions. They are really very kind people, though more like animals. They are very un-enterprising too. We see many fields propped up by walls but uncultivated; they do not fish or build boats. At Levkos they said they had a boat 'but the captain was dead'.

I think we have got to the end of our 7 days here and are no longer great wonders, but every Sunday we always are one of the amusements of the day. We however had a great amusement of our own. The Schoolmaster during his visit asked us 'if we knew Captain Hatteras?' We said no. He told us he was a great English traveller and had been, as we thought, to Constantinople. We both imagined he said 'Eis ten Polin' 'Εἰς τῶν πόλεν', 'To the town' as they call it, and he thought we might know him.

I said to T I was sure I had heard the name, so T said 'we know the name but are not personally acquainted with him.' 'He has written a very interesting book' said our Host, 'Have you read it?' We had to confess we had not. After a little he said 'By the bye, I have Captain Hatteras's book, a translation, should you like to see it?' So at our request he brought forth a book of Jules Verne's – 'The English at the North Pole.'[34] We did not then take in that he really believed this book to be true, so we never undeceived the poor Pedagogue, but talked lightly of Jules Verne's other books and then of other things. Afterwards it dawned

---

[34] Jules Verne's *Les Adventures du Capitaine Hatteras*, later translated as *The English at the North Pole* (1864).

upon us that what we had taken to be 'Eis ten Pólin' was 'Eis tón Pólon' ('Εἰς τών πόλον'), to the Pole.

As an instance of the stupidity of the people, we ordered a lot of milk to be sent daily, and a lamb on a certain day, but though we have given this order at 2 *mandhras*, or shepherd's dairy, no notice is taken of us and preserved milk is our portion. Easter Monday. Dreadfully rainy, many inundations in the room. Every house is full of dairy produce, for every shepherd gives every house 3 small curd cheeses and a lot of cream and each house returns a loaf and a *kouloúri*. Each godchild of a shepherd receives a lamb and cream.

We have only one joke of our own, made by T, now an old friend. They commonly call cream here, instead of *dhrilla* or *anthógala*, by the Turkish name *kaïmak*. T's joke is to call it *kaïmakam*. We suppose the word must mean something superior, but our knowledge of Turkish is limited. Such is the force of example that I have just had the joy of hearing M ask for *kaïmakam* to be sent us. I laughed and he is dreadfully confused and says it is very hard to understand the people and that he has ordered *dhrilla*. It was a dreadful slip. He does not understand as quickly as we do, for, of course, our ears are used to so many dialects and they use such odd words.

We always get up without difficulty about ¼ to 6. It is better to do like the rest of the world and we go to bed very early. It is now about 12.30. We have short gleams of sun and try to dry up our clothes – then violent downpours. We have bought a little very pretty marble head, larger than an egg and a wee bronze cow. We have also had patients. The schoolmaster, who is 'doing nicely', brought us a bottle of very welcome ink – a suitable fee – and the news that a woman with a pain wished to be cured. So his little girl of 9, Maroukla by name, was duly despatched to say that T was ready, and soon a young woman was led in by her husband.

I really was inwardly convulsed with laughter at the very home-questions T had the courage gravely to ask her; the schoolmaster pursuing the investigations even further. It is really no use mincing matters here, for no one wishes to have matters minced and indeed the lady cared no more than if the enquiries were about a cold in the head. Well! We did our best but we must always confine our prescriptions to available remedies, such as the herbs we see on the mountainside (always avoiding poisons) – rice, oil, and hot water, the latter a difficult thing to get.

It is a sad thing to see these poor creations depending on such ignorant people as we are, but there are only 2 or 3 doctors who, they say, know nothing, besides which they must pay them 3 or 5 pounds (18f the pound), pay a mule and wait till it is convenient for him to come. Sometimes they say they have to pay more but I can hardly believe it.

Our next patient was a very small baby, 2 years old with a fever. These people sent us: one, 6 eggs (red) and the other 2 large pieces of *mesethra* pastry and sesame seeds and honey. After that came the schoolmaster's mother-in-law with a gift of a dish of *kaïmak* and 2 more pies.

We then went all together to a ball in the outer room of the church. We sat in a heap of people in the middle and round the edge sat mothers, each with a babe and a string of men screwed round in the narrow space left, preceded by the *sampouna*, pronounced *sabouna*, or bagpipe, and the *lyra*, a thing like a mandolin played with a bow strung with little bells. Only little tiny girls danced in this string but tomorrow is the great day when the young ladies will be dressed smartly and dance. When it got too hot inside we went outside and there being more space the dance was much prettier, but we found it too cold to remain long.

I went home and when T returned from a walk he found me doing my best to entertain 6 visitors, 2 clergy and 4 laymen, giving my very humble opinion on old coins of which I know nothing, but T endorsed all I said, showing them maps, etc. They had really come to see T's sketches and were delighted at the portraits of Papas Manolis of Mesochório and Marigó of Spiliés.

Tuesday April 7th. Very fine day. This is a very busy and gay day. There is to be a ball and, as it is a holiday, we have many visitors. I was going to the ball in my ulster,[35] but a crowd of women discovered a white dressing gown of mine covered with yellow lace and blue bows. They begged me to wear it for the ball, so of course I agreed. Over this, flowing open and with the sleeves tucked up to show the lace and bows of the dressing gown, is a flannel gown made extremely plainly for sleeping in in damp places. We have each one and I call them Flood-gowns, as Noah and his family had the same for the Ark and all that wet weather. My Flood-gown has only a little bit of lace round neck and sleeves and down the front, but then it is crimson so it has a fine effect with the blue, yellow and white.

Everyone has a display of jewellery today, so have I. The trumpery bracelets and brooches brought as presents were shown and I was made to put on gold, silver and garnet bracelets. Over my hat, with blue and yellow tuft in it, is a large white lace handkerchief, which I always wear for the sun, but 3 brooches, one a blazing diamond, are under my chin. A bunch of marigolds and geranium leaves in front, and over this is *trained* by my friends my steel watch-chain. I had 3 plain gold rings on one hand and one has been removed to the other hand, and they insist and implore that I shall not wear gloves, for it is a pity to hide such pretty white hands, which they liken to those of Maroukla, who is really only 7 years old and evidently the spoilt darling of the town.

They are quite delighted with me, and T and M are in fits of laughter. I am very smart indeed, but not a bit gayer than my neighbours with dresses of scarlet, orange, green, and blue. At the ball we sat in the middle of the court of the church with the mothers and the older men. No married ladies dance or boys, but grown up and very little girls and young men.

The circle had just room to get round sometimes at a visible pace and sometimes hardly perceptibly. The first man only danced and jumped, according to his fancy. The men *occasionally* spoke to each other but without causing any change in the expression of the girl they talked across. No one seemed in the least to care who he or she was next to, for with rare exceptions none of the dancers spoke and all the girls looked nothing short of sad. How they could keep jiggling round and round I know not. They seemed untiring. We and the sitters were merry enough. They sat on stones about the size of one's head or smaller that they brought in for the occasion.

The married women were all plainly dressed, but the very ugly girls had all sorts of brilliant colours and had their heads and necks loaded with silver gilt necklaces and ornaments. It was a great comfort to us to have secured a set. The little girls and babies were also a mass of chains, etc. I sneaked into my gloves, but on all sides I heard what a pity it was and many turned down my gloves to look at my wrists, and my sleeves were often pulled up to show off my bracelets.

I took a photo, as they said I 'telegraphised' them, which I daresay is as good a word, and returned home with the instrument, followed by some men, and as M almost immediately slipped out with a mustard leaf to bear to the sick, it was eagerly hailed as the result of my operation.

Wednesday [April] 8th. T has gone off to sketch. A very dirty and poor looking woman has just been to ask me to sell her an orange for a halfpenny. I could not do it as the four

---

[35] A sleeveless cape/coat.

Ólymbos, Kárpathos.

oranges had just been brought by Maroukla and her sister Eirenió as a gift and Maroukla was in the room, so I referred her to M. He was very angry and said she was to go. She begged for the orange as medicine. M loudly shouted that it was good for no illness, no medicine at all, and if she were to offer ever so much we would not sell neither an orange nor anything else. They screamed for a long time but I watched my opportunity and beckoned to her and said 'Take it quickly and say nothing about it; it is a present from Maroukla', and of course I could not give it before her, and stuffed it into her coat, the usual and only pocket. She thanked me warmly and offered the halfpenny but I said 'Típote! Típote!'[36] and refused it; so

---

[36] 'Nothing! Nothing!'

then she hugged and kissed me and begged me to come to her house when my man came home and she would give us cream. Oranges are rare here. 3 visitors came.

On Thursday [April] the 9th, being tired of Elymbo and finding it very damp, we determined to go to Dhiapháne on the coast, more especially as there was to be a pilgrimage and great festivities. So at about 6.30 we opened our door and a multitude rushed in, amid which we packed under the guidance of the schoolmaster who tried to make us pack the very boots and hats we wanted to wear. However thanks to the hurrying at 8 our baggage started, a wonderful thing considering the 7 women who carried it were always laying down one thing and taking up another and requiring great screaming at by M. It is such a comfort to have him; we never could 'phonasé'[37] loud enough.

The room looked bare enough when the beds were gone but we remain there till 2, T sketching and I working, and the schoolmaster talking and people bring clothes to sell. We bought 3 dresses. When we started we had a horse, or rather pony, laden with our food and cooking things and a little donkey, which I rode. M in both his hats and holding a sort of honey-pot which he never quits, and T holding a Rhodian jug which is our tea-pot and our washing jug.

We had two boys. One about 16 for me and one about 14, Manóli, for the pony. He had never been this road before and was quite excited about it. He carried the frying pan. He gave us a great description of the road, always ending with 'etsi legé' (so he says – meaning Michaél, the big boy). It is an awful road; the worst we have been. I began by walking a good way, then I mounted the little donkey who is quite the most courageous beast I have ridden in this island and a good jumper, which was needful as the path was gone in some places. We came down a river and the donkey was very much frightened of the waterfalls and once rushed up a bank but I was easily able to get off. I do not the least know how many times we crossed the river or how many times we had to walk down the middle of it. It was not deep enough to wet one's feet except in some deep pools and the walkers had to wet their boots some times.

Once my ass seemed so frightened that I got down and what he might have done with me on his back can't be said, but the pony fell on his side and we 3 saw a sack full of our goods lying in the water while the boys were busy with the beasts and we were clinging with hands and feet to the rocky wall of the river, scrambling along. No harm was done but the pony had shed everything and took some time to reload. We were glad the women had taken the precious packing cases.

Another time Michaél took off his boots and we went down the smooth bed of the river while T and M scrambled into the height above, but the donkey began to slip about and I thought I had better slip off, so I did onto a dry rock in the middle and to T's surprise my head appeared out of a thick bush of oleander which I forced my way through. We then got among pine trees and into a really pretty enjoyable part where one could spare one's eyes from one's feet for a few steps at a time, and in 2 hours reached the end of what we think to be our last land journey with beasts of burden.

We found that our luggage had been placed in the abode of the Protopapás, or first priest, and were well content with our dwelling, which offers some advantages we do not always enjoy. It is a small shop up an outside stair with a balcony on 2 sides and a door on each and from this we can get onto the roofs of 2 houses, about 10 feet from the ground. We have also a window which we can dress by as the balcony is public property. The room is small and the upper part does not do much more than hold my hammock, so T has his

---

[37] 'Shout'.

bed on the *pátoma*, or lower floor. A little high and very dirty counter, a fire place as high as a table, where we have a good basin, and are well lighted by the chimney; 2 chairs and some fixed boxes along the wall are the furniture of the room and we have added a pile of packing-cases by way of a table.

The boxes contain various wares for sale and we were induced to examine them by various mysterious sounds, caused we found by hundreds of live snails crawling up and falling down. T wanted to eat some but M says these large and shut up snails are not wholesome, and they add to the smells from which we suffer.

M takes his bedding and sleeps in a boat on the shore. There are very few houses here but it is a charming situation in a bay with rocky headlands and such beautiful walks up numerous branching valleys, and trees too, not very fine or close, but a great relief to the eye.

We had not sat down when a man rushed to us for advice for a very mysterious complaint that we do not understand, so we could only be guided by our natural instincts and as in a similar case in Elymbo order poultices, hot. In about 10 minutes I went out on the roofs and an old woman directed my attention to a little girl who I desired her to take to bed and I at once went and was soon cooking arrowroot in her cottage. The grandmother is called Hadji Mangaphou, as she has been to the Holy Sepulchre. (Hadji being a Turkish word with 2 letters that the Greeks cannot pronounce, θ and κ, they say Χάδσι (Chátsi)). The child is Mangathoula. She soon was well and the old thing tried to give me 3 eggs but I refused them and afterwards brought a *koulouri*, but it was also sent away. We gave her our washing to do but had to provide soap and next day they brought some of the clothes, tied up in one of T's pocket handkerchiefs, dry, and the rest to hang in our balcony.

By the time it was night the pilgrims began to arrive with mules and many bundles and after our dinner we wandered out, as there were no rocks to clamber over, to see what was going on. The master of the house was giving the feast and 8 or 9 lambs were hanging round the middle post which is in each house. Everyone was also making *kolivá*, or a sort of pudding, placed in the church all night as an offering to the departed relations and distributed after the liturgy in the morning. This is a round heap of boiled barley and sesame and sugar, with heaps of white sugar on the top, and some stock flowers stuck in.

We were asked into a house where a good fire of pine-chips was blazing. I and the men sat in a circle round it and the women on the outskirts. We stayed there for some time. About 8 they began to dance, all very smart, and continued dancing and singing till the liturgy, about 6.30. Then they sat outside the church, close under our balcony, and everybody handed round the *kolivá* and by the time everyone had taken a handful or even a few grains of every dish, they must have had a good substratum for the feast which soon began.

We in the meantime breakfasted and were summoned to visit our patient who seemed really very ill. She was a stout woman of about 50, with her shoulders, sides and back robed in a grey woollen garment. A most animated discussion over the complaint took place, with young men and maidens, old men and children all very noisy, and they got T's sketch book and really recognized people before they were told by us who they were, in a very satisfactory way with loud exclamations of 'It is himself!' I asked the patient if she did not mind the noise but she seemed to think it as inevitable as the roar of the sea.

We had the greatest possible advantage for seeing this feast, for we could see both the eating and the dancing from our roof. Inside the men squatted round and gnawed lamb in their fingers, and outside sat a man beside a huge cauldron, ladling out a sort of stew to

'We had the greatest possible advantage for seeing this feast, for we could see both the eating and the dancing from our roof...'

any woman who brought a plate. We knew so many of the people that it was quite pleasant. The Protopapás and many others sat with us and we were brought a good many presents of food. Some one had told of the sketch book and they were equally able to recognize the subjects and most cried 'Panagiá' (All Holy, The Virgin) and one cried 'Dhiávolos!', and the Protopapás constantly exclaimed 'Kyrié eleïson!'.

At ½ past 10 the dancers began to tuck up their smart skirts, pull off their best shoes and stockings and put on their ordinary ones, and shouldering their bundles and saying 'Apó chróno' to their friends, set off to Elymbo.

In the afternoon we took a beautiful walk along the cliff towards the S. and returned inland into a pine wood and then we got down a watercourse and, finding we could go no farther, we determined to climb up the hillside but it was awfully difficult as there was absolutely no foot hold on the crumbly schist, all slippery with needles. As T's big boots gave him firmer hold he crawled up a bit and lay down, and I pulled myself up by his legs and then he crawled up again, and could lean on me a little as I lay. When we could gently, gently, catch a branch of a tree we never left that friendly tree till we had got above it, carefully handing each branch to each other; then another crawl to another tree, and so we reached the top, and returned home bearing a good salad of sorrel leaves.

Saturday [April] 11. At ¼ past 7, having duly made our beds, we walked up the watery way towards Olymbo. Indeed, as M said, a boat would have been useful but I got on very well with my galoshes to put on for water and take off for rocks. T took a sketch and we remained till luncheon. In the evening we saw a boat come in with the shepherds who had been to Saría and many dead lambs and kids, cheese, cream and milk, but though we have offered to pay a boy to bring milk and to buy it besides, we have to use 'preserved'. We thought to have had a variety on lambs and that we would take the opportunity of the baking day and have a fowl filled with sage, which grows wild here, and onions, also rice, but such is the manner of baking here that when dinnertime came it was not ready and we ate M's dinner, which was a great disappointment but it was excellent at luncheon today.

Sunday 12th April. This morning on looking out and seeing the people smart and idle, I remarked to T that this seemed to me to be some kind of a holiday, but he only said it was Sunday, to my surprise. We went and made our liturgy in the pinewood and after lunch T made a sketch and all day we have been anxious about the weather, as it is so stormy that we had fears of not getting to Saría tomorrow but now we are full of hopes and are expecting our dinner. In has just walked a lady who sat down and announced to T that she also is a victim to this mysterious complaint that we never came across in England and here we have been consulted by a cow and 3 women. The coolness with which she broached the subject very nearly made me laugh in her face. No one minds talking of anything here more than if they were all cows.

Monday 13th April. After being kept awake a good deal by anxiety as to the wind which howled furiously, here we sit at 7 o'clock quite ready to start and waiting for the 6 men to come down from Elymbo. They are to row the boat which we shall keep during our stay at Saría. The sea is much better though noisy still. We have to take every kind of provision we want except lambs and milk, which we hope to get, so we have laid in a good stock of bees wax candles, petroleum, lamps for the tombs, matches, bread, coffee, oil, etc., and with the tools, all our 9 beds, the tent and the necessary raiment, we have plenty to fill a boat. We leave behind an additional packing case of curios.

We have various plans for our voyage to Syra. Here at this moment we have 4 cases besides other luggage, and at Pegádhia we have 1 case, 1 sack, a 'carpet bag', and a little statue[38] still at the house of the seller. The Turks have a disagreeable habit of examining outgoing luggage and we fear that the sight of so much together, and all we *hope* for from Saría, may excite them.

One of the plans is to start from Pegádhia in the dirty little steamer *Roúmeli,* which is supposed to be going to call on May 3rd to carry off some of the male population, in this case we must go there by boat.

No 2 plan is to get the steamer to call here, and in that case M is to go and gather up the 'goods and chattels' taking coverings for the little statue, 3 or 4 ft long, and meet us here.

No 3 is that we go to Syra in a sailing boat, not yet finished, with 20 other people; 24 hours at least. M fetching the things from Pegádhia and keeping them in the boat he comes in, and changing them into the big boat, then keeping them in the new boat in Syra harbour till we can get them on board a Liverpool steamer, for fear the Greeks should wish to have a look.

No 4, which seems to me the best, is to take a private boat and go to Khalki or Simi, and let the things remain in the boat till a steamer comes and then ask Mr. Binney at Syra to protect the transfer.

---

[38] See page 152.

Certainly we have had no difficulty as yet with the government here. They are all very kindly and the Pasha of Rhodes' letter was very civil, as we heard. He certainly did not write it till the last minute and after we had loudly expressed our surprise at such rudeness to his friend Mr. Aristarchis, but whether we have been forgotten and were never considered quite as dangerous as Mr. Aristarchis would have us believe, nothing bad had happened; still it will be nice to get our things safely to Syra. If we take a boat to ourselves, we can pick up things at Saría on the way, wind and weather permitting, for from this day out they are our masters.

About ½ past 8 we began to contemplate the fact that there was probably more wind up at Elymbo and that the men would think it too rough to come, and to look sadly at our beds and think how horrid it would be to have to unpack them again that night in that dirty room, and at last T went up the river to meet people and get news. He returned about 9 and told me he heard they were coming.

He found me having a *tête-à-tête* with the Turkish *zaptich*, or soldier, who is here as *Chorophylax*, or guard of the town. He had wandered up into the balcony and when I said 'Kal'eméra'[39] to him he came in and sat down and had been with me a quarter of an hour. He said he was from Cyprus and now English; his Greek was not of the best but we got on splendidly. This poor man appears to have nothing in this wide world to do. I pity him as I see him wandering about, now helping to pull up a boat, now digging a little, if he can find an idle spade, at the foundations of a house that is going to be built, opening on to the shingle and which will certainly often have the sea in it. But his pet amusement is to catch one of the 3 lambs, who browse in a field of quite high barley, in the ear and to nurse it walking about in the barley. There is an immense variety in the forwardness of the various crops – some barley is only just springing up.

We created great astonishment during these hours by getting out books, work, and this book to write, instead of sitting idle. They can't understand why I who am so rich should work. M shrieked at the men, of course, for being so late, and not till 12, after much more shrieking, were we 3 lifted into the boat: once there we all had our work, T to mind the honey-pot, I to steer, and M to bale incessantly. As these boats live up on the shore they are all very leaky. As for our luggage, as it lay on the shore it looked like that of gypsies. I tried to count it but gave up after 30. Cooking pots, frying pan, an immense wicker-covered bottle of wine, a huge jar for water, etc.

In 2 hours and a half we reached a place in Saría called Ta Palátia, the palaces. I felt so glad when we got past those draughty places, where our mast was broken. The coast scenery was very beautiful and the little bay here is quite invisible from the sea. It is all rocky, but a very small beach, then the land slopes very gradually back to a wall of mountains. As it is sheltered the mastic grows high and there is lots of green and actually the birds sang in the early morning, a rare sound. We thought of pitching our tent down by the sea as there is a well there but it seemed a windy spot, so we went further back near a little chapel, and, as it turns out, the digging place.

As we had built the beds and unpacked the sack which contained many things beside the tent, these were laid on the beds and carried up while we all followed laden; I with an earthen pan of *khalvas*. Our floor is level but stony. Under my hammock T can contemplate mallows, poppies, yellow clover, and a white flower as he lies in his bed.

As soon as the tent was pitched, T went round to choose a digging place, M to settle himself and his pots in the chapel where he cooked the dinner and sleeps. This is not considered irreverent by the Greeks and, indeed, it is the chief use of the chapels in these

[39] 'Good morning!'

isolated spots. We dined about 7, outside off a very pretty table, an old capital of a pillar, a comfortable size. We had not much meat and were to keep it for luncheon, but now there is a lamb taking his last meal tied to a bush.

[Tuesday] April 14th. We had a soup composed of onion, the only vegetable cultivated here, and wild turnip, flowers and all, and a little oil and some water – then a red herring – an omelette *aux fines herbs* and a sorrel salad from the same kitchen garden – *khalvas* and honey.

We felt quite at home in our tent; it was nice to feel it our very own and so sweet and clean. It rained heavily at sunrise and I remembered my gaiters were out, so I flew out of bed, flung my mackintosh round me and screwed out of a crack, as I could not unhook the door. I ran round to see that the pegs, etc., were all right and got very wet in the operation, but I retired to my warm bed till T dressed. He bathed in the sea, a mere tub however in the rocks for fear of dogfish (i.e. sharks 'σκυλόψαρα') and we breakfasted at 6.30, a trifle damp under foot but very jolly, and now there is a hot sun; we have the lamb, milk, cream, and M out partridge-shooting with a gun longer than himself, borrowed from the *zaptich*. It has crescents and stars and much other brass inlaying, single barrel and muzzle-loader – a picturesque weapon.

Altogether we should be very happy if we did not fear we should move tomorrow, for *Byzantine* is all we find. The little chapel is inside what must have been the apse of a Byzantine church, for the semicircular tiers of seats are behind it and we thought to find a temple among the ruins round, but as yet we have only found holy inscriptions.

Thursday April 16th. I will continue our life in its proper order, though I now write from a different camp.

All that morning they dug at what certainly was a temple but the Byzantines had destroyed everything, so after luncheon, about ½ past 11, T carried the men off to dig some tombs high up the mountain side, where, however, he found nothing but the bottom of a plate with two little raised heads kissing; he thought they were snails at first.

I did not go. First there might be no tombs, 2nd, it was excessively difficult to get through the jungle of mastic, between which were beds of nettles and thistles masking heaps of stones, and 3rd, it was not very safe to be far from the tent, as a family of shepherds had brought a family of bulls, cows and calves of all ages to have a good stare. They sat quite close and if I went into the tent, squatted at the door and I had to sit as near it as possible to prevent them and their fleas entering.

I could only take little walks, or rather climbs, as the chapel was not in sight from the tent and M busy. First I picked a salad then I went in another direction and read, but perceiving the cattle grazing among the tent pegs I had to descend and drive them out often. First I went into the tent followed to the door by a boy of 14 and a big girl called Sophilda, but I soon went out and hooked up the door and had turned my back on it when I heard the boy say 'To mandhiláki tes Kyríes!'[40], and the girl make a warning grunt. I turned round at once expecting to see my red-bordered handkerchief on the floor or to be handed it, but not seeing it I looked into the tent in vain for it and felt sure they had it, so I sat near to see what would happen.

After a long time Sophilda brought me a lump of cheese and I said 'I cannot find my handkerchief; do you know where it is?' 'Oh no!' she said she didn't. 'I thought you had seen it,' I said. 'No she had not' and here she made all the signs of negation, drew in her closed

---

[40] 'The lady's handkerchief.'

lips, threw up and closed her eyes, turned head, shoulders and hands up and remained a few seconds in this position.

I gave it up as a bad job and took the cheese to M that I might not have to eat it then and there and returned to have another try but they were gone, so I went back to M and told him my tale. He rushed up and down till he discovered their direction and with much shouting on both sides brought them to a standstill and demanded of Sophilda the Kyria's handkerchief. She utterly denied having it and M drew out his knife and said 'I shall cut your throat if you do not give it up at once'. And then she said 'Oh! There it is! There it is!' and M brought it back in triumph, but rather dirty.

M then went to fish, and about 3 minutes after the old woman of the party came to me and spoke much of 'klephtes' and 'psevtes' – thieves and liars – and I thought of course she was alluding to my handkerchief, so I told her kindly to think no more of it, to forget it, that it did not matter, but she loudly screamed that it did matter and matter very much. Then she spoke of the Elymbites that were with us, so seeing that we were at cross purposes, I told her I could not make out what she was talking, whereupon she said 'Ela'do Kyria'[41] and led me to the sacks of our men which the family had been sitting amongst and evidently examining, and drew out a blanket and told me our men had stolen it, so she carried it off and we have heard no more of it. They are certainly not very honest. As an instance, at that dance T saw one of the cheap brooches with which I was adorned fall out and be picked up by the father-in-law of the schoolmaster, a most respected man called *Diáko* Nikóla, because he 'knows letters'. I was occupied and thought he was waiting to give it to me but he never did. Both his wife and the schoolmaster remarked the loss, but we did not like to make a fuss as they were so civil.

Well, yesterday morning, [Wednesday] 15th [April 1885], we had packed our personal goods, T had taken a sketch, and bathed, and we were at breakfast at 6.15, and in an hour and a half, that is at ¼ to 8, we were off, alas!, without the spoons that did duty for egg and tea – *quite* irreplaceable in this island for they are not used.

At first we were in calm water with the bottom of the sea deep blue and light green and the red and coppery reflections of the rocks broken up by the ripples into feathers; I never saw the sea look so like a peacock's breast. But when we got to the strait between Saría and Karpathos it was very rough and we got a tremendous tossing. We landed at 10.30 in a little bay below the place called 'Tas Philakes', the Prisons, with 4 workmen, the others coming over and soon joining us.

We had caught several large fish on the way and M at once set up a kitchen on the rocks where we landed at one side of the bay. T walked up ½ an hour with 2 men and their tools to the Prisons. He found that there were only a few walls and a flat *kampo* and the ruins of a tower, as in many similar situations, to guard or *phylax* the crops. He did not think it a good place, which is well for he said it was hideously ugly.

In the meantime I went to bathe, having spotted from the sea a cavern to be reached bare-legged at the other end of the 50 or 60 yard long beach. I left my foot gear on the beach and ran round getting my petticoats a little wet to be sure, though I thought I held them high enough, but what was that compared to so private a dressing room? It was very large with the sea light into the mouth and so like the Lion's Den, lighted from above, that I could not help looking up to see if Nebuchadnezzar was there. As he wasn't, I had a very good time and a jolly swim, always looking for sharks though, but there was only a porpoise

---

[41] 'Come here lady.'

Rock-cut tomb, Vrykoúnda, Kárpathos.

and some pretty diving ducks. M told us he was once stripped and just jumping into the sea at Antiparos when he saw a shark – so he dressed again.

After luncheon we sent off the boat with the 6 men, 4 to be landed at the north of Karpathos and the 2 walkers to return to row us to Vourgounda, saying that if it were too rough we would stay at Tristoma, for one of the excitements of yesterday was that we knew not where we should camp. It was near sunset when we landed at the bay of Vourgounda and chose a camping ground just above the beach, near the work and with a greater water supply, though brackish, and plenty of driftwood.

We are in a square field of stones chiefly open to the sea, and 2 walls are full of tombs all cut smooth. The 4th side has low rocks and under it is our kitchen, also of tombs square cut. By the time we had pitched and furnished the tent and arranged the kitchen it was too dark to seek a dining room so we sat on sacks at the door of the tent with the lamp burning in the still air.

[Wednesday, April] 16th. This morning we rose at 5.30 and now 2 men are digging in the corner of our square – T has taken the others on the point. I soon went to bathe, having found as I thought a quiet little bay but when I reached it I found clothes being washed, so I took off my shoes and stockings, put on galoshes, and getting through a little water climbed up and then leaving my shoes and stockings I climbed down a little precipice, as T says, good footing if you are not inclined to be giddy. I reached a ledge 18 inches wide just under water. Then stuffing my mackintosh into the rock, hanging my galoshes up and throwing my hat,

I was ready for the water. It was very deep and I had a good swim, no fear of sharks, and I put on my cloak afterwards and walked home with my galoshes wet, to dress in the tent.

We have been very successful in finding unopened tombs with better things than we found before. We had a baking day. Just after our first sight of the sun our dining room was almost unbearable, but we just got the shadow for luncheon.

[Wednesday] April 17th. We had such a fearful storm in the night that we could not sleep. The wind playing the drum on the tent and we were every moment thinking it would be rooted up, but morning came and found us still there and the wind still violent and a black gloomy day. We had heavy rain in the middle of the day but I was in the tent and T softly lying on a heap of fresh dug earth regardless of his clothes. We have now for some time ceased to fear that our raiment may be spoiled. We are indeed like the Gibeonites[42] now and it is funny to see T's last year's suit, hat and all getting shabbier and shabbier on M. The trousers, supported by a red sash, have a large blue check patch in them, M having sat on a sharp rock, but we hope in about a week to start home. A dog in the night broke a tumbler so it is time to refit.

More tombs and more basketsful of things. We had to place our stores in the kitchen and eat there as it was so windy. Our news from England is now a month old.

Saturday April 18th. A fine day and hot. We went to bed with great confidence last night, the tent having stood the night and day and slept well and found the wind gone down when we woke. The sun only greeted our last mouthful of breakfast! We are so glad it is Saturday and that Sunday will be tomorrow. It is very fatiguing climbing from tomb to tomb to see that the men are not sleeping or smoking. After today we dismiss 2.

On Monday we mean to go to Tristoma. I do not know why this point is all terraced up and divided into fields for there is nothing but stones in them, like a newly mended road or worse.

Who would think that the next place I should have an opportunity of writing my Chronicle should be Crete! and further more at Kalé Liminas or the Fair Havens! where we, like St. Paul are sheltering from the tempest.[43] We are still so surprised to find ourselves here that we can hardly understand it. All sorts of things have hurried on that we have been in quite a dizzy state. Well, that Saturday we found very little and in the afternoon had the greatest difficulty in finding work for the men and it became clear that Vourgounda was quite exhausted, so we got home more than an hour before sunset and putting our 3 heads together decided it was impossible to go to Tristoma under the nose of the man-of-war and announce ourselves as excavators to the idle crew thereof. And then we bethought ourselves that finding anything at Tristoma was problematical. In fact the Greeks at Tristoma grew sour and so we then and there determined that nothing remained for us but to return to Diaphane and if possible get on all together to Pegadhia; then it was said that Vourgounda was a most hard place to leave, and we had better leave in the morning if the wind were fair, for else we might remain a month.

The remaining daylight was therefore spent in getting the bed things into T's large handbag and the small portemanteau and others into a large 2-handled pot with a lid which we left to the workmen; about 6 big pithoi, etc., remained out and we went to bed sorry to think it might be our last night in our dear little tent, but half undecided whether we should pitch it at Pegadhia. We decided that as it was Sunday and as there was no hurry and only

---

[42] See Joshua, 9 (3-15).
[43] On the southern coast of Crete, a little east of Cape Mátala.

4½ hours to Dhiaphane, we would take it very easy! So consequently it was not till 7.30 that we were lifted into the boat.

[Sunday] April 19th. Surely Karpathos is the island of imaginary fear! Just as we were starting the men begged us to get out our flag, that when we passed the man-of-war our boat might be taken for an English one. We said that it did not matter and in spite of their implorings we declared it was in the tent-sack, in the bottom of the boat and could not be got out. They said 'If the Turks take us, what shall we do?' We said they will only ask who we are and let us go. We laughed at their fears and could not understand them but they told us that on account of a murder just committed at Volatha they feared being taken for the murderers. 'But you, *Aphentikó*,[44] will say you are our master and that we are your men and this is your boat, won't you?' They were really alarmed. I told them we would say we were all English and this comforted an auburn-haired one called Andreas. They even spoke of our being carried to Constantinople and we said it would be delightful to get there without paying our passage.

It had been settled that if it were too stormy we should stay at the bay of Almiró (salt) in Saría till we could proceed, living in the tent. When we got near Tristoma, we hugged the rocks of the 2 small islets that mask its mouths and eyed the masts of the man-of-war, put in there as the engines are broken. When we got to the open S. mouth they rowed hard and greatly did they rejoice that we had been unseen, for they had been saying 'If she makes a sign to us we will row straight to the ship' but we intended merely to stop and let them send a boat.

In the strait the wind was so favourable that by hoisting a cloak and 3 umbrellas we really made way and the men were highly satisfied as we perceived some sentinels on the heights, for they said 'the umbrellas are quite as good as the flag; people with umbrellas they will know are English!' We passed these sentinels quite safely and when we came to more the men rushed for the umbrellas again and however little our enemies may be intimidated it is a fine thing to feel how safe our friends felt under the protection of the British Umbrella!

We reached Diapháne about 12, at once lunched on tinned lobster, no time for cooking, and packed all our things, for we believed the *Roúmeli* was to call at Pegadhia on Monday afternoon, but everyone said she would be late on account of the storms. When we got all done we set off with prayer books and towels, meaning to 'make our Liturgy' and bathe, but when we got to a little beach a mile off, the first place we could descend to the sea, it was 5 so we had a very cold bathe, our 5th, and found it quite too cold for an out-of-door liturgy. At one end of the beach a charming bathing-box was walled off by rocks.

Monday, April 20th. We said we would start at 5 to frighten our men, but did not get up till 10 to 5 and did not start till 8. 26 packages I counted. The schoolmaster came down and brought letters of March 4th. We had later ones. At last we started to continue our voyage home, all in the highest spirits, M quite as pleased as we were. I little thought that when they lifted me into the boat I should never touch Karpathos again!

Shortly after we started we heard great shouting after us. These were really 2 Cassiote[45] carpenters wanting a passage, but in the distance their European dress caused them to be taken by the men for *zaptiehs*, so the men said they would not stop; they should not get into a scrape for the boat was T's. It was said they had something in their hands, perhaps it was ours, but we thought seriously of all our things and said it could not be and even if it were it was not worth returning for and running the risk of our things being examined. These

[44] 'Boss!'
[45] I.e. islanders from Kássos, between Crete and Kárpathos.

people can shout and hear at great distance, so requests and refusals flow through the air and still we were pursued. Then a suggestion that it might be letters made us a little regretful, but still we determined to push on.

At last it was settled that we should go under a cliff where they could not come down, not go very near but stop till we could really hear what was wanted. By this time the carpenters were recognized but still the boat was so full that we had to persist in our refusal till one of our men offered to land and give up his place. The carpenter embarked with many thanks and many polite excuses on our part. 'Had we seen who it was, etc.', but M scolded him well, called him brother, and asked why he had not told us before.

We were all regretting the half hour wasted in the 7 hours' voyage, when 'To Atmópleion!' burst from every lip. There was the steamer, steaming north and away from Pegadhia. We at once steered towards her with shouts and cries, no doubt unheard. M in the prow waved his big white hat. 'Your parasol, put up your parasol!' said the men; we said 'What good would that do?' 'Oh never mind. It will do no harm and as you have been on the steamer of course they will know it.'

We were tremendously excited as the steamer still went on and real tears came into my eyes with anxiety and I am sure if they had asked me to kneel in the bilge water I would at once. We comforted ourselves with knowing the captain and his son/mate to be civil people. At last they stopped and took us on board, leaving our whole lamb to the men and taking a large open jar of wine, as that of the steamer is bad. The captain was implored to return to Pegadhia after calling at Diapháne and was undecided, but as we saw 5 cases placed in the hold and other things, including the jugs under the saloon, besides our good-sized cabin paved, and the passage choked, we felt pretty easy, but happiest when a symphony had been come to for £13; he asked £20 for the 3 passages, and return to Pegadhia for our luggage about £5 extra.

The passengers, all deck, or in the hold, were not pleased and no wonder. '£13' was buzzed on all sides. The ship was full of acquaintances and we seemed to have to shake hands all round. A large group dragged me from the ladder to enquire all sorts of things and as for the men, T said it was sad we had so many drunken friends. The carpenter was just as pleased to be on board as ourselves, though all his luggage for a voyage to Syra was a little round basket with food on his arm, a saw in one hand and 4 feet of plank in the other.

The next excitement was getting the things at Pegadhia. I decided to remain on board and became a perfect queen-bee. I gave up moving at last for I was always followed. I eagerly watched the proceedings on shore. M set off to run to the house where was a very hideous statue, more than the size of a baby, half a mile off.[46] T and the Turks sat down at the café.

People came to the steamer and said 'Why have you returned?' and shouts of 'Oi Angloi, oi Lordhi', 'The English, the Lords'. And 'Dekatris Lires! Lires kavalkamenes!' Or '£13 on horseback' – meaning with St. George on them – and they could not make out why I said our luggage was in the custom house when they saw M run away. 'Where are your things? They must be at Apéri (2 hours off) for your servant is running there.' I laughed at them well and began to read, so that was a great entertainment. 'Now she has turned a leaf' they said.

---

[46] Now in the British Museum, Room 11. Registration No: 1886,0310.1 (PRN: GAA49603); catalogue Xref: Sculpture: A11. Described as 'Limestone female figure with beak nose, pointed breasts and raised pubic triangle. Height 66.00 cm. Period: Neolithic (late). Excavated/Findspot: Europe, Greece, Dodecanese, Karpathos, Bourgounte.' Mabel's testimony indicates that this unique idol, curiously modern, was acquired in the vicinity of today's harbor town. The figure, thought to be Neolithic (4500-3200 BC), if genuine, remains the earliest stone sculpture found in the region.

At last I saw M tearing back with the burden on his shoulders and very soon they reached the ship and all was on board. We sat almost speechless in our cabin but I said 'We are not off yet. I can't stay here'. At the door I hear 'O Lordhos. Pou einai o Lordhos?' 'Where is the Lord?' For all English who appear to be independent gentlefolk are lords here. I could have been knocked down with a feather but no one tried to do it, so I asked what it was and was told – letters and newspaper. They were fetched and we were safely off.

'Oh!' I could not help exclaiming 'How thankful I am to be under the Greek flag'. And indeed with 3 umbrellas in the cabin, though all in disrepair, what now had we Britons to fear from Turks?

We sat down to luncheon at 12 in gay frame of mind and then I heard how M had run to the house and found it locked and had broken the door open, found the statue, wrapped it up in what he carried for the purpose, and ran back. T was in the meantime drinking much *raki* with the Harbourmaster and other Turks, having been to the custom house and told an old woman to take a long time carrying the three things, one by one, very slowly to the boat and thinking M would never be back; as I could see M I was luckier.

A 'very hideous statue, more than the size of a baby'. The limestone figure acquired by the Bents on Kárpathos.

When M appeared, T could see that the statue showed behind and told him so, but he said 'No matter' and rushed on to the boat and then came back to say goodbye to the Turks. T saw them spot the statue and whisper together and shrug their shoulders, so now we are in possession of the most hideous thing ever made by human hands. We mean to deposit it in bond at the customhouse of Syra with all the cases and things we do not want. We also talked of how the delay caused by the carpenter, which annoyed us so much at the time, was really a great blessing, for had we not been delayed we should have been deep in a bay, hugging the shore and never have caught the steamer.

The longest way round is evidently the shortest way home for us. For having started 8 in our boat we went N. to Diapháne, S. to Pigadhia and on round the island; goodbye to Karpathos and N.W. to Kassos, where we remained 3 hours with all the captain's relations on board, as this is his home. He introduced us to one just as he was going ashore, and we found him to be Kyriós Nichólas Mavrís, for whom we had a letter, so T rushed and got it just in time.

Tuesday [actually Wednesday] April 22nd. After this we turned S.W. and sailed under Crete…[47]

---

[47] Under Crete, the Bents leave the Dodecanese behind them and make a long journey home by sea, via Kýthera, Sýros and Malta, returning to London in May 1885 with a considerable cargo of finds, much of which

My Fourth Chronicle
1886

March 1886
Monday, March 1st. We hope to go to Lipsós and Agathonisi tomorrow and to Patmos if the wind becomes good. A good big ship is engaged and Demetrós comes with us. It has been made clear that no wages are to be expected so he may not turn up. As for digging, we can do nothing till we have the leave of the council of 4, not yet elected and not to meet till the middle of April, and that will be rather late for us –

I take up my pen again in a cell, up many flights of stairs in the big monastery in 'the isle that is called Patmos'[48] on March 7th [Sunday, 1885]. I had better continue our history in due course.

Tuesday [March] 2nd. Contrary wind and rain so we had no hope of leaving Samos, so made our beds and prepared to spend the day in the house, but at 11 a good wind came and we summoned the captain and it was agreed to start at once. M rushed to prepare food for the journey and we packed and were all ready by 12 – but the ship was not. We had been going to start that morning but they had to get oil, bread, tobacco, water, their papers, etc., so at two only did we embark. Suddenly a violent storm of rain came on and the wind went down so we had to land and sadly make our beds again. We decided to start at dawn next morning and were to be called at 3, but of course they did not come till 5.

We started at ¼ to 6. It was not very cold and the sunrise was most lovely. The very new moon was sailing about in the blue. The morning star (Αυγερινός άστρα) was shining through pink and the mountains of Anatolí (the Sunrise) were quite black. Watching the sunrise occupied us till the ship, a schooner, was all in order and then we got out our breakfast things and made some tea. In four hours we got to Agátheonisi, or Gaidáronisi, that is Good or Donkey Isle.

It is a small low, barren spot inhabited by an old man and woman with 6 sons and 7 daughters – 3 sons and 1 daughter married and some children – in all 22. They live in the most wretched huts and the greatest poverty, drink brackish water in winter and buy it from Samos in summer and pay £127 to the Turks.

They keep sheep and goats and we bought a lamb and a *mysethra*, and lunched off eggs and *chloro*, a kind of junket or curd, and bread which we had carried with us. We examined the houses and a woman gave T an old knapsack of goat skin for which she of course was given a return, and at 1 we set out for Lipsi. We also had a good voyage there of about 4 hours.

We were very despondent about our lodging there and took the trouble to ascertain on the way to the little scattered village that a church was open in case we wanted to return there. The real harbour was the other side of the island but we could not get there. We all were laden. T had a basket of provisions and an earthen pan containing the lamb's fry. I clasped a large flat loaf in my arms. The path was very smooth and not very steep and we crossed the island in half an hour, getting into deep and unavoidable mud near the village.

This is the first place where the people have not been hospitable, at least in word. The man at the café said we might sleep in his shop, but there seemed no other place and no one offered anything though we said we would pay. A Kalymnos man begged for us and M took the café man out and argued with him and the result was that we got a little room at the back

is now in the British Museum.
[48] Revelations 1:91.

with a window about 6 feet from that of the café where they drank and played cards all day long. They are certainly very idle people.

We remained there 2 nights and caught fleas and did not read, for our books could not be got from the ship. From the bible to the Chronicle[49] we were utterly bookless and surely, before we knew the alphabet even, we can never have been 48 hours without seeing the outside of a book in some language. I fortunately always have a little bit of needlework in my pocket.

In getting the boat round they nearly got on a rock and then lost one anchor. We went to all the ruins and were glad to find that there was nothing of such interest as to keep us in Lipso. On Friday the wind turned N. again so we gathered up our goods in a hurry and set off for Patmos about 12. I travelled away bearing a plate with some *mysethra* on it. We had 4 hours' sea again and at last had to tack a good deal to get into the bay.

I hate tacking. This bay is only separated from another by a very narrow isthmus and the island is divided in 2 nearly equal parts. The monastery, which looks like a great castle and is surrounded by the town, is about ½ an hour's climb from the sea. The cave of the Revelation is a little way down off the road. We came straight up here guided by a funny little Deacon who we met on landing. We had 2 letters, one from the Prince of Samos and the other a circular to all the abbots of Patmos and Samos from the chief Archimandrite in London, Jeronomos Myrianthos.

These were sent before us by a man but did not arrive before 2 little boys, one carrying the pan containing the heads of 2 fish and their tails, and the other a little common earthen brazier, had audaciously taken them into the Abbot's own house. We found him scolding them and he really seemed very cross with us. We begged his pardon and said they ought to have kept these things at the door while we visited him and our servant was seeking a house. We drank coffee, ate jam and were introduced to all the dignitaries, and at last the heart of the Holy Egóumenos was softened and he said it would be hard to find a house at this hour and they would manage well enough for a night and we should be put in the cell of Gerásimos. We were delighted, and still more so when, on being led up many stairs and over and under many places, we found the cell consisted of a little house containing a hall, kitchen, bedroom for M, a sitting room 25 feet long, and a bedroom within for us.

T slept in the monkish bed. M is charmed with his kitchen and is never still. He went out yesterday morning, 6th, and shot 3 partridges and a little bird and I took 4 photographs inside the convent with one ragged old monk and a few deacons. We inspected the library and saw some beautiful old books which the awkward old *Bibliophylax* turned over very roughly. We had a visit early from the old Egóumenos and we asked to stay till Tuesday. I visited him in the evening.

We also took a walk in the town and met a little tailor called Janko who has undertaken to seek for various things we want. He took us into several large houses furnished with Dutch cabinets and chairs, a little inferior Chinese china and some of the most awful daubs of pictures ever seen: their owners or their fathers having been merchants. We also went to a nunnery. The nuns were in church in long black coats and skirts and their heads in black handkerchiefs. We went to visit the Lady Superior but she was ill in bed. Soon however we were taken to her bedroom and there the poor old thing was in all her greasy old black clothes. One nun, a fat rosy person of 55, was delighted to find we could talk French and carried me off to her cell, 3 very comfortable rooms and she told me she had been brought

---

[49] Mabel styles this *Chronicle* her 'fourth', but it is actually the third of her notebooks in the Hellenic Society's archive.

Pilgrim, the Cave of St John the Divine, Pátmos.

up in the French convent of Santorin. She spoke very well. T and Janko joined me after they had visited the other cells, some poor, some otherwise.

Sunday [March] 7th. Tremendous S. wind and rain so we did not get out till after noon. We had a most peaceful morning. We took a little stroll on the roofs before luncheon and then went down to the Cave of the Apocalypse. The highway was a roaring brawling stream with eddies and waterfalls but with galoshes quite passable.

The cave is one of a great many which we have not yet explored. It is the highest up and must have been a wide, rather shallow, cave with an overhanging roof. Of course now it is not very easy to see the shape as it has divisions to make it a church. In fact it is a double church, one side, the right, the cave and the other a church of St. Anna. Of course no one could really know which cave St. John saw the Revelation in because the island had been uninhabited for so long before the Holy Christódoulos came here with his monks to make this monastery.

This cave has in the floor some little cut channels to let water run off. Now only a little water flows when it rains and from a little cavity near the floor, where they think St. John was silly enough to put his pillow. And there are some holes high up which look as if meant for lamps, so that this cave may have been inhabited. Of course every crack in the cave has some marvel attached to it. An old ragged woman, a most kind creature, the sister of the

Papas who keeps the place, bawled all these things at the top of her voice and gave us some little chips of the cave and after we left took us to her house, part of a once flourishing but now ruined school. We both agree that this is the most interesting place we have yet been in.

When we returned to the monastery we were shown the skull of St. Thomas, bound in silver, and that of 'Antipas, my witness, my faithful one',[50] who was of the Church of Pergamos, enclosed in silver. St. T's skull is in a huge silver cup. We saw the walking stick and shoes of St. Christódoulos. His real name was John, but he took this name, i.e. Christ's servant. We saw his embalmed body with a sort of box to show his head. Then we retired up to the roofs again and T and M went out and I had a visit from the Holy Pro-Egoúmenos, who was Chief last year and will be next. He remained with me about half an hour and was very happy looking with all our things. He caught sight of the legs of my bed through the door, so we hurried into the bedroom that it might be thoroughly explained.

Monday [March] 8th. T and M are gone out again this morning and I am quite happy alone. We might really as well be in our own house as in the very top of this castle. I rather expect the Egoúmenos, but not till evening as the Greek Lent begins today, 2 days before ours, and there is much to do in Church. I shall be very sorry to leave this, but if we dig this would be too far off. By the bye, Demetrós never turned up.

In the afternoon T and I walked and scrambled and paddled to a little church called the Garden of the Saint Képos tou Osíou, i.e. Christódoulos. It was dreadfully wet and we were glad to get home, climbing up the narrow rocky lanes, in one place 10 inches wide.

Tuesday morning, [March] 9th. A new plan came into T's head in a dream! So we quite determined to go to Kalymnos and began to pack in order to be off that day, but the weather was too bad to leave the island so we settled down for another night and in the meantime changed our idea and went back to the plan of visiting Ikaria or Nikaria next. We went down to the 'Apokalypsin'[51] again and there bought a very pretty old *eikon*, much better painted than most. The first time we bought a little wooden pot, very like a Scotch quaich[52] which the old woman kept incense in.

We had a visit from the Pro-Egoúmenos, who had come to show off our things to the Ekonomos and one of the Papadhes, who photographs with wet plates. The art of photography with dry plates had to be explained to him by me. It is a thing I am ill-fitted to do in English even. Someone in Patmos has now a good umbrella, for T left his in some respectable house where he had been visiting, but everyone denied it so we had to come away without it.

Yesterday, Ash Wednesday, [March] 10th, we actually did leave Patmos, with great regret on account of the comfort and quiet we had enjoyed. The floors were not washed and the rooms were bare but, as the owner had betaken himself to a hermitage, the native fleas had died. But we found digging would not repay so we said farewell and departed, I on a small ass and stirrupless and perfectly devoid of any kind of bridle. We got down to the harbour and there a fearful shower came on and we had to scramble about ¼ of a mile to our captain's house.

There we remained about an hour and a half, not at all sure of getting away at all, but at about 11 we did get off and were a very long time getting out of the many capes of Patmos…

---

[50] Revelations 2:13.
[51] The famous cave of St John below the monastery.
[52] A shallow drinking cup, typically with two handles.

[Sunday March 14th, Ikaría] ...This morning we were, about 7, going to start for one place or another, according as the wind suited, by boat, as the land ways are too difficult, but in the course of 3 hours we changed our plans several times and this evening are here still, after a day of some excitement. M went for the permission to the Kaïmakam who lives next door and the Kaïmakam refused to give it so T went and offered him money; he had had presents, but this, to everyone's surprise he refused and told T he would prevent his digging or even visiting any ruins – T told him he was an Anglos and therefore could not be prevented travelling where he would, etc.

After all this it was settled that it would be useless to remain here, and, hearing from an Astypalitis, Giorgios Morphino, a favourable account of his native isle, we settled to go there and a boat is engaged to start early tomorrow morning, the ship's papers being made out for Kalymnos! to deceive the Kaïmakam. It is between 50 and 60 miles and we shall have to sleep on board *if* we go.

This horrid old Dr. Andreades is, I believe, at the bottom of it all and I believe he plans to make private diggings himself – he pays us frequent visits. The Astypalitis advised, and it was done, that T should write to his most excellent worship the Kaïmakam and say that as he had refused his written request to dig for the English archaeological societies and was told that he was not even allowed to travel through the island, T begged that he would give him this refusal in writing to show when he got home. 4 stamps were affixed to this as to the request.

The Doctor was annoyed and the Kaïmakam said he would give the answer this evening, but now he said to M, who went for it, he should give it tomorrow morning. T instantly went and found the Kaïmakam at dinner but could not extract it so he demanded the *teskerehs*, or passports, from one island to another and got them. I do not believe we shall go tomorrow as there is every chance of a calm. The inhabitants are very angry with 'that dog', for preventing them earning money. The sum began with £1000 and had got to £200,000. There have been excited little meetings. We had a visit of 7 or 8 of the judges, advocates and their families, who amused themselves with our belongings.

The Astypalitis called about dinnertime and was asked to join us – a magnificent repast of pease soup and 2 courses of kid, boiled and stewed, and walnuts and honey. He is a nice little advocate.

T saw the sunrise in his 'camera obscura'[53] this morning.

If they only knew it is almost more amusing than annoying to have such a fuss made about us.

Monday [March 15th]. We went to bed in a very doubtful frame of mind but are so accustomed to these ups and downs that we slept in peace and this morning, as a Greek calm seemed to have set in, we did not get up earlier than usual, about 6, and then made every preparation for a night at sea, with books, blankets, food, etc.; everything we could think of.

The ship was put in the water and ballasted and it was thought we would go, but then the wind changed and there was for many hours uncertainty. The ship cannot now remain here as there is no harbour and if we do not start must go to the Phournoi Isles to shelter and the question was whether we should go in her, live on the ship and wait until we could get to Astypalaia, or wait here till she returns for us. We could not leave Agíos Kyríkos as we must not waste the opportunity and we can go nowhere by boat on account of the wind, or by land because it is 6 hours on foot to the nearest place. Then we thought of going to Vathý in Samos and all were disgusted with the idea. The steamer which could take us to

[53] Mabel is referring to an accidental trick of the light they noticed previously.

Kos, whence we could get to Astypalaia, is most irregular and we might be a fortnight there in great discomfort.

It feels like 2 o'clock and M has gone to make luncheon, but it really is ½ past 10. We have decided to go to Karlóvassi in Samos and shall start about 12.

In the meantime they are in a nice fright here. Cassim Effendi now refuses to give the written refusal and his friends are telling him T is going to prosecute him in Chios. The Doctor came here and asked T why we did not go and visit him in his house and T snubbed him rather. He has been telling M that he (M) is a civilized man and he can speak to him and asked him if the Chios notion is true. M says we have not told him anything but he can very well take in that this must be T's idea – i.e. to inquire into this new law which forbids travellers to pass through an island.

M says he will make the Doctor come that T may cram him with terrors for Cassim Effendi. There is talk of shooting the Kaïmakam! We wrote some letters yesterday but find they could not go to the post for 13 days, so keep them.

Vathý, Samos. Tuesday, [March] 16th. We eventually left Agios Kyrikos at midday on Monday and in 8½ hours reached Karlóvassi in Samos. We got a horrid room at a café. Yesterday morning we went on foot to the 3 villages of Palaio (Old) Karlóvassi, Meseon (Middle) and Neo (New) Karlóvassi, and visited the Vorgias family with whom we had stayed in '83 in Meseonkarlóvassi.

We settled first to wait for the *Roúmeli*, which will go to Kalymnos, and then at dinnertime determined to go to Vathy, by the little *Giorgios*, and wait there for the *Roúmeli*. So we went to bed at once and slept and caught B flats till 2.30.[54] We then were hurried on board but did not start till 5.30 and got here in about 2 hours. We heard that nothing could be done about the digging till after Easter, so we got everything ready to abandon this island for this year, asking the permission for next, but T has now seen several people who tell him there is not any doubt about the permission and that nothing need be said about dividing the finds, if any, with the Government. So now we have re-arranged our luggage and are leaving things here. It is raining.

T has spoken to Mr. Mare of the rude conduct of the Kaïmakam. The Prince had sent a letter to him after us but we never got it. We got a bundle of letters.

I am most curious to see a young lady of Kalymnos, aged I hear about 16 and just married to a Mr. William Paton of Granholme in Aberdeenshire.[55] Her father's name is Olympites, a sponge merchant and very rich. Everyone has heard of 'O Ouiliermos' in the neighbouring islands.

I took a photograph of a Samiote soldier at Karlóvassi, focusing with a bit of paper. It blew away with all its pins. I have today got my frame back with a very bad glass from Smyrna, but at all events it won't flutter about like the paper.

Kalymnos. [Thursday] March 18th. We were lucky enough to fall in with a clean little English steamer, *Ianthe*, where we had a most comfortable flealess night and a very calm passage here. We started about 6 and arrived about ½ past 12 yesterday. The captain, on our asking to see the charts and saying we had left ours at home, has lent us one to be left at any port here.

This is a very populous town of large houses filled with rich sponge fishers who have a reputation in these regions of being thieves, liars and cheats. We were sorry to hear that Mr.

---

[54] Bedbugs and fleas.
[55] Classical scholar and archaeologist, William Roger Paton (1857-1921).

Paton had returned to England 2 days ago, leaving his wife at her father's as she does not wish to undertake the long journey till the summer of next year.

After a very public examination of our luggage by the Turks in a heavy shower, we and the crowd adjourned to the coffee house. Here M was kissed by a friend from Antiparos and we speedily made some acquaintances. I was puzzled by hearing behind my back 'Oh! Mrs. Virginia! how are you? Welcome.' 'Well have we met!' I exclaimed and wondered who on earth it was. This was the schoolmaster from Tilos.[56] We are always having these meetings.

There is no inn but a suite of rooms was given by a jolly old boy whose name I must find out and write down. It is a very cold place, for few broken panes remain to prove that many windows once were glazed, and as the doors have never had any fastening the draughts are great. We lunched off limpets and pina, a huge shellfish, and afterwards went out for a walk.

We were very much amused on landing to hear 'William has returned'. 'No, it is his brother.' 'He is exactly the same.' 'How very like he is.' 'No, it is *not* him.' And these sentences never cease to be buzzed round wherever T goes. At the British Museum they have been taken for one another and a gentleman came and shook hands with and said 'When did you come' and then 'Oh! Excuse me. I thought you were the son-in-law of Olympidis'.

A tall young man just like a Jew in the Constantinople bazaar accosted us in English and said, 'This is the father-in-law of Mr. Paton and I am the brother-in-law of Mrs. Paton'. So on invitation we entered the café and gave our history, in Greek, to the crowd. The brother asked us to come and take a walk in their garden, so we were removed to an orchard of young lemon and orange trees. Chairs were procured and we sat on ploughed beds, damp, so that one had never to forget to be always trying to sit on the highest leg of the chair for fear of overturning. He would talk English which we had constantly to help out with Greek so we sat silently for a long time till I shivered loudly and we were led silently home.

We announced that in an hour we would call on Mrs. Paton. Accordingly they prepared themselves. We entered a mud-floored hall littered with broken machinery, up dirty marble stairs with a rusty banister and reached a drawing room where some matting had been thrown down, but rolled up where it could not pass under the chest of drawers. A quantity of pieces of embroidery bought during the honeymoon to Simi and Rhodes were plastered round in an absurd way. The chest of drawers had a green table cover falling over the front of it, over that a large cotton antimacassar and on top a large pier glass smashed in 4 bits, some hanging out.

Mrs. Paton is a fine big girl who might pass for 20 but some say 14. She had a pretty new dress, quite out of keeping with the place, her wedding ring and a splendid diamond one on her middle finger and a pink coral one on the other middle finger. Her face is good looking but not very pretty. She was very quiet and very much more ladylike than her sister, a coarse rough girl with a dirty snuff-coloured handkerchief on her head, a loose black jacket and a green skirt, much too long in the front. She brought us coffee and jam and seemed very respectful to Mrs. Paton. We could see some dirty little brethren in the general living room. It is very sad to see such relations for an English gentleman.

We have been warned not to go to Rhodes as there is a Pasha there who is well aware of our digging in Karpathos and angry that the packing cases were not opened.

There is little doubt that the big pot the workmen stole from us and buried is here. T and M hearing the description went to see it but some lies were told so they did not succeed. The Kaïmakam sent for T this morning and pitched into him well and asked him many questions as to his intentions. Truly the balmy days of excavators are over.

---

[56] From the Bents' 1885 trip, this was Kýrios Spirídonos.

A certain Mr. Logothetis, who is the richest man in Astypalaia and who has a daughter who he hoped I will love like a dear sister, and who has been obliged by M's fawning [?], begs us to dig on his property and is most polite but it is evident he does not wish us to dig without him. We are to send for him if we think the place looks likely. Well! we shall see how it all turns out. It is midday; we are just going to lunch and embark for Astypalaia.

[Sunday] March 21st Astypalaia. We did not start till 3, though we were ready at 12 but, of course, the papers were not. We had a very rough but good passage on a large schooner, 5 sailors, us, a *zaptick* (a Turkish policeman) and a man who keeps a café. We reached this at ¼ to 2. 50 miles across open sea, and as usual first went to the café. We only took 20 minutes climbing to the town – fortunately there was a bright moon.

After a meal of our own food, with some coffee, we were conveyed to a small room up an outer ladder and most awfully dirty. A dusty desk or writing table and the usual divan made of trestles and boards with a dirty mattress on it was the only furniture. My hammock was set up and we lay down amid the mingled smells of petroleum lamp and earthen water jar – T had his own bedding.

We went to the café to eat our breakfast, not yet having a fire of our own and hoped for a better lodging, but finally found out this was the best to be got. A woman called Virgó scrubbed under my directions, used much water and got off an immense deal of mud, having previously removed a great deal of loose dirt in her petticoat as a dustpan. Then she left it very wet and was considered done, but I asked the son-in-law of Mr. Logothetis if she might have a cloth to dry it a little and much more mud departed. Now it is raised to the rank of a very dirty English floor – and the fleas did not die.

This book is so full of fleas that it must make people want to scratch themselves, but they are a matter of such awful importance to me that I hope for forgiveness.

We were lent a table, some chairs, a covering for the sofa and some very grand bedclothes for T, so we are pretty well off. M has a kitchen underneath. We live in the greatest publicity. A good view can be had through the open door and we have constant visits.

The women here wear a beautiful dress. Their heads have a long yellow scarf wound round and hanging in loops below the waist, behind and in front, over a little cap covered with beads and spangles and very large earrings of silver; a shirt with embroidery round the tail and very large sleeves like those of Nisiros. These they tie up to their shoulders when at work.

Their dress is made of a fine cherry-coloured cloth; a full skirt, echoing the embroidery of the skirt, down the front is let in about half a yard of blue cotton. Round the tail of the skirt is turned up about 8 inches of course white flannel and above that about 8 inches of the blue, so really there is not so very much red. The jacket is of the same red, square backed to the waist, where it branches out to 2 points which are left open and above the slit 3 big silver buttons all tight together. A sort of bib is worn in front, 5 or 6 inches wide, and down to the waist, embroidered and spangled and sometimes covered with gilt coins and a bit of white calico sewn to the end, which looks as if meant to tuck in but is not.

I photographed a bride. Her head was covered with a sort of mitre of gold and seed pearls and gauze scarf; dress velvet, silk shirt, jacket fringed with immense silver buttons and big blobs of glass which looked crystal, and on the back there was a quantity of silver. 3 pairs of silver gilt and pearl earrings larger than bracelets. She had 2 holes in her ears. I took 6 photographs. I have now a wretched glass but it is an improvement on paper.

The inner part of the town is walled in, a mass of narrow, crooked dirty passages, some about 16 inches wide. Altogether there are here in and out 400 houses. The people are friendly and pay many, many, long, long visits, very good for our tongues, but tiring.

Three linked chapels, Hóra, Astypálea.

On Monday [March 22nd] T and M left me, T to examine Mr. Logothetis's property and M to shoot. I poached some eggs for lunch and had many other good things to eat. And Mr. Logothetis's only sister, Maria, who lives opposite, came with her daughters, Smaragda and Marigo, to do their work with me. I am sure they meant to be kind but I became very weary of them. After luncheon we went for a long walk together to the Livadhi and they were constantly calling 'Virdzinia! Sit down you go too fast; we cannot cut along like you'. I was so much amused at hearing them use that very expression.

T did not think Mr. Logothetis's field a good place. He is quite a prince here.[57] A quarter of the island belongs to him and *all* the cattle. And all the inhabitants are his relations but even his sister speaks of him as 'Kyr. Ianní', Mr. John.

His only daughter is a very nice woman indeed – Eirenakí, or Renatzí as they pronounce it here. He and his daughter adore each other and she says her husband is a soft man (in island dress) and the only consideration he obtains is being father to the little prince and princess. The sister of Kyr Ianní lives in a small mud-floored windowless hovel with poultry and cats and wears patched, ragged dirty clothes, and her daughter goes bare legged. His brother, Kostí, is a rough but pleasant man who looks like the mate of a ship, and his dirty babes go bare legged too. They have a brother, a doctor in Adalia and no doubt a very smart man.

Kyr. Ianní has more property than money. He has £1000 in a church and his son-in-law told T he had heard of banks, but T quite failed to make him understand the banking system.

---

[57] On nearby Sámos the Logothetis name was a prominent one. Lykourgos Logothetis (1772-1850) led an uprising against the Turks in 1821. The remains of his 'tower' are still to be seen in Pythagório.

Yesterday we paid several visits here preparatory to our intended departure this morning. We went to see Eirenaki, and as her house is on the same pattern as the others here I will describe it. About 6 feet from the end of the room is a high wooden settle with a step. On this at one end is a trunk or chest. When you have gone up the step, up the settles and on to the chest, you have only about 3 feet to climb to get into the bed. Care must be taken not to fall through the valance into the kitchen part of the room.

When you are in the bed there is a sort of closet at the end of it, the outer side of which is a kind of dresser for plates and under which is the entrance to the kitchen. No man's house is his castle here, or in other islands, because all the tag rag and bobtail rush in wherever we go and the mistress says 'Go out! Go out! Children!' But they always stay. They screech at their children a good deal but they never obey.

The old Bishop of Malatyeh,[58] having travelled as far as Lyons, has come to the conclusion that the children of Europe do not cry so much as the children of Asia, but they seem much the same.

We were all ready to start when the wind changed and became contrary and very violent indeed, so here we are, the house rocking and no hope of departing tomorrow.

Friday, March 26th. Here we are still. The wind has been banging and rattling night and day and these 2 days we have to keep our shutters shut. The house quakes fearfully and wind comes in at all sorts of cracks. It is not very lively; we are now hearing a good deal of gossip. People seem very jealous of Kyr. Ianní and say he is a most mean man to his relations, but I heard from one woman that they never lend anything without taking a pledge. Another funny thing that they wear their skirts wrong side out every day and right side out for great feasts. The white flannel border that I have described is the lining.

We are rather under a cloud here with one family for the supposed embezzlement of seven Turkish pounds. Giorgios Morphinos, who we met in Nikaria,[59] gave us letters to his wife and then asked T to carry Turkish pounds, for which T gave him a receipt. He then wrote another letter to his wife and gave it to Theodore. At the last minute Theodore said 'Now we cannot go straight to Astypalaia but must go round by Kalymnos and Samos and we might not get to Astypalaia before you do, so what shall be done about the money?' He said he would have it back, so requested the last letter and opened it, took out the receipt, returned it, put the letter in another cover and off went we. On getting here we delivered the letters and had numerous visits from Mrs. Virginia Morphino's mother and at last she asked for the money. We explained but in the letter Giorgios said he wasn't sending 7 Turkish *lires* and no explanations would satisfy her. And Mrs. Virginia has never been near us. Her husband was to be here in a week from now so we shall be cleared.

Sunday, March 28th. Two days more of this wind have gone by and we are now at the end of the 5th day. There is an idea that we may get away tomorrow but they say there will be a difficulty about collecting passengers and we may not start till late. I do not much relish a night on board. There is a little cabin with 2 bunks and about a foot and a half in height and 2 cats and 2 dogs on board. On our way here a cat got into the cabin and finding there was some fish in one of our baskets, tore the Turkey-red mouth of it and devoured most of the fish. M threw away all the remains he could find at once, but on arriving here some

---

[58] A fellow passenger with the Bents on the ship to Constantinople in February: 'There were not many passengers. The most remarkable was the Prince Bishop of Malattiah, in the middle of Armenia, an old gentleman wrapped in many dressing-gowns which he varied daily, not so his shirt that he had made a vow not to change. He wore red, blue, green, violet, brown, and was very cheery and talkative in Italian.' (*Chronicles* I, 132)
[59] Ikaría.

fragments tumbled out. He surveyed them then with satisfaction, murmuring 'They can be cleaned', but I am glad to say they were not presented to us.

I do not believe we shall start tomorrow.

It was a very evanescent satisfaction to me next day to have been the only person who thought we should remain, but we never got away till Wednesday, March 31st, when we reached Kalymnos in 9 hours and remained the night with no adventures but that I was given a very nice sponge ...

My Fifth Chronicle
1888

On Thursday February 24th [Thursday was February 23rd] about 4 we left 'The Town'[60] in the *Alphée* for Syra, picking up letters at the post on the way. We had no remarkable fellow passengers and reached Syra on Saturday morning about 4. As we passed the Dardanelles we got our case and opened it in a spare cabin, got out some things, put in others, and consigned it to the ship for England.

At Syra we met Matthaios[61] and he had all our goods from the hold in Andoni's boat by the time we appeared. We did not go to Matzis' Hôtel d'Angleterre in the Platea, I am sorry to say, as M had taken beds at his old hotel, now the Aigyptos, thinking well to be near the port. They were very civil and clean but the cooking not nearly so good.

Theodore at once took to visiting ships to put into practice our plan of chartering a ship and becoming pirates and taking workmen to 'ravage the coasts of Asia Minor'. Everyone says it is better to dig first and let them say *Kismet* after, than to ask leave of the Turks and have them spying there.

In the afternoon the nicest captain they saw, and of the best vessel, came and sat in our bedroom and signed a 'symphony'[62] and now all we had to do was to prepare to set sail in the *Evangelistria* schooner with Kapitan Nikólaos Lambros, whose countenance speaks volumes for his excellent character. We had a large room, but none too large for our baggage, that part of it which we opened I mean.

Who now more busy than M victualing for 2 months and engaging workmen! We got 11, of whom one Vasilis is the chief, who are all from Antiparos and worked for Mr. Swan at his mines, and some have already dug for Theodore in that island 4 years ago.[63]

We have sacks and sacks of biscuit flour and other provisions and we also have plenty of arms, bills of health from England and the Greeks, and I think all we can require – except our beautiful hydraulic winch and 6 yards of chain, etc., which by someone's stupidity, not

---

[60] Constantinople. The couple had journeyed directly there from England in January 1888 in the hope of returning to excavate on Thásos in northern Greece. By 14 February, however, Theodore had admitted defeat as regards returning to the island, where he had made substantial discoveries the previous season. He writes as much to Cecil Smith at the British Museum: 'Our negotiations with Hamdi have entirely broken down; he is quite inexorable about the knotty point of allowing anything of value to go out of the kingdom...Consequently we have with much regret abandoned Thasos for this year. We stay here until the 23rd and after that go to Syra with the intention of "going on a cruise" for a couple of months... Seriously though I am thinking of Capo Krio and the Doric Chersonese ...' The Bents steam away from Constantinople on the Messageries Maritimes vessel Alphée (2095 tonnes), built 1861, and 'de 1881 à 1888 revient en Mediterrannée entre Marseille et l'Egypte'. (http://www.messageries-maritimes.com/alphee.html).

[61] Manthaios Símos, the Bents' dragoman.

[62] Agreement or contract.

[63] In 1884 Theodore 'excavated' with the Swan brothers on Andíparos.

'February 24th about 4 we left "The Town" in the Alphée for Syra.'

ours, has not reached our hands. We went to church on Sunday to a tidy little chapel, which they say will be closed if Mr. Binney[64] is no longer there to keep it up.

It was not till the afternoon of Wednesday February 28 [Wednesday was 29th February 1888] that we started, having previously got all our beds and big baggage on board, so we had only a few trifles, which looked sufficient for a 'tour on the Continent' to take with us. We had a fair wind and all sails set till evening, when some were reefed up and it rained and we retired downstairs.

I ought now to describe the ship. She is blue and has high bulwarks and a queer little stumpy figurehead. In the stern the cabin is situated where we abide. We go down a ladder and can stand up in the middle. There are 2 wide bunks; 7 feet of floor between. T sleeps in the one facing the stairs and the other is full of luggage. There is a high seat round the stern end full of things and some little cupboards above; one, a glass one, contains the holy pictures and a little lamp hangs there at night.

At the opposite end is my hammock. In the middle our 2 chairs and table which can stretch half on to my hammock and all are easily folded by in stormy weather. Next comes the hold, a very roomy place filled with sand. Here M and the 11 have their beds and also cook. In the middle stands our little cooking stove and M can sit and cook in his folding chair with great dignity.

The four shipmen, Kaptan Nikólaos, Andreas the *Devtero Ploiarchos*, or Mate, Gregorios and the large stout 'boy' Stavros (which means cross) sleep in the fo'c'sle. There are 2 large boats, one within the other in the middle over the hold, and a little galley on deck. There is a dog called Zouroukos, who was at first terrified, and us and the little tortoise, Thraki.

Now to return to that miserable evening [Wednesday 29 February?]. M, as usual, was incapacitated and the excellent sailors did not understand cooking for us or waiting at table, so we began by a soup which tasted as if it were made of the sea and rice. After a few mouthfuls I said I had no appetite and would sooner lie down. T was furious. He only got some very nasty mush and no coffee and found himself some walnuts.

He wished the chairs and table at the bottom of the sea and complained bitterly of his size and wished he were no bigger than me, 'and now', he said, 'I shall be *most wretched* if

---

[64] He died on Sýros on 12 March 1888; his grave is in the atmospheric cemetery on the way up to Áno Sýros.

you take to being seasick! And you *know* you *needn't*. You are going to do it on purpose! *Eat*!! And I'm so beastly hungry and can't get enough to eat!' Poor thing I pitied him very much and myself worse for I thought it a dreadful beginning for a Pirate Bold, but my seasickness ended by this refusal of a very horrid dinner.

T spent the night saving himself from falling out of his bunk, for the little ledge which holds in a sheepskin is of little use for his luxurious bedding. I like my hammock better on dry land than at sea for it waggles and shakes and jumps and trembles at every ripple, so of course in the storm I had a fine tossing.

We continued our journey all night but when morning came the captain said we had better make for Myndos[65] on the coast and shelter there. We consequently were at anchor till the following morning but in just as rough water. We were like in a lovely lake between Kos, Kalymnos and the mainland with many islets round but it was too windy to stay on deck. M had recovered and we had a more comfortable dinner. In the morning breakfast was a great struggle as we could not get at the things we wanted.

We were off again on Friday morning and had a really delightful sail, turning to our right round Kos where we could plainly see the square fortified town with the newer one spreading round and even distinguish the top of the plane tree which was there B.C. and was supported by marble columns now grown into it. …We want to go to Agios Jannis, south of Astypalaia, a small island inhabited only by shepherds.[66] …On Thursday 8th at 5 o'clock we arrive in Dacha Bay. Here the cape is so low and narrow that Kos appears over it. Seeing the village full in sight but about an hour off we decided that nothing could be done there and that it was not even safe to land, so, as it was also very tiresome having to seek places for ourselves, we settled to go to the island of Symi and pick up a guide.[67]

Accordingly on the 26th 9th (I am always writing the Old Style dates)[68] we started before sunrise and reached the bay called Panormos [Sými], or shelter for all, which is landlocked and where a large white monastery is situated on the shore. This contains very few monks but all the labourers and their families abide there, and as it is the only house of call for any who enter the bay, the great pile of buildings is a lively place.[69]

M was at once dispatched to the town[70] to see what antiquities he could pick up 3 hours off; so he was to stay the night. We went ashore and landed on the quay and went up some steps and in at a great door into a court with 2 storeys of cloisters and one other row of rooms above round it, and the church standing in the middle as usual. We ascended a staircase and were received at the corner of the cloister and seated on a divan and given coffee and jam by the Ekonomos or Holy Housekeeper, the old Egoúmenos   being asleep.

Presently he came out and seated himself in a passage which runs away from the cloister to the garden. A fireplace was there and cupboards and there were 4 or 5 steps from the cloister and there sat down the Holy Egoúmenos Macharios, with a brazier before him and our chairs were put round and we talked a long time, and after refusing to sleep and eat in the monastery we said we would return to our ship after vespers or *Esperinó*, which we did.

---

[65] The ancient city of Mydos/Myndus, modern Gümüslük, some 25km north-west of Bodrum.
[66] Ag. Ioannis or Sírina, the uninhabited islet due west of Tílos and south of Astypálea; they visit the island later.
[67] Theodore and Mabel it seems never disembarked at the Knights' city of Kós. She is probably reading of the famous tree from *Murray's* guide. It would have told her that Hippocrates' plane tree is 12m around and that it was said to have been planted by the great doctor, who used to teach under its shade.
[68] There was a 13-day difference between the calendars.
[69] The Bents have landed on the southern point of Sými, at the celebrated monastery of Taxiárhis Mihaïl Panormítis.
[70] Sými town on the north of the island.

Saturday March 10th. Great bustle on board. The ship was to be blessed. The *eikons* were brought up and dusted, lanterns lit and a clean towel spread above the companion, and they upon it, with a bowl of water.

Presently Kapitan Nikólaos came on board with a priest and a deacon and a red bundle, out of which came the stoles, books, a bunch of basil and a splendid large, silver dyptich: the Holy Virgin and Child and the Lord Michael, the Archangel, the Judge, and Archgeneral, to whom the place is dedicated, also a lantern. Then we all took our places, bareheaded all but me. The crew stood first and 'the boys' one side and we on the other, amidships.

It was a beautiful, interesting and solemn sight. There were many prayers to many saints, but also many in which we could join, 'for the safety of the ship and the living therein'. Nikólaos and all his companions, from every kind of misfortune at sea, and that our souls and our bodies might be blessed and that we might all abide peacefully together.

All this time Gregorios had been standing with a silver censer and the deacon came round and incensed us all, and then the priest who had been reading the Gospel about the Angel, troubling the water and blessing it and stirring it with his hands, came and sprinkled us and all parts of the ship with the basil and when that was done the priests turned round to chat and drink some wine, while the bundle was re-packed and Kapitan Nikólaos divided the remains of the water between our two largest water casks.

About 10 o'clock we went ashore and were gaily greeted by the Holy Macharios, who exclaimed, 'I'm looking a bit to pass the time and amuse myself'. He had had a pot brought him from the kitchen and put on his brazier, and there he was peeking and stirring and skimming, and I am sure I think it was a very nice occupation for an old gentleman, don't you?

I forgot to say that the day we landed was Friday of the Souls, so after the service a small table was put in the middle of the church with a white cloth on it and a high dish of *kollyva*, boiled wheat with sugar and raisins in patterns on it, and a candle stuck in the midst. This was blessed and afterwards handed round. Everyone had to take a handful and it was supposed to benefit the souls in Purgatory.

The church is frescoed all over inside and the carving is very fine. There is a huge 6 feet high silver Archon (Lord) Michael with only his face painted, a sword in one hand, a good little swaddled soul in the other, and some wicked person under his feet. On the other side is a curious representation of the Entombment of our Lord, made in Russia. All the figures are on wood, in very low relief and painted. They have clothes of cloth of gold with embroidered borders. The sheet is cloth of silver, also embroidered and it is all very well executed.

Well, to return to our muttons, or really lambs, we were invited to luncheon and accepted and a most tremendous meal it was. The table was round, covered with a blue-checked cotton cloth and drawn up to a sofa. There were plates for 8 and scattered round were 19 lumps of torn bread. In the middle a large round bowl of soup, with rice and egg in it. T sat in the middle of the sofa, I on his left, and the jolly old Egoúmenos on his right, perched on a bolster, with his left stockinged foot on the sofa and his right on the ground.

He was not very near the table, but with a loud sigh of 'Ahhh! Good luck to us all!' he set to work to give us brimming plates of soup. Next we saw a large iron pie-dish with a very young roast lamb lying in it. This was brought to the table and dished by a Papas, taking it by the legs and putting it in a dish, the Egoúmenos crying out, 'take care that the little thing don't cry!'

Now he set himself to work with a knife and fork and cut off the legs. These he deposited with his fingers at the other end of the dish and began to cut the sides, revealing a stuffing of rice, chopped liver and raisins. He helped us liberally you may be sure and very delicious it was.

He constantly added to our supply some tasty mouthful torn off with his fingers and while helping us, helped himself to a spoonful of stuffing and when the 4 other eaters began to help themselves, 'Stop!' he said to one, 'I want to steal a bit of that' and tore off 2 mouthfuls for me. T being next to him he could thrust bits into his mouth.

Then 4 heads on a baking dish were presented; the old gentleman seized the jaws of one and tore out the tongue and offered it but we assured him we could eat no more. 'You'll eat some mesythra and honey?' said he. 'Willingly' said we.

But fancy our horror at seeing the attendant youth bearing in the roast leg of a larger lamb on a long spit. This the Egoúmenos seized and cutting off bits with his knife delivered them to us in his fingers, having first been made to eat some peculiar pickle to keep up our appetites. We had to eat a little, also some salad.

Finally we had *mesythra* and honey, of which there were dishes out of the comb, and then *yaourt*, a sour milk, with honey. 'You must take some Kyriá Verghiniá, it will make all you have eaten sit down comfortably.'

Just as this excellent meal was ended, in came M and he took his place and dined while he told us he had heard of lovely antiquities at Symi but could not even see them. The Turks have made such strict laws and one is afraid of the other telling of him if he sells them.

We thought there was no use remaining and anyhow it was better to be out of that port, hard to leave, so having engaged a man called Joannis, as a sort of pilot or guide and picked up the loaves of bread made with our flour, and borrowing a ship's chart (English) we bade adieu to our kind entertainers and with much tacking sailed away.

As the anchor was coming up we looked at each other and said 'Whither?' So we looked then at the chart and chose a bay called Aplotheka (or simple receptacle) on a large promontory south of Cape Krios and where are the ruins of ancient Loryma. We arrived there in the middle of the night.[71]...

...On Friday [March] 23rd, we set sail early but were long in getting out of the 'lake'.[72] Then after much calm we had great contrary winds and we changed our destination 8 times between Myra, Kastelorizo, and Leviza.[73] Every time we changed to please the wind it changed too and there we stuck in the same hole in the sea and neither back nor forward could we get 2 days and nights.

By the time the first night came I did not feel so well as could be wished, so stayed in bed next day. There was no pleasure in being up and it was hard to dress and everything was banging about, so I read and had tea and arrowroot biscuits.

Next morning, Sunday [March] 25th, we had violent wind and reached Myra with great difficulty. We were all on deck holding on hard and getting ducked and wondering what was going on in the cabin, but it was impossible to look and see till we anchored in the wildly tossing water. Thus we found the table had not fallen, only turned round and shed all that was on it, but nothing was broken.

We soon landed on some rocks on the edge of a desert of some miles. First we sat and rested, then having brought our prayer books we pretended the rocks were a cathedral. Next

---

[71] Aplotheka Bay (below 'Kavo Kryos', on the Turkish coast, northeast of Rhodes, and an access to the ancient cities of Loryma and Sigas).

[72] The Bents have been at anchor off the little island of Tersane across the bay from modern Fethiye.

[73] The area of Myra and Leviza is one of the main regions for classical antiquities and, above all, the famous Lycian rock tombs. The present-day island of Kastellórizo (Megísti) is the southernmost Greek island, although just a nautical mile off the Turkish coast, opposite Kaş.

we roasted chestnuts and afterwards walked over the desert. There were great things like railway embankments running in all directions and all carved into ribs down the sides by the wind, very hard to climb up if not down. There is a great shingly beach between this and the sea and under it a great city. In between this and the mountain is the present village of Myra. In the night, that anchorage not being safe, we voyaged some miles and found ourselves at the I. of Kakova, in a lake again but bare and rocky, not wooded like our last.

Monday [March] 26th. Off with M and all the 'boys' to go to Myra. We were in the big boat. We tried to land at another place where a dismal swamp which joins the desert runs down to a sandy beach. At each side of a pretty wide bay close to the rocks ran down a small river with a sandy bar. We tried both sides and ran aground, got off, and at last clambered on to quite the outside of a mountain, where it was deep enough for the boat and had to scramble round it, over rocks and through bushes, up and down, as we could, then down on to the sand and finally struck into this path on the left bank of the left river which led us to Myra.

We did not know that a wider river was in the middle, over the bar of which we could have got the boat and had only about a mile or so to walk. But if we had we should have missed seeing a huge palace wanting only roof, windows and wallpapers to make it quite comfortable. It had an inscription about the Emperor Trajan. The whole swamp is crowded with ruins of fine buildings and great sarcophagi stick up in the water (oh! how the ship waggles!). This river smelt strongly of sulphur and indeed all the bay. When we left the swamp there was a great cracked plain and then Myra.

By the bye, a horse had been awaiting me at our first anchorage, so he was found and we lunched from our basket at his owner's house in a balcony, which serves as a kitchen, with the addition of some eggs and milk, at 10.30 and none too early for our appetites. Then, I bestriding my steed, which I can now do nearly as well as Jeanne d'Arc, we went first to the theatre, the best preserved I have seen, very nearly perfect, but a little earthquaked and much sunk.

I forgot to say that on our arrival at the village we met the *Egoúmenos* of a monastery of which he is the only monk. St. Nikolas was born here so it is considered a very holy spot.[74] The Russians therefore spent 4 years and £T 2000 on digging out the old church 18 or 20 feet full of earth. There are still some of the old vaults and domes with frescoes and pavements tessellated. Now it is re-roofed. It reminded us of S. Clemente in Rome. We were so hot we were thankful to have a shady seat and some coffee.

The women here all wear the dress of Kasteloriso: long full coloured cotton trousers, then the shirt fastened down the front with 5 large round silver buckles, and then married women wear a gown slit up to the waist at the side. The 2 front bits are often tied back as they become mere strings. Then a jacket with sleeves ending above the elbow and very long-waisted, and very low is wound a scarf. The girls do not wear the gown. They have a fez on the head and a turban round it or not.

But the strangest and most wonderful thing in Myra is the mass of rock-cut tombs, just like houses, one above the other on cliffs around. One stands quite free on a jutting point. Certainly things cut in the live rock are more awe-inspiring than anything built. They made quite a little door, then dug away inside as large as they like and made a slide for a slab of rock to slip along, and when the funeral was over drew this door shut and chiselled off the handle, so these doors only look like one panel of a large one. I had

---

[74] Nicholas of Myra (AD c. 270–c. 350). His relics were removed from Myra in the 11th century and ended up in Bari, Italy. A tiny fragment of his finger has recently (2006) been donated to his eponymous church in Ermoúpolis, Sýros.

seen pictures of these but was perfectly delighted to see them actually. I never thought I should be in Lycia.

Before leaving we returned to the house where our basket was. A little girl of 6, fully dressed, ran out to see us. When we got into the sitting room she retired to a carpet with some pillows on it and a blanket, which she held up to her chin as she sat by a window down to the floor. Her mother complained that she had seen the doctor, who, as she has a fever, told them to keep her in bed. We said they should keep her covered and lying down and not in such a draught, with 2 windows and 2 doors open. The mother shrugged her shoulders and said, 'You see she does not like it'. All children are treated like this, also dogs.

We returned much better than we had come. How glad I was not to have to walk; it was bakingly hot. Not long after we had got among the rocks which skirt the plain we came to the river, where was our boat, which 2 'boys' had fetched. When we arrived at the bar, we alone stayed in; with much heaving and many fears of upsetting, we were lifted over into the sea. We brought an inhabitant with us as guide and interpreter who brought his bedclothes.

Tuesday [March] 27th. We went in the other direction, westwards, down a strait and landed at a mass of ruins (Kakova) where the Austrians spent 2 years, 4 years ago, with 2 ships taking anything they liked, lucky Austrians!, and they painted their flag very large on the rocks. Here, of course, we found nothing to dig, but were very much interested with all we saw. This town had sunk in the sea a good deal and we could see foundations under water. There were high sarcophagi everywhere about and the remains of houses cut in the rocks. They evidently never put a loose stone in when they could cut a wall from rock and acted as if it were soapstone. There is a Turkish village and we persuaded a man for about a shilling to remove his wooden lock from his door for us. We lunched ashore and returned to the ship about 12 and we commenced a holiday, which for me is now at its 4th day.

We now decided not to go to Cyprus,[75] whither our papers were made out, as we have not enough things to make a great fuss about and transshipping would be difficult, but to go back to Syra. First to go to the island of Kasteloriso, where there is a Greek consul, and have a manifesto made that we came from Turkey so that the Greeks may not touch our things in Syra, and then who is to know where we call on the way.

Now all was preparation for this civilized place. T assured himself that his collar and tie were at hand. I hung out my best Ulster[76] and produced respectable gloves and shoes and M came to ask if the Kyria has not a pair of scissors to lend for the barber. Kostandinos cuts hair very well, that of others, not his own, and shaggy locks 2 inches long were cropped to the roots, beards shaved and trimmed. We really made a very tidy party when we reached our goal. They are a very clean set of men and most obliging and hard working. What the hold would have been like with 12 Bulgarians in it is awful to think. The 'boys' speak of it as '*to káto kósmos*', the lower world.

We had a very dreadfully calm voyage. An average time from Myra to Kasteloriso is 6 hours, though in our storm we did it in 2. We took about 26. We did not land in the regular harbour. The captain said questions would be asked as to why there were 18 people in such a boat. We landed about 8 [Thursday, 29 March?]. It is a flourishing looking little town, divided by a point on which rise the ruins of a red castle. The name should be Castelrosso, but first the Greeks have made it 'orso' and then stuck in an 'i'. The Genoese or Venetians made it.

---

[75] A fascinating aside. No previous indication exists of the Bents having planned to explore on Cyprus. There are no records of them ever having set foot on the island (although Theodore published an article on a visit there by Oger, Lord of Anglure ('A Pilgrimage to Cyprus in 1395-6', *Fraser's Magazine*, Vol. 103 (23), Issue: 618 (1881: June), pp. 818-821)).

[76] Mabel's sleeveless cape/coat.

The harbour of Kastellórizo.

Kaptan Nikólas was greeted wherever he went by friends. He did not seem anxious to be questioned much and once when asked where he had come from gaily answered, '*Apo to pelago!*' (from the open sea). I was delighted at this answer and so, when some women, sitting spinning on rocks, called out, 'Welcome Kyria,' to which I answered, 'Well met!' and then asked, 'Whence have you troubled yourself?' '*Apo to pelago!*' I smilingly replied and swept on round a corner where we could laugh, and who more than Kaptan Nikóla. We went on board for luncheon and I stayed and T did not go on shore till evening. We lunched and now behold Mr. and Mrs. Theodore Bent kneeling at the washtub!!

I think if we had planned it beforehand the idea of so large an undertaking might have frightened us and we might have put off this evil day till a more evil day still fell on us. But it was not so very evil after all.

Stavros was amazed at seeing the india-rubber come up wrapped round the clothes. We made him fill it over and over again from the sea and we knelt and kneaded where a sail gave shade and had soap and soda in our basin and when we had washed enough we together and in unity wrung. Then T started off to the starboard side to hang them up. He soon came back asking, '*How* many towels did we wash?' and '*How* many have you there?' Well we counted and counted but there was no making the clothes come home right from this wash. T had gone down for pins and away a towel had flown to the fishes. They were very soon dry and folded and smoothed and stroked and fondly patted and proudly contemplated.

When night came we became rather anxious about the 'boys', they were so late. Not till half past 8 did they appear, gay enough, and usually by that time snores resound all over the ship. As we get up about 5 and always have a great hurry over our dressing, breakfasting and bed-making, it is not to be marvelled at…Yesterday morning, Good Friday [March 30th], we had a very quiet voyage hither to Patara,[77] not too rapid by any means…We found nothing but inscriptions. Altogether 14 in Patara.

Tuesday [3 April] it appeared too rough for the boat so they went overland and I had to stay behind and as before I got on very well and only landed to bathe, which was delicious. When they returned at dark they had brought the tools and done with Patara and now today, April 4th, we are off to Sirina, a small island called also Agios Ioannis, south of Astypalaia. We are to go north of Rhodes, but are being becalmed I fear, a mixture of gentle contrary winds too.

April 5th, Thursday. Dreadfully quiet all yesterday. We worked at the inscriptions, 37 in all, copying out, sewing together, etc., and by evening had not passed the place we could reach by rowing 1½ hour.

It is now near 5 and we have got on gently today and passed the n. point of Rhodes, *Koum* (sand) *Bournou* (head) and close up along the town, very pretty in the evening light. These 2 days we are lunching and dining on deck, not proudly on our chairs, but on the ground where we shall not be in the sailors' way. I wonder what we shall have for dinner. We have no meat, as we could not obtain a kid from the Yourouks at Patara, our last chicken consumed yesterday. No milk. We have some eggs and bacon still. We had potted lobster and some arrowroot pudding for luncheon. We started with the largest piece of Gruyere I ever saw in a private family, or even in a grand hotel; a foot long, high and wide in proportion. It is less now.

The ship is kept very clean and there are no native fleas, but bugs abound. The captain however takes no more personal shame to himself at being their proprietor than to the hosts of mosquitoes or mice. They drop out of the deck and I always keep my mosquito curtain up (for we have them too sometimes) and that saves me a good deal.

April 6th, Friday. The wind got up in the night and in the morning became too strong for us, so here we are back rolling in Aplotheka[78] again. Our only consolation is that we now possess a kid, milk, eggs, a *mysethra*, and a salad of sorrel. The 'boys' and the sailors dine in a very simple way. First the biscuits are soaked, huge and many broken in big bits, then a bowl of lentils, beans and onions, or fish broth, is put in the middle and they all sit round on the deck and those who have no spoons scrape up with their knife on a bit of bread. The crew have a little table 6 inches high and tiny stools as high. They always sit near the steersman. Afterwards all crumbs are swept up and the place and the pots washed, and then they stroll to the water and drink. Indeed everyone is always drinking…Sunday [April] 8th. Well, this morning we set sail, but not before dawn, for Sírina, as we thought and with the *scirocco* we should have sailed s. of Telos, which lay directly in our way. We were busy in the cabin but I peeped up and saw we were steering straight for Nisiros, north of Telos. So I told T and he proposed to go up and row the captain, but I said I would make less formal enquiries. I said to Grigorios, 'We are going n. of Telos it seems?' 'Yes,' he said, 'But *very* far n! We are going to Nisiros.'

'We are keeping up to Kavo Kryos.'

'Well! I suppose we shall tack soon, for we shall no doubt pass Telos as close as we did Rhodes.'

The wind was quite fair for Telos. He shrugged his shoulders as if to say *he* could not help it, and I said 'How soon shall we tack for the south?'

---

[77] Located on the mouth of the Xanthos River, Patara was the major port of Lycia. St Nicholas was born there.
[78] The winds force the Bents again towards the Turkish mainland and Aplotheka Bay (Kara Buran), the long spit of land across the water, north of Rhodes.

'We are going inside Nisiros.'
'But why?'
'To go to Kos!'

So T went up and there was a frightful, awful row. Now he said he did not wish to go to Sírina at all, and would not go there, and there was no water or harbours and many rocks and no lighthouse and he was always considered a most noble man, and honourable, and so on. 'Very well', said T. 'Go straight to Syra and we will go to the judge and the consul,' etc.

Later with M as a go-between we said if we could not go south, we did not mind going to a small island called Levitha[79] on the way to Syra. This was agreed upon and we did not care a bit. It rained. I looked out again and saw that now we were going s. of Nisiros and close to Telos, past Kavos Kryos and Kos, where we had agreed to anchor for the night far to the dim north.

'Where are we going now, Andreas?'
'To that place,' very sulkily.
'What place?'
'To Sirina!'

Of course we have lost hours by going so far north and are now fearing a calm. Next morning [Monday, 9 April] about 10 we reached Sirina and landed after luncheon.

We walked across the island to the sea at the other side, where there is a deep bay. Here was a sort of farm, a very irregular enclosure of loose piled stones and very thick walls. The only thing with mortar was the oven. An old woman came out of the dark hut where she was shut in and brought us out little square blocks of wood to sit on and she directed T to where there were some old stones and so I returned to the ship with one man and the rest went off, but finding the earth all gone and only foundations on rocks they returned and we set off again in the afternoon.[80]

We appeared to get on very well and rushed up past Nisiros, Kos and Kalymnos, nearly up to Leros, and we also seemed to be getting on well during the night, but when morning dawned we were down at Astypalaia.

All day [Wednesday, 11 April] we tacked and got up to Amorgos and in the morning, instead of having got round west of Tenos, we found ourselves far too much n.e., at Nikaria, and soon the wind got so bad that we had to go for shelter to Patmos. We were not near the town but a place they call the Kambo. We landed with great difficulty and some very poor and kind people asked us into their cottage, which was very clean, and gave us coffee and I entrusted to them the photos I had done 2 years ago of the monks and the monastery to take to the *Egoúmenos*.

We got very wet in returning to the ship, so I never landed again and T only to take some quinine and little gifts to our entertainers. By this time we were not on speaking terms with the captain, or rather he with us. We set sail again about 11.30 and had been gone about 20 minutes and were at luncheon when suddenly we found ourselves shut up, all down on one side. The captain had thrown the rug and books down on us and when T asked, '*vroché*' (rain), he replied '*borá*' (squall).

On looking out an awful scene presented itself. All the sails and sheets were flying wildly and all our men were helping the sailors to loosen them. Behind a black wall was advancing and just on the extreme stern heavy drops were falling. Waterspouts and spindrifts were rushing along and we were tearing back to the rocks. The sailors looking anxiously for the

---

[79] One of two islets between Léros and Amorgós, the other being Kínaro.
[80] The island is uninhabited now but for summer shepherds and yachts.

Grand Hôtel d'Angleterre à Syra   Ξενοδοχεῖον τῆς Ἀγγλίας ἐν Σύρῳ.

The Hôtel d'Angleterre in Platía Miaoúli, Sýros, where the Bents liked to stay.

moment to cast anchor, and glad enough we were to hear it go down. Soon torrents of rain fell and there was no more hope of leaving Patmos that day nor the next and it was not till the morning of Sunday 15th that we started.

We had 7 of these squalls and had we not had so many men on board we should have fared like a rather smaller ship a little further out, which had all her sails torn to ribbons. This voyage was very quiet and a little slow and we had not very much to eat. We got near Syra at sunset but did not get to anchor till 2.30 [Monday, 16 April]. They had to row in...[81]

---

[81] April 1888 was the last time the Bents sailed and explored in the Dodecanese (although in 1890 they excavated in 'Rough Cilicia' on the Turkish west coast). After Sýros now the couple headed once more to Constantinople and returned to London via Berlin.

Sidetrack 1

Some related extracts from other articles by J.T. Bent

Theodore it seems travelled frequently to the Dodecanese in his thoughts, inclining, when appropriate, to add paragraphs touching on the islands in more general articles referring to regional customs or topics. Several of these paragraphs are reprinted below, amounting, as they do, to a small corpus of asides and footnotes. They often repeat ideas he had previously published in extended articles.

'The Three Evils of Destiny'[82]

This is the general term given by an inhabitant of the Greek islands to express the three important events of life – birth, marriage, and death…

Marriages are almost invariably celebrated on the Sundays immediately preceding the great Lenten fast. This is a distinct survival of the ancient custom of marrying during the first month of the year, from which fact that month was formerly called Gamelion; and in the islands where men are often absent during the summer months in search of work abroad, the betrothals usually take place shortly before Christmas, with a view to the marriage being solemnised on one of the Sundays of the great marriage month. On the remote island of Telos, which is inhabited by semi-barbarous Greeks, they retain the most extraordinary and elaborate system of wedding festivities, which continue for the space of a fortnight, during which time the village enjoys one long holiday and cessation from work,

The first ceremony takes place ten days before the crowning, with what they call the 'little flour,' when each household brings a handful of meal to the bride as an earnest that more will come presently, and as an intimation that all know about the wedding, and are prepared to share in the coming festivities. On this day and on every day before the wedding, the female friends of the bride assemble to assist in preparing the trousseau. Two days afterwards the 'greater flour' takes place, when large quantities of grain are brought by all the friends for the wedding-cakes. This is distributed by the young men to all the houses which possess a grindstone, to be ground, and late in the evening, accompanied by the sound of the bagpipe and lyre, they go round to each house to collect it, and deposit it in that of the bride, where a table is spread, and great festivity and dancing ensue.

---

[82] Extracts from Bent's article in the *Scottish Review* (10:20, 1887: Oct, pp. 369-387). This apparently was the original article that motivated Theodore to write more extended pieces on these events for other periodicals – relying on his own notebooks, his wife's journals, from memory, or other written sources. There is some doubt as to whether he witnessed all these activities firsthand.

Celebrations, Megálo Horió, Tílos.

The Sunday immediately preceding the wedding is called the 'maccaroni day,' when the female friends go each to the house of the bride with their low wooden tray to assist in making this commodity. But on the Wednesday before the wedding the festivities begin with real earnest. The young men go on this day to the mountains for brushwood to heat the oven for baking the wedding-cakes, and are accompanied for part of the way by all the villagers, and are met in the evening on their return with music, and the night is spent in dancing and revelry. Next day the same ceremony is gone through with regard to providing fish for the wedding banquets; all day the young men cast their nets into the sea, and again pass the evening in festivities. On Friday they go to the mountain farms for the kids and lambs necessary for supplying the table, and thus the preparations are concluded.

On Saturday the bridegroom moves to the house his bride is bringing to him as her dower; he is accompanied by his young male friends to the sound of the lyre and song; his bride is there to greet him, and both of them have brought their luggage. Then follows a very curious ceremony, when the stone walls are hung with embroidery, and the clothes of the happy couple are suspended one by one from a pole which has been hung for that purpose just over the door; first a pair of trousers is hung up, and then a dress, and as each garment is suspended a song appropriate to each is sung by the young men and maidens who have assembled. When all are hung up the priest blesses them, and then the nuptial couch is decorated, a sort of tent being formed over it with an old piece of embroidery, called a *sperberi*, which is handed down in families until quite worn out. This *sperberi* is commonly known as 'the heaven,' and is most elaborately blessed by the priest on each occasion that it is called into use.

When all this ceremony is over the marriage contract is signed; the most worthy men of the village are called in to append their signatures to it; congratulations follow, and then a little dancing, but the party breaks up much earlier than usual this evening, the key is turned by the best man in the door, and he is left thus to meditate over the second evil of destiny which the Fates have ordained for him.

At Telos, where they have such very long prolonged festivities, the Monday after the crowning is jocularly called the bridesmaid's wedding day, and is consumed in singing and dancing. If the day is fine the party repair to the bride's threshing-floor – for of course every bride counts a threshing-floor among her other belongings – where they eat, and sing, and dance as only sturdy island Greeks can dance, without ever thinking it necessary to take any rest.

The following day is the 'cook's day,' that is to say, in honour of those who have assisted in preparing the victuals for the wedding festivities, when the entertainment is usually given at the threshing-floor of some near relative of the bride's; and as it is the last of the series of entertainments, it is kept up until a late hour in the evening.

And yet there is one more festive gathering before the whole of the wedding festivities are over. This takes place on the fortieth day after the crowning, when the priests come to bless the embroidered garments as they are taken down from the walls and the pole over the door. It is considered highly essential to have this ceremony performed, and many cases are on record of misfortune having ensued from its omission. Then the *sperberi* is taken down from off the nuptial couch, and packed away till the wedding of the bride's daughter. They sing once more and dance once more, and then the bride and bridegroom sink altogether into insignificance...

In different islands they have many and various ceremonies attending the home-coming of the bride after the knot has been tied in church. In Karpathos the bridegroom's mother meets them, as after a christening, with the incense of the share as described above...

Families of the better class have their own tombs, where the bones of one deceased member are left until it is necessary for them to make way for the incoming tenant. In the island of Karpathos they put plates into the tombs; why, no one seemed to know. But it is an obvious continuation of the ancient custom, for in some old tombs we excavated close to the spot, we found as many as sixteen plates laid out with the remnants of a feast for the dead, which had been there untouched for perhaps two thousand years...

'Parallels to Homeric Life Existing in Greece To-day'[83]

Progression is slow in all primitive societies, and no more primitive society can be found existing in modern times than amongst the Greeks of the remoter islands off the coast of Asia Minor. Here we may find parallels without end to the life as recorded to us by contemporary Byzantine, Hellenistic, and classical writers, but the subjects of comparison on this broader basis are so numerous, and fraught with so many philological and ethnological intricacies, that I propose now to take exclusively the poems of Homer, and from the experiences of several winters passed amongst the peasants of these remoter islands to give parallels which I have gathered, and which, I think, will establish quite as clear a continuity of custom and myth, as could be obtained from a perusal of Chaucer with regard to the continuity of custom and myth in England.

---

[83] Extracts from Bent's article for *The National Review* (Vol. 11, Aug. 1888, pp. 825-836).

The festive and commemorative poems, and the death-wails of these people, which have been handed down from generation to generation, will prove of great assistance to us in this study. Individuals are still chosen as bards amongst them, whose vocation in life gives them leisure for composition and committing to memory; the blind man plays the lyre and sings for the dancers in the village square, the women as they work at their looms learn and invent death-wails...

The Turkish islands...are the most primitive. Many of them for long years have been left entirely to themselves, and in the mountain villages we were surprised to find complete autonomy, and the assemblies, the βουλαί, by which they govern themselves, partaking of quite an Homeric character. At Astypalæa, for example, the assembly of δημογέροντες, old men of the people, meets in the one broad gateway which leads into the town, just as in Troy, 'at the Scæan gate sat the elders of the people;' these elders are elected by voice and the acclamation of the people, no balloting, no other civilized process, only the form of the ayes and the noes which follow the proposal of the name; and furthermore they are like the Homeric 'old men of the people,' not necessarily old, not all Nestors, but ὠμογέροντες, men of weight, and recognized respectability. There is, however, generally a Nestor in these assemblies, who always speaks first, and whose opinion is almost law. No one dares to interrupt him; but when he has done, their tongues are loosened, and like the members of the Homeric assemblage in the third Iliad, they are extremely loquacious, like grasshoppers, which, sitting upon a tree in a wood, chatter with a shrill, small voice.'

When on the island of Karpathos, we accompanied the peasants of a mountain village to one of their pilgrim festivals, which, like the panegyris of old, is a curious blending of religious solemnity and mirth. After the service in the church was over, they set to work to cook their meal in huge cauldrons outside the church. The meat was cut up into tiny portions before boiling, as in the Iliad it is described: 'On a tray they placed the portions of meat, and Antomedon held them whilst the noble Achilles cut them up and divided them into pieces, whilst Menætiades, a hero resembling the gods, lighted a fire; then Achilles sat opposite to the noble Ulysses against the other wall, and charged Patroclus, his companion, to sacrifice to the gods, and he cast the first morsels into the fire, and then they stretched forth their hands to the prepared food which lay before them.' This is an exact picture of what we saw, except that, instead of Patroclus, the priest cast a morsel into the fire, to propitiate the saint whose festival they were celebrating, and then, without aid of fork or spoon, they stretched forth their hands to the savoury morsels before them.

'And when,' says Homer, 'they had removed the desire of eating and drinking, the young men of the Greeks all day propitiated the god with singing, chanting the joyful pæan, and celebrating the far-darting Apollo, and he heard them with joy.' Thus did our pious peasants celebrate in song, for hours after the feast was over, Saint Demetrius,[84] in whose honour they were making merry. 'Nay, as for me,' says Ulysses, 'I say that there is no more gracious or perfect delight than when a whole people makes merry and listens to the singer. This fashion seems to me the fairest in the world.'[85]

---

[84] Theodore's reference to the saint here is puzzling. The great Saint Dimitrios Myrovlitos has his name day on 26 October. The Bents were on Kárpathos for Easter 1885 and Bent is probably recalling one of the associated Orthodox events.
[85] *Odyssey* IX, 1-20.

'On Karpathos there is, in the mountains, a shepherds' village. In the summertime these shepherds disperse over the mountains to pasture their flocks...' Ólymbos, Kárpathos.

When the singing was over, our festive peasants played games on the level space outside the church door, as the suitors in front of Ulysses' palace 'took their pleasure in casting weights and spears.' A game called *omades* or *chermades* indiscriminately, is the favourite modern game for the men at these feasts, and it consists on throwing a heavy flat stone so as to knock the coppers off a certain mark. In the fifth Iliad we read how 'Tydides seized in his hand a stone (the same word χερμάδιον is used), a mighty deed, which no two men could bear, such as men now are, but he shook it easily all by himself.'...

But to return to our pilgrims; when tired of games, the men and women began to dance, the blind bard was placed on their midst with his lyre, an admiring crowd gathered round, and men and maidens joined hands alternately in the circular wavy *syrtòs*; sometimes they moved slowly; sometimes the leader of the circle indulged in acrobatic feats, sometimes they sang part-songs, sometimes they were silent; but as Homer has described this circular motion and the interlacing steps to the life, I cannot do better than quote from the eighteenth Iliad his description of it. 'There danced the youths and maidens, worth many oxen apiece, holding each other's hands near the wrist; of these the maidens wore fine linen dresses, and the youths were dressed in well-woven coats, slightly shining with oil; these also had beautiful garlands, and those wore golden swords, suspended from silver belts. Sometimes with skillful feet they nimbly ran the circle, as when a certain potter sitting shall try a wheel, fitting it in his hands to see if it will run; and at other times they retreat to their ranks. But a great crowd stood around the pleasing dance delighted.'

Curious, too, is the phrase 'worth many oxen apiece,' ὑλφεσιβοῖοι. A shepherd still will dower his girl with flocks, and one of the shepherds of this very village at which the pilgrimage of which I have spoken took place,[86] had a daughter whom he promised with a dower of many sheep and goats to any young man who could beat her in a foot-race – the story of Atalanta over again; and this coy Karpathiote maiden is as fleet of foot as any nymph who accompanied Artemis to the chase. Until her prime is past she will certainly not be caught...

Female life in the islands exhibits many parallels to Homeric days...In Karpathos washing is done by the feet in wooden trenches... Two women sit at either end of this trench and tread the articles with their feet, continuing at this work all day, and to while away the time, and soften the labour, a man will often come and play the lyre to them. In Telos each woman has her washing-trench, which she takes to the seashore, and all day long treads her linen in it...

On Karpathos there is, in the mountains, a shepherds' village. In the summertime these shepherds disperse over the mountains to pasture their flocks, and live for the most part with their families in caves called *mandras*. On visiting some of these we realized how well Homer must have known them when he sang of the cave of the great Cyclops Polyphemus. Outside are the pens, walled in and topped with brushwood, in which the lambs and kids of different ages are kept; inside, the receptacles for milk are ranged, the cauldron for boiling milk are ranged, the cauldron for boiling the milk is simmering in one corner, the cheeses are drying in baskets of wicker-work on a ledge above, still called by their **classical name of** τυροβύλια. When the shepherd and his family are absent, they just roll a big stone to the cave's door to prevent any animal from straying in. They sleep on thick goatskins, spread on the mud floor, and their shoes are made of pieces of untanned oxhide, fastened to the foot with thongs of the same material, just like those of the swineherd described in the Odyssey thus: 'Now he was fitting sandals to his feet, cutting them out of fresh-coloured ox-hide.'...

Perhaps the most perfect parallel of all those which modern Greek life presents to that pictured to us by Homer, is to be found in the conceptions concerning death... Death, the lord of the lower earth, is known now, as in olden times, by the name Charon... The modern Charon has a wife, Charontissa by name, Queen of the lower earth, who rules in what Homer would call 'the groves of Persphone.' She is, in fact, Persephone herself, and assists her lord in his effectual endeavours to prevent the dead from escaping their prison, which is illustrated by the following mœrologue[87] from Astypalæa: –

Who is the King of the lower earth? Who is the Queen of Hades?
Who are the key-keepers who keep you locked up?
Make for the King a throne, for the Queen a canopy,
And for Charontissa also a golden mantle,
That they may allow you to come back for three feasts a year;
For the raising of the Cross, for the blessing on Epiphany,
And on the Sunday of Easter, for the resurrection of Christ.

---

[86] Mabel notes in her diary: 'On Thursday the 9th [April], being tired of Elymbo [Ólymbos] and finding it very damp, we determined to go to Dhiapháne [Dhiafáni] on the coast, more especially as there was to be a pilgrimage and great festivities.'
[87] Laments.

'Personification of the Mysterious Amongst the Modern Greeks'[88]

During many visits to the Greek islands, and constant intercourse with the inhabitants, I have often been struck with a trait in their character which they have inherited, with slight modifications, from their ancestors. This is the personification of mysteries which they do not understand, atmospheric phenomena, curious-shaped rocks, mysterious diseases, and death; and in their personification they have followed much the same line that characterized the myths of ancient Hellas...

The mystery of death and a future existence, perhaps, offers us the most perfect parallel between ancient and modern beliefs. The personage called Charon, who ferried the souls across to Hades, is altered in very few respects today;...they tell you of the gardens of Hades, where the souls of the departed are planted and come up as weird plants...The same idea is conveyed in ...a popular death wail in Karpathos, which runs as follows; 'Charos wished to plant a garden; the old men he planted, and they came up as lemon-trees, with tortuous stems; the young came up as tall, erect cypress-trees; but the little children he placed as flowers in his vases.'...

After death the spirits if wicked men rest not in peace, they become vampires (Βρουκόλακες), more especially if, at the time of death, they have not made peace with all their enemies; for this reason, dying people often ask for a glass of water in which to melt a pinch of salt for each enemy they can remember, saying, as they put it into the water, 'As the salt has melted, so may my curses melt.' They only leave bodies in the earth for a year in many islands, and when they exhume them, and the flesh is not decayed off the bones, they imagine that the deceased is still wandering in ghostly form, eager to suck the blood of man or beast. There is no peace for him in Hades, no peace for his relatives, for he returns to his home, and 'feeds on his own,' as the expression goes; he brings with him plagues, typhus, cholera, etc. The grass dies near his grave, the flowers wither and are eaten by worms, ruin comes on the herds, and dogs wander ominously about the streets howling at night. This idea of vampires is an ancient one. Homer tells us how the shades in Hades had an idea that by filling themselves with blood they could return to life, and, consequently, eagerly supped up the blood of slaughtered sheep. So now a poor ghost is supposed to suck the blood of his relatives, that he may gain strength for his nocturnal wanderings.

Some terrible scenes are witnessed on these occasions, at which the priests secretly connive: the bones are burnt, and the ashes are scattered to the winds; or else they are packed in a bag and carried to some island rock, the idea being that ghosts cannot cross water. Sometimes, however, they are satisfied that the spirit is put to rest by the priest who reads a prayer over the grave, and sprinkles it with sacred oil.

In Karpathos they call these beings 'Cains,' affirming that Cain, who slaughtered Abel, on his death became the first wandering vampire. They here mix them up with another species of hobgoblin, evil spirits formed like men, with asses' or goats' feet, which appear on the earth for ten days only, from Christmas to Epiphany, during which time they subsist, like the Amazons of old, on snakes and lizards. They come down the chimney at night; so a careful housewife is bound, during this time, to keep embers smouldering on the hearth. When crickets come to a house, they say it is a sure sign that Cains will come and play all

---

[88] Extracts from Bent's piece in the *National Review* (Vol. 9, April 1887, pp. 224-233) and reprinted in *Littell's Living Age* (May 7, 1887, No. 2237).

sorts of horrible antics with the food and household utensils. Cain was a huge man, they told me, taller than the tallest chimney, with the feet of goats, and wooden shoes; in short, the satyr of ancient days. In like manner they imagine Lazarus to have risen from the grave an abnormally tall, thin man, with a round, flat head; for this reason they call the pole with an oval board at the end of it, which they use for putting their bread into ovens, a Lazarus.

'The Carpathiote Dialect'[89]

A pastoral village to the north of Carpathos has a population of Greeks which speak a dialect of remarkable purity. Ludwig Ross mentioned it as a regret in his 'Inselreisen'[90] that he could not visit this village. We made a point of going there, and besides curious customs and folk-lore I collected several interesting words and expressions, amongst which are the following.

The shepherds speak of their mules as κτήματα, or possessions, and do not understand the use of any such word as ζῶα or μουλάρια, common elsewhere in Greece; this use of the word must date from classical times. Their goats they call χίλια, or thousands – a word suggesting patriarchal life, and flocks which could not be counted for numbers; and in distinguishing their goats they have many curious words. Πολιομούρι is used for a goat with grey face and ears, retaining the classical use of the word πολιες, which in the vulgar is ψαρός; ρουσσύμερτος expresses a goat with red cheeks; here we find the word ρούσσεος, unknown in modern Greek, but common amongst the Byzantine authors, who appropriated the Latin word *russeus* for red. For an apron they use the New Testament word λέντιον, instead of the common podia or 'μπροστελὰ; and the narrow alleys of the village are called ῥύμαι – again a New Testament word, which is used in the Acts for the street which is called Straight, and recalls the celebrated oracle to one's mind, ἔσται μὲν 'Ρώμη ῥύμη καὶ Δῆλος ἄδηλος.[91] A young man they speak of as ἄωρος, 'unripe,' reminding us of Herodotus's ἄωρος θανεῖν and Plutarch's ἄωρος πρὸς γάμον. Κανάχια is a word in use for caresses, kisses, which strikes one as a possible survival of the classical words κανάσσω, κανάχη, a sharp noise. Though in classical times the meaning was confined to the sound of water, there is no reason why after the lapse of ages it should not be applied to the noise produced by the lips.[92]

These are only a few amongst the many strange words in use still in this mountain village of Carpathos, which is cut off by the difficult passes from communication with the other villages of the island; but the most curious thing of all in connexion with the dialect of this place is the existence of a gamma under circumstances which are at once suggestive of the old digamma in real life. This is especially remarkable in a dialect which drops the ordinary gamma on every possible occasion, for ἐῶ is used for ἐγὼ, ἤτρωα for ἔτρωγον, &c. Before the word υἱός, 'a son,' they place a hard gamma, which I have not only heard, but seen written in marriage settlements. A mother calls her son Γυιέ μου. Then this gamma is inserted after the diphthong εὐ; for example, they say πιστεύγομεν and δουλεύγομεν. Whenever this occurs this intrusive gamma is hard and perfectly distinct from the modern use of the *g*, reminding

---

[89] See page 56. Published in *Athenæum*, 3011 (1885, July), p.48.
[90] For Ross, see page x.
[91] A reference to the strange *Sibylline Oracles* (lines 428-9, and elsewhere), and the play on the names of Rome, Delos, and Samos: "ἔσται και Σάμος ἄμμος, ἔσεται Δήλος ἄδηλος, και Ρώμη ρύμη τα δε θέσφατα πάντα τελείται. Σμύρνης δ' ολλυμένης ουδείς λόγος, ἔκδικος ἔσται, αλλά κακαίς βουλῆσι και ηγεμόνων κακότητι..."
[92] See note 51, page 58.

one more of the change which has converted the Latin *rastare* into the *guastare* and the French *gâter*.

'Modern Life and Thought amongst the Greeks'[93]

We will now proceed to take examples of the educational work that is in progress from various points of the Turkish Empire. Where the monastic resources are sufficient, and where help is not urgently required, matters are allowed to pursue their old course. On the island of Nisyros, for instance, we found the Archimandrite Cyril, of the monastery of the Holy Virgin of the Cave, the chief mover in the diminutive society on this island; besides acting as banker for the peasants and issuing cardboard notes, an inch and a half square and of the value of one penny each, signed by his name, as a medium for exchange,[94] and, besides paying for a doctor, who attends the poor people free of charge, he has likewise, with the income of the monastic property, established a boys' school and a girls' school at Mandraki, the chief village on the island, which are presided over by efficient teachers, who have been sent out thither through the agency of the Society;[95] the books of instruction have likewise been provided from the same source. But all this has been done at the expense of the monastery, which is a prosperous one; and to realise the real benefit of religious institutions on mankind, and the readiness with which even effete monastic institutions work for the advancement of the Greek race, one ought to travel in the out-of-the-way corners of the Turkish Empire.

In Greece proper, the work of the monasteries is practically over, since the Government has taken upon itself the sole superintendence of education, and is alone responsible for the improvement of the people. What monasteries once were, and what good they have done, can now only be realised in Turkey; the smaller ones, as the one in Nisyros, for example, have provided education for the masses; the larger ones, as Mount Athos,[96] have provided instruction in the higher branches of learning, and act as universities; and it is a question open to much doubt, as to whether the Greeks have benefited by the transfer of education from the priests, who have acted for ages as their protectors from annihilation and barbarism, to the Government schools; in Turkey, as we have seen, they provide for the better education of the clergy, and, if this can be effected, the priesthood will continue as the natural instructors of their flocks.

On the neighbouring island of Telos, which is inhabited by semi-barbarous Greeks, living in a state of shocking ignorance and superstition, the monastery, in a similar fashion, has of late years commenced to work for the good of the people. Five years ago, the monks decided to expend £25 per annum on the maintenance of a schoolmaster, who gave us a lamentable account of the ignorance he found there, and which still exists among the elder inhabitants; but when we visited the school, each boy had in his hands the books which the Society has printed for educational purposes, and the elder ones could read Xenophon quite fluently, and translate it into modern Greek. The monastery of Telos is far from being as rich as that of Nisyros, so the inhabitants have to die without physic, and the girls have to

---

[93] From 'National Life and Thought of the Various Nations Throughout the World: a Series of Addresses' (New York, MDCCCXCI, Chapter XVI, pp. 287-302).
[94] This token is exhibited by Mabel later; see page 185.
[95] The contemporary 'Hellenic Philological Syllogos' of Constantinople and Athens.
[96] Theodore never stepped foot on the Holy Mountain – Mabel would not have been allowed to accompany him.

grow up without instruction; but doubtless, in good time, the Society will step in and see to the rectification of the latter deficiency, for such ground as this is the field on which the Society has done such admirable work elsewhere. But the island of Telos is only thinly populated, and as remote a spot as well could be found from any centre of civilisation.

Sidetrack 2

On Insular Greek Costumes: an Appendix by 'Mrs. Bent'

The Bents were keen collectors[97] of fabrics and costumes and sought to acquire all manner of things on their travels, making frequent references to such material in their writings.

Some of the outfits Mabel purchased (often having to pay top-dollar for them as vendors knew the market well) have survived. Some of her island costumes were featured in a major 1914 exhibition at the Burlington Fine Arts Club[98] and found their way later, and tortuously, to the Benaki Museum in Athens.[99]

Some 25 years before this event, Mabel proudly displayed a selection of her Greek costumes at a lecture given by Theodore for the Royal Anthropological Institute. Her 'catalogue' featured as an Appendix in the subsequent publication.[100]

Appendix by Mrs. Bent

The following is a description of the articles collected during three winters in the Sporades and Cyclades which I have the honour to lay before the Institute for inspection:-

A figure dressed as a woman of Niseros, in a short narrow dress of white cotton, embroidered round the tail and round the square neck, and with wide sleeves, embroidered in stripes of various coloured silks, and with silver embroidery on the shoulders; over this a very wide dress of turkey-red, half a yard shorter, and sleeveless. A black kerchief across the forehead, and a yellow one over that, hiding the mouth.

A figure dressed as a woman of Karpathos 150 years ago; raw silk embroidered with a wide border in green, dark blue, and red silks, also all round the neck and down to the knees. The sleeves are square, and the pattern mostly a chequer. The dress is 8 or 9 feet long, and

---

[97] They were also dealers. The Victoria and Albert Museum has some relevant correspondence, including a nominal file MA/1/B1149, linked to two associated files: RP/1913/1748M: 'Embroideries [lent] for photographing [Greek embroideries to be photographed to "give in as simple a manner as possible a series to illustrate the uses of Greek embroideries"]' and RP/1929/6460: 'Re embroideries & tiles property of the late Mrs T. Bent.'

[98] See Sir William Matthew Trevor Lawrence and A.J.B. Wace, *Catalogue of a collection of old embroideries of the Greek islands and Turkey*, Burlington Fine Arts Club, London 1914.

[99] For a wonderful presentation by Ann French on the background to this (with illustrations), see http://patternsofmagnificence.org/

[100] J.T. Bent, *Journal of Royal Anthropological Institute*, Vol XV (4), 1886, pp. 391-403.

Lace sample brought back from Greece by Mabel Bent.

a great tuck forms it into a double skirt. Embroidered trousers. Round the waist a silk scarf, embroidered, and on the head, over a black kerchief, a long silk scarf called βομια (νιδοκια): three or four silver and gilt chains, &c., round the neck, and chains with drops across the brow, also pear-shaped silver-gilt ornaments with glass garnets hooked on the top of the head, with several chains coming down the cheeks, and rings about 4 inches across hanging from them.

Sindhonia [sheets] of Karpathos, one cotton and the other silk, and both embroidered very similarly in red and dark green. These are 2 yards deep; 18 inches at the bottom is more handsomely embroidered, and separated from the rest by a gold insertion 1½ inches wide. In this island, where they have no bedsteads, they are used as wall hangings for festive occasions.

A Sindhoni of Niseros worked in brown, light yellow, and blue, and with a pattern resembling that of Karpathos.

Two pillow covers from Karpathos, silk, with a green and blue border on both sides, that they may show when the pillowcases are stored in piles.

Two towels of Karpathos, cotton, with woven coloured ends.

A swaddling band from Karpathos, 150 years old, cotton closely worked with black and red silk on the outer end, and with a small sprigged pattern on the rest.

A bank-note, a card 1¼ inches square, covered with paper with the name of the Monastery of Spiliane and the signature of Kyrillos, the Prior, who issues them – legal tender in the Turkish island of Niseros.[101]

---

[101] See page 182.

Sidetrack 3

The itineraries in the Dodecanese

The Bents in the Dodecanese – their itineraries (and J.T. Bent's subsequent writings).

The travellers record no landings on Kos, Léros or Hálki (although they sail close by and refer to them). No references are made to the small islands of Arkoí or Psérimos.

Rhodes [1885: Feb 7-20]

'Rhodian Society', *Macmillan's Magazine*, Issue 52 (1885: May/Oct), pp. 297-303.

Nísiros [1885: Feb 23-24]

'On Insular Greek Customs (With an Appendix by "Mrs. Bent")', *Journal of Royal Anthropological Institute*, Vol. XV (4), 1886, pp. 391-403.

Tílos [1885: Feb 25-Mar 4]

'A Protracted Wedding' *The Gentleman's Magazine*, October 1888, Issue 265:1894 (1888: Oct), pp. 331-341 (also slightly modified for *English Illustrated Magazine*, 93 (1891: June), pp. 672-676).
'The Three Evils of Destiny', *Scottish Review*, 10:20 (1887: Oct), p. 369-387.
'The Islands of Telos and Karpathos', *Journal of Hellenic Studies*, Vol. 6, 1885, pp. 233-242.
'Parallels to Homeric Life Existing in Greece To-day', *The National Review*, Vol. 11, Aug. 1888, 825-836.

Kárpathos [1885: Mar 5-Apr 20]

'On a far-off island', *Blackwood's Magazine*, Vol. 139, Feb 1886, pp. 233-244.
'The Three Evils of Destiny', *Scottish Review*, 10:20 (1887: Oct), p. 369-387.
'A Christening in Karpathos', *Macmillan's Magazine*, 54 (1886: May/Oct), pp. 199-205.
'Idyls of Karpathos', *Gentleman's Magazine*, 260:1862 (1886: Feb), pp. 185-190.
'Rock-Cut Tombs of Carpathos', *Athenæum*, Issue 3002 (1885: May), p. 606.
'On Insular Greek Customs (With an Appendix by "Mrs. Bent")', *Journal of Royal Anthropological Institute*, Vol. XV (4), 1886, pp. 391-403.
'The Islands of Telos and Karpathos', *Journal of Hellenic Studies*, Vol. 6, 1885, pp. 233-242.
'The Carpathiote Dialect', *Athenæum*, 3011 (1885, July), p. 48.
'Personification of the Mysterious Amongst the Modern Greeks', *The National Review*, Vol. 9, April 1887, 224-233.
'Parallels to Homeric Life Existing in Greece To-day', *The National Review*, Vol. 11, Aug. 1888, pp. 825-836.

Agathonísi [1886: Mar 3]

'Greek Peasant Life', *Fortnightly Review* 1886, 40:236 (1886: Aug.), pp. 214-224.

Lipsí [1886: Mar 3-Mar 5]

Pátmos [1886: Mar 6-Mar 10]

'What St. John saw on Patmos', *Nineteenth Century: a monthly review*, 24:142 (1888:Dec.), pp. 813-821.
'Revelations from Patmos', *Blackwood's Magazine*, Vol. 141, March 1887, 368-379.

Kálymnos [1886: Mar 18-Mar 20 (and Mar 31)]

Astypálea [1886: Mar 21-Mar 31]

'Astypalæa', *The Gentleman's Magazine*, Issue 262:1875 (1887:March), pp. 253-265.
'Parallels to Homeric Life Existing in Greece To-day', *The National Review*, Vol. 11, Aug. 1888, pp. 825-836.

Sými [1888: Mar 9-Mar 10 (?)]

'A Piratical F.S.A.', *Cornhill Magazine*, Vol. 58 (11), December 1888, pp. 620-635.

Kastellórizo [1888: Mar 27-Mar 30]

'A Piratical F.S.A.', *Cornhill Magazine*, Vol. 58 (11), December 1888, pp. 620-635.

Sýrna (Sirina/Agios Ioannis) [1888: Apr 9]

'A Piratical F.S.A.', *Cornhill Magazine*, Vol. 58 (11), December 1888, pp. 620-635.
'Sirina', *The Classical Review*, Vol. II, No. 10, 1888, p. 329.

Pátmos [1888 Apr 11 (?)-Apr 12 (?)]

'What St. John saw on Patmos', *Nineteenth Century: a monthly review*, 24:142 (1888:Dec.), pp. 813-821.
'A Piratical F.S.A.', *Cornhill Magazine*, Vol. 58 (11), December 1888, pp. 620-635.

Bibliography

Theodore Bent's monographs, articles and papers relating to this volume

Bent, J.T. 1885. *The Cyclades, or Life Among the Insular Greeks (London)*.

Bent, J.T. 1885b. *The Cyclades, or Life Among the Insular Greeks (new edition edited by Gerald Brisch, Oxford 2002)*.

Bent, J. T., 1885. 'Rhodian Society', *Macmillan's Magazine*, Issue 52 (1885: May/Oct), pp. 297-303.

Bent, J. T., 1885. 'Rock-Cut Tombs of Carpathos', *Athenæum*, Issue 3002 (1885: May), p. 606.

Bent, J. T., 1885. 'The Carpathiote Dialect', *Athenæum*, 3011 (1885, July), p. 48.

Bent, J. T., 1885. 'The Islands of Telos and Karpathos', *Journal of Hellenic Studies*, Vol. 6, 1885, pp. 233-242.

Bent, J. T., 1886. 'On a far-off island', *Blackwood's Magazine*, Vol. 139, Feb 1886, pp. 233-244.

Bent, J. T., 1886. 'Idyls of Karpathos', *Gentleman's Magazine*, 260:1862 (1886: Feb), pp. 185-190.

Bent, J. T., 1886. 'On Insular Greek Customs (With an Appendix by "Mrs. Bent")', *Journal of Royal Anthropological Institute*, Vol. XV (4), 1886, pp. 391-403.

Bent, J. T., 1886. 'A Christening in Karpathos', *Macmillan's Magazine*, 54 (1886: May/Oct), pp. 199-205.

Bent, J. T., 1886. 'Greek Peasant Life', *Fortnightly Review* 1886, 40:236 (1886: Aug.), pp. 214-224.

Bent, J.T., 1887. 'Astypalæa', *The Gentleman's Magazine*, Issue 262:1875 (1887: March), pp. 253-265.

Bent, J. T., 1887. 'Revelations from Patmos', *Blackwood's Magazine*, Vol. 141, March 1887, 368-379.

Bent, J. T., 1887. 'Personification of the Mysterious Amongst the Modern Greeks', *The National Review*, Vol. 9, April 1887, 224-233.

Bent, J. T., 1887. 'The Three Evils of Destiny', *Scottish Review*, 10:20 (1887: Oct), p. 369-387.

Bent, J. T., 1888. 'Parallels to Homeric Life Existing in Greece To-day', *The National Review*, Vol. 11, Aug. 1888, 825-836.

Bent, J. T., 1888. 'A Protracted Wedding' *The Gentleman's Magazine*, Issue 265:1894 (1888: Oct), pp. 331-341. (also slightly modified for *English Illustrated Magazine*, 93 (1891: June), pp. 672-676).

Bent, J. T., 1888. 'What St. John saw on Patmos', *Nineteenth Century: a monthly review*, 24:142 (1888: Dec.), pp. 813-821.

Bent, J. T., 1888. 'A Piratical F.S.A.', *Cornhill Magazine*, Vol. 58 (11), December 1888, pp. 620-635.

Bent, J. T., 1888. 'Sirina', *The Classical Review*, Vol. II, No. 10, 1888, p. 329.

Mabel Bent's *Chronicles*

The Travel Chronicles of Mrs. J. Theodore Bent:

Volume I, *Greece and the Levantine Littoral* (Oxford 2006).

Volume II, *The African Journeys* (Oxford 2012).

Volume III, *Southern Arabia and Persia* (Oxford 2010).

Other related works of interest for this volume

Travel writers and guides

Ayliffe, R. *et al.*, *Rough Guide to Turkey* (2003).

Baedeker, K., *Greece: Handbook for Travellers* (1905).

Barber, R., *Greece, Blue Guide* (1995).

Byron, R., *Europe in the Looking-Glass* (1926).

Dubin, M., *Rough Guide to The Dodecanese and East Aegean Islands* (2005).

Dubin, M., *Trekking in Greece* (1993).

Durrell, L., *The Greek Islands* (1978).

Durrell, L., *Reflections on a Marine Venus* (1953).
Ellingham, M. et al., *Rough Guide to the Greek Islands* (1995).
Hogarth, D. G., *A Wandering Scholar* (1896).
McDonagh, B., *Blue Guide: Turkey* (2001).
Murray's *Handbook for travellers in Greece: including the Ionian Islands, continental Greece, the Peloponnese, the islands of the Aegean, Crete, Albania, Thessaly, & Macedonia* (1884).
Murray's *Handbook for travellers in Turkey in Asia: including Constantinople, the Bosphorus, Dardenelles, Brousa and Plain of Troy* (1878).
O'Connor, Scott, V. C., *Isles of the Aegean* (1929).
Ramona, P., *Les paquebots vers l'Orient* (2001).
Ramsay, W. M., *Historical Geography of Asia Minor* (1890).
Ross, Ludwig (ed.), *An Account of the Travels of King Otto and Queen Amalie* (1851).
Ross, Ludwig, *Inselreisen*, Tübingen (1840-1843).
Strabo *Geography* (Books 12 and 14) (Loeb Classical Library, trans. H. L. Jones).
Torr, C., *Rhodes in Modern Times* (1887) (new edition edited by Gerald Brisch, Oxford 2003).
Torr, C., *Rhodes in Ancient Times* (1885) (new edition edited by Gerald Brisch, Oxford 2005).
Tournefort, de, J. P., *Travels in the East, Voyage into the Levant* (tr. John Ozell, 1741).
Tozer, H. F., *The Islands of the Aegean* (1890).
Travis, W., *Bus Stop Symi* (1970).

History and archaeology

Barber, R., *The Cyclades in the Bronze Age* (1987).
Broodbank· Cyprian, *An Island Archaeology of the Early Cyclades* (2000).
Droop, J. P., *Archaeological Excavation* (1915).

Gardner, E. A., *Greece and the Aegean* (1933).
Manolakakes, E., *Karpathiaká* (1896).
Smith, C. L., *The Embassy of Sir William White at Constantinople 1886-1891* (1957).
Stoneman, R., *Land of Lost Gods* (1987).

Natural history and geography

Polunin, O., *Flowers of Greece and the Balkans* (1987).
Rackham, O. and Moody, J., *The Making of the Cretan Landscape* (1996).

Mythology and folklore

Graves, R., *Greek Myths* (1955).
Lawson, J. C., *Modern Greek folklore and ancient Greek religion: a study in survivals* (1910).
Rodd, Rennell. *Customs and Lore of Modern Greece*, London (1892).

19th-century travel equipment

Opie, R., *Rule Britannia: trading on the British image* (1985).
Opie, R., *The Victorian Scrapbook* (1999).
Victorian Shopping: Harrods 1895 Catalogue (1972).
Yesterday's Shopping: The Army and Navy Stores Catalogue, 1907 (1969).

Finds

There are two main online reference collections for the Bents' finds and acquisitions held in the UK:

The British Museum, London: http://www.britishmuseum.org/research/collection_online/search.aspx.
The Pitt Rivers Museum, Oxford: http://www.prm.ox.ac.uk/databases.html.

List of Illustrations[1]

Portraits

Facing title-page. Mrs J. Theodore Bent, 1847-1929: a studio portrait (detail), presumed taken in Cape Town or Kimberley in 1891. ©National Archives, Harare (Ref. No. 7677). J. Theodore Bent, 1852-1897: an undated portrait (detail) credited to the Lafayette Studio and used for the frontispiece of the Bents' monograph *Southern Arabia* (private collection).

Page iv. Mabel Virginia Anna Bent. Reproduced from *Hearth and Home*, 2 November 1893. From the Studio of H.S. Mendelssohn, South Kensington (private collection).

Page iv. James Theodore Bent. Obituary photograph from the *Illustrated London News*, 15 May 1897. Reproduced by permission of Bodleian Library, University of Oxford (shelfmark ref. N.2288 b.6).

Maps

Front section. The Bents in the Eastern Mediterranean. Drawn by Glyn Griffiths.

Front section. The Dodecanese and other islands. Reproduced from the 1885 edition of Bent's *The Cyclades, or Life Among the Insular Greeks*.

Page xiv. The Dodecanese and other islands. Drawn by Glyn Griffiths.

Page 67. 'Loryma', 'Lissæ', and Lydæ' on the Turkish coast. Theodore Bent's own details from a contemporary Admiralty Chart. Originally published in E.L. Hicks, 'Inscriptions found by Mr. Bent at Casarea, Lydae, Patara, Myra'. *Journal of Hellenic Studies*, Vol. 10 (1889), pp. 46-85.

Illustrations

Facing title-verso. Under sail in the Dodecanese: the straits between Rhodes and Turkey.

Page vii. 'Beauparc – Lady Lambert's House'. Mabel Hall-Dare was born here, in County Meath, Ireland, in January 1847. From a watercolour by Garrett Scanlan. Reproduced with the artist's kind permission.

Page xii. Theodore and Mabel's grave and memorial (right) in the churchyard of St. Mary's, Theydon Bois, Essex.

Page 2. The 'D'Amboise Gate', one of the entrances to the Old Town of Rhodes. © Nikos Kasseris.

Page 4. Turkish cemetery, Rhodes Town.

Page 7. Lindos, Rhodes.

Page 11. Acropolis above Megálo Chorió, Tílos.

Page 12. The Bents' Greek friend and *dragomános*, Manthaios Símos, in old age and among his family. © Andreas Michalopoulos.

Page 13. The small monastery below Megálo Horió, where the Bents roomed on Tílos.

Page 14. Megálo Horió, Tílos: 'I tried to sketch some of the women... No bribe whatsoever would induce any of them to stand for a photograph.'

Page 17. Theodore Bent's *lýra* acquired in the Dodecanese in 1885, and now in the Pitt Rivers Museum, Oxford (1903.131.18.F151). © Pitt Rivers Museum, University of Oxford.

Page 17. Theodore Bent's *samboúna* acquired in the Dodecanese in 1885, and now in the Pitt Rivers Museum, Oxford (1903.130.23.

---

[1] All photographs © Gerald Brisch unless otherwise acknowledged.

PR342Q). © Pitt Rivers Museum, University of Oxford.

Page 18. Local produce for sale, Tílos.

Page 21. Easter goats at Ag. Andónios, Tílos. The Bents also landed here.

Page 23. Tílos landscape.

Page 24. Antique altars in a ruined chapel, Tílos.

Page 25. Diafáni, the small harbour for Ólymbos, Kárpathos.

Page 28. The east coast of Kárpathos.

Page 32. A *tsamboúna* player at Easter. The cockerel is killed for eating when the music stops.

Page 33. Ólymbos, among the clouds.

Page 36. Above Diafáni, Kárpathos.

Page 39. Rhodian baptism.

Page 41. Picking olives, Diafáni.

Page 44. Beekeeper's store, Diafáni.

Page 45. '[A] plough such as Homer would have seen if he had not been blind. The chief requisite for a Karpathiote plough is a tree with a trunk and two branches: one branch serves as a tail, whilst the other, tipped with the share, penetrates the ground, and the trunk serves as the pole.'

Page 51. Easter and the windmills of Ólymbos. © Nikos Kasseris.

Page 59. The extensive, ancient site of Vrykoúnda, on the northern tip of Kárpathos, near Trístomo Bay.

Page 61. Red-figure *oinochoe* removed by the Bents from Vrykoúnda, Kárpathos, and now in the British Museum (AN538131 Registration No: 1886,0310.12 (PRN: GAA8083). Catalogue Xref: Vase: F28). © The Trustees of the British Museum.

Page 63. Rock-cut tomb at Vrykoúnda, Kárpathos.

Page 68. The polymath and overseer of Turkish antiquities, Osman Hamdi Bey (1842-1910).

Page 73. 'Donkey Island'. Traditional inter-Dodecanesian transport.

Page 79. Pilgrims on Pátmos.

Page 81. Plaque at the Cave of St John the Divine, Pátmos.

Page 86. Pátmos harbour, looking up to the Monastery.

Page 93. The caldera of Santoríni (Thíra).

Page 95. View over the Panayía Portaïtissa, within the Kástro of Hóra, Astypálea. © Marc Dubin.

Page 102. Distaff acquired by the Bents from the islands, and now in the British Museum (EU1972, Q.2511). © The Trustees of the British Museum.

Page 106. Mabel Bent's *Chronicle* covers for the years 1885 and 1886. Reproduced courtesy of the Joint Library of the Hellenic and Roman Societies, London.

Page 108. Along the lanes of the Old Town, Rhodes.

Page 111. Sými harbor.

Page 113. The small monastery below Megálo Horió, where the Bents roomed on Tílos.

Page 117. The ruined village of Mikró Horió, Tílos. In the Bents' time a thriving community.

Page 119. Trístomo Bay, where the Bents first landed on Kárpathos.

Page 121. Forks from Mabel Bent's travelling canteen, engraved with her initials (private collection).

Page 125. Plates and saucers acquired by the Bents from the Turkish coast and Rhodes (private collection).

Page 130. Interior scene, Ólymbos, Kárpathos.

Page 133. Vrykoúnda, Kárpathos, the subterranean cave-shrine of John the Baptist.

Page 137. 'This the men shot at, getting nearer and nearer till he got on fire.' Modern islanders shooting an effigy of Judas Iscariot at Easter. The Bents witnessed a similar traditional event in 1885.

Page 140. Ólymbos, Kárpathos.

Page 143. 'We had the greatest possible advantage for seeing this feast, for we could see both the eating and the dancing from our roof...'

Page 148. Rock-cut tomb, Vrykoúnda, Kárpathos.

Page 152. A 'very hideous statue, more than the size of a baby'. The limestone figure acquired by the Bents from Kárpathos, and now in the British Museum (EU1972, Q.2511. Room 11. Registration No: 1886,0310.1. PRN: GAA49603. Catalogue Xref: Sculpture: A11). © The Trustees of the British Museum.

Page 155. Pilgrim in the Cave of St John the Divine, Pátmos.

Page 161. Three linked chapels, Hóra, Astypálea. © Marc Dubin.

Page 164. 'On...February 24th about 4 we left "The Town" in the *Alphée* for Syra.' © Philippe Ramona (http://www.messageries-maritimes.org/alphee.html).

Page 170. The harbour of Kastellórizo.

Page 173. The Hôtel d'Angleterre in Platía Miaoúli, Sýros, where the Bents liked to stay: the building still stands. A reproduction adapted from a postcard of the time.

Page 175. Celebrations, Megálo Horió, Tílos.

Page 178. 'On Karpathos there is, in the mountains, a shepherds' village. In the summertime these shepherds disperse over the mountains to pasture their flocks...'

Page 185. Lace sample brought back from Greece by Mabel Bent (private collection).

The small motif that appears throughout is a design adapted from a Rhodian silver *didrachm* (two drachma) coin of c. 300 BCE. The bud is often cited as a rose, but more likely depicts a pomegranate flower or even hibiscus variant. It was drawn by Patrick Harris.

Index of Place Names[1]

Adalia (Antalya): 161
Aden: viii, xi, 11 n.10, 107 n.5
Ægean (Aegean): vi, 25, 38 n.32, 41 n.34, 71, 72, 73, 92
Agathoníssi: 73-75, 153
Agíos Kyríkos (Ikaría): 157, 158
Alexandria: x, 1, 42, 71, 77, 106, 116, 118
Almiró (Saría, Kárpathos): 150
Amorgós: 29, 72, 172
Anáfi: x, 11 n.10, 35 n.26, 72, 94 n.108, 107 n.5, 108
Andíparos: 59, 72 n.81, 148, 159, 163
Ándros: 72
Apéri (Kárpathos): 26 n.23, 120, 122, 123, 126, 127, 151
Aplotheka Bay (Kavo Kryos): 167, 171, 172
Argolid: 49 n.43
Arkássa (Kárpathos): 59, 64, 123, 124
Arkoí: 186
Asia Minor: vi n.6, xi, 10, 55, 68, 71, 74, 77, 108, 163, 176
Aspronísi: 88

Astypálea (Astypalæa): 71 n.75, 72, 94-104, 157, 158, 160, 161, 162, 165, 171, 172, 177, 179
Atabyros, Mount (Rhodes): 6
Athens: 50, 96, 135, 182 n.95, 184
Áthos, Mount: 10, 126, 182
Ay. Andónios (Tílos): 21, 112 n.15, 115 n.18

Babylon: 93
Berlin: 173 n.81
Bodrum: 111 n.13, 165 n.65

Cairo: 2, 106
Caria (Karia): 3, 72, 109
Cave of the Apocalypse ('Apokalypsin') (Pátmos): 75, 78, 81, 83, 154, 155, 156
Chíos: x, 29, 42, 90, 108, 109, 110, 135, 136, 158
Constantinople (Istanbul): x, xi, 69 n.66, 159, 162 n.58, 163 n.60, 173 n.81, 182 n.95
Corfu: 118
Crete: 15 n.14, 25, 38, 47, 48, 50, 64, 65, 76, 94 n.108, 110, 149, 150 n.45, 152
Cyclades: v, x, xi, 34 n.26, 48 n.42, 49 n.43, 57, 67 n.63, 72 n.79, 105, 107 n.5, 111, 135, 136, 184
Cyprus: xi, 62, 69, 145, 169

Dacha Bay: 165
Damankoor (Egypt): 106
Dardanelles: 90, 163
Delos: 181 n.91
Delphi: 6
Dhiafáni (Kárpathos): 36, 37 119, 126, 129, 141, 149-152, 179 n.86

Egypt: x, 2, 87, 92, 116 n.25

[1] The usual difficulties present themselves with place names. Phonetic variations result in frequent spelling inconsistencies, especially with accents. Generally, the author's first choice has been adopted for future references, but where there may be justification to vary them their later preferences have been included. These often differ from contemporary references.

Eleusis (Santoríni): 91
Embona (Rhodes): 6
Emborios (Níssiros): 112
Ephesus (Temple of Diana): 65, 92, 101
Euphrates, River: 93
Évia (Eubœa): 49, 50, 85, 114 n.19

Fethiye (Turkey): 107, 167 n.72
Filérimos (Phileremo), Mount (Rhodes): 6, 109 n.7
Foúrni (Phournoi) Islands: 101 n.114, 157

'Graham's Island' (Sicily): 87

Hálki (Chalki): 9 n.6, 110, 111, 144, 186
Holy Sepulchre (Jerusalem): 142

Ialé (Yali): 111
Ialyssos (Rhodes): 109
Ikaría (Nikaria): 156, 157, 162, 172
Ithaca: 47

Kakova (islet): 168, 169
Kalé Liminas (Crete): 149
Kálymnos: 103 n.119, 111, 113, 153, 156-158, 162, 163, 165, 172, 187
Karlóvassi (Sámos): 158
Kárpathos (Carpathos): x, 16 n.15, 25-68, 72, 109, 110, 114 n.19, 115, 116, 118-152, 159, 176-186
Kaş: 167 n.73
Kássos: 150 n.45, 153
Kastellórizo (Megístri): xi, 68, 71, 105, 167-170, 187
Kavo Kryos (see Aplotheka Bay)
Kéa: 48 n.42, 66 n.63
Kínaro: 172 n.79
Kolombo (islet, Santoríni): 89, 90, 92, 93
Kos: 22, 111, 113, 158, 165, 172, 186
Kum Burnú (Rhodes): 108, 171
Kyriá Panagía (Kárpathos): 29, 30, 120-123
Kýthera: 152 n.47

Lastos, Mount (Kárpathos): 29, 48, 127
Léros: 107, 172, 186
Levant: 69, 82
Levitha (islet): 167, 172,
Levkós (Kárpathos): 128, 137
Límni (Évia): 85 n.92
Lindos: 7
Lipsí: 153, 154, 186
Liverpool: vi, 144
London: vi, xi, 5, 22 n.20, 40 n.33, 56 n.49, 63 n.57, 69 n.66, 123, 152 n.47, 154, 173 n.81

Loryma: xi n.14, 167
Lycia: 169, 171 n.77
Lyons: 162

Makri (ancient Lycian Telmessus): 107 n.5, 108
Malatyeh (Armenia): 162
Malta: 152 n.47
Mandraki (Níssiros): 9, 111, 182
Megálo Horió (Tílos): 11-14, 112-118, 175
Menités (Kárpathos): 124, 126
Mesabounò (Santoríni): 88, 92
Mesochorion (Kárpathos): 38ff, 127, 128, 134
Mikró Horió (Tílos): 114, 116, 117
Monastery, Astypálea (Kástro): 111, 112
Monastery, Ayíou Pandelímona (Holy Pantaleomonos) (below Megálo Horió, Tílos): 12 n.11, 13, 23 n.21, 112, 114
Monastery, Ayíou Pandelímona (Tílos): 112 n.16
Monastery, Panormítis (Sými): 69, 70, 165
Monastery, Spiliane (Holy Virgin of the Cave) (Níssiros): 9, 10, 182, 185
Monastery, St. John the Divine (Pátmos): 75ff, 153ff, 172
Mýkonos: 100 n.113
Myndos (modern Gümüslük): 165,
Myra: xi n.14, 167-169
Mytilíni: 110, 136

Náxos: 72
Neohóri (Neo Maras) (Rhodes): 2 n.3, 108
Níssyros: 9, 10, 110-112, 114 n.18, 136, 160, 171, 172, 185, 186
Nysyros (ancient city, Kárpathos): 64

Odessa: 39
Œa (Santoríni): 91
Ólymbos (Elymbo) (Kárpathos): 25, 33, 51ff, 66, 118, 119, 126, 129ff, 179
Othíos (Othos) (Kárpathos): 31, 121, 124-127

Paleokastrizza (Corfu): 118
Panormítis (Panormos) (Sými): 69, 165
Páros: 72, 73 n.82, 74
Patara (ancient city): 171
Pátmos: xi, 72, 75-94, 153-156, 172, 173, 187
Pheníki (Kárpathos): 124
Pigádhia (Pegádhia) (Kárpathos): 60, 118-120, 126, 144, 149ff
Poseidonia (ancient city, Kárpathos): 59, 64
Profítis Ilías (Prophet Elias), Mount (Astypálea): 101
Profítis Ilías (Prophet Elias), Mount (Kárpathos): 129

Index of Place Names

Profítis Ilías (Prophet Elias), Mount (Pátmos): 85
Profítis Ilías (St Elias), Mount (Santoríni): 88, 92
Profítis Ilías (Prophet Elia), Mount (Tílos): 112 n.16
Psérimos: 186
Pythagório (Sámos): 161 n.57

Rhodes: x, xi, 1-9, 11, 12, 15, 20 n.16, 22, 25, 38, 47, 48 n.41, 51, 64, 65, 71, 106-111, 120, 125, 135, 136, 145, 159, 167 n.71, 171, 186
Rome: 84, 168, 181 n.91

Sakkarah (Memphis): 116 n.25
Saloniki (Thessaloníki): 126
Sámos: x, xi, 73-75, 108-110, 133, 136, 153, 154, 157ff, 181 n.91
Santoríni (Thera): 40 n.34, 87-93, 155
Saría (Kárpathos): 62, 63, 118, 126, 134, 144-147, 150
Sériphos: 34 n.26
Sigas (ancient city): 167 n.71
Sírina (Sýrna): 72, 165 n.66, 171, 172, 187
Smith, Mount (Monte) (Rhodes): 4
Smyrna: 1, 4, 92, 106, 107, 110, 135, 158
Sókastro (Kárpathos): 128
Spiliés (Kárpathos): 40 n.34, 121, 124, 127, 139
Spinalónga (Crete): 15 n.14
Spoa (Kárpathos): 128, 129
Sporades: x, 38, 106, 184
Stavlalonia (Kárpathos): 57

Syme (Gulf): xi
Sými (Sími): 9 n.6, 69, 111, 117, 144, 159, 165, 167
Sýros (Syra): xi, 56 n.49, 63 n.57, 69, 70, 72 n.79, 111, 126, 135, 136, 144, 145, 151, 152, 163, 164, 168 n.74, 169, 172, 173

'Ta Palátia' (Saría, Kárpathos): 145
'Tas Philakes' (Saría, Kárpathos): 147
Tersane (islet): 167 n.72
Thásos: xi, 69 n.66, 163 n.60
Therasía: 88
Tílos (Telos): 10-24, 110-118, 128, 136, 159, 165 n.66, 171, 172, 174, 175, 176, 179, 182, 183, 186
Triánda (Rhodes): 6 n.5, 108
Trístomo (Tristoma) (Kárpathos): 59, 60, 118 n.28, 119, 131, 148-150
Troy: 177

Vathý (Sámos): 157, 158
Venice: 79
Vesuvius, Mount: 87
Volátha (Volá) (Kárpathos): 26, 27, 29, 31, 33, 34, 50, 120, 122, 125, 150
Vróndi (Brontë) (Kárpathos): 120
Vrykoúnda (ancient Bourgounta, Bronkounti, Brykountios, Vourgounda) (Kárpathos): 59ff, 131ff

Xanthos, River: 171 n.77